Imagining
the Kingdom

The "End" of Worship:
① to be over, done
② Purpose, intent,
      completion

telos vs.

? aesthetic in worship ?

p 12
Worship
a pedagogy
of desire

p 81 98
Community
habitus

p 117
Metaphor

ISA 6
The holy imagination
(p 14)

p 141
to become habituated
to the way of life
GOD intends !!!

p 151
WORSHIP
& DISCIPLESHIP

p 153
WORSHIP
→ mission

telos

We are not all at back to the past
or even pushed into a future —
but God's future pulls us forward —
continues to found in time and —
refuses yesterday, today, tomorrow
Not in our practices

Jesus has
already sum?

Imagining the Kingdom

How Worship Works

Volume 2 of Cultural Liturgies

James K. A. Smith

Baker Academic

a division of Baker Publishing Group
Grand Rapids, Michigan

© 2013 James K. A. Smith

Published by Baker Academic
a division of Baker Publishing Group
P.O. Box 6287, Grand Rapids, MI 49516-6287
www.bakeracademic.com

Printed in the United States of America

Library of Congress Cataloging-in-Publication Data
Smith, James K. A., 1970–
    Imagining the kingdom : how worship works / James K. A. Smith.
        p.   cm. — (Cultural liturgies ; v. 2)
    Includes bibliographical references and index.
    ISBN 978-0-8010-3578-4 (pbk.)
    1. Worship. 2. Liturgics. 3. Liturgy and the arts. 4. Imagination. 5. Philosophical anthropology. I. Title.
BV15.S485 2013
264—dc23   2012032893

The internet addresses, email addresses, and phone numbers in this book are accurate at the time of publication. They are provided as a resource. Baker Publishing Group does not endorse them or vouch for their content or permanence.

13   14   15   16   17   18   19   7   6   5   4   3   2   1

For Jackson:
in memory of long walks—
    in the fenlands of Cambridge,
    in the forests of Lowell,
    among the sheep with Yorkminster
        towering over the field—
your curiosity and chatter
    the soundtrack of my joy,
your companionship
    the song of my heart.

These beauteous forms,
Through a long absence, have not been to me
As is a landscape to a blind man's eye:
But oft, in lonely rooms, and 'mid the din
Of towns and cities, I have owed to them,
In hours of weariness, sensations sweet,
Felt in the blood, and felt along the heart;
And passing even into my purer mind
With tranquil restoration:—feelings too
Of unremembered pleasure: such, perhaps,
As have no slight or trivial influence
On that best portion of a good man's life,
His little, nameless, unremembered, acts
Of kindness and of love. Nor less, I trust,
To them I may have owed another gift,
Of aspect more sublime; that blessed mood,
In which the burthen of the mystery,
In which the heavy and the weary weight
Of all this unintelligible world,
Is lightened:—that serene and blessed mood,
In which the affections gently lead us on,—
Until, the breath of this corporeal frame
And even the motion of our human blood
Almost suspended, we are laid asleep
In body, and become a living soul:
While with an eye made quiet by the power
Of harmony, and the deep power of joy,
We see into the life of things.

William Wordsworth, from
"Lines Composed a Few Miles
above Tintern Abbey" (1798)

Contents

List of Sidebars   ix
Preface   xi
Acknowledgments   xv
How to Read This Book   xvii
 For Practitioners
 For Scholars

Introduction: A Sentimental Education: On Christian Action   1
 The End of Christian Education and/as the End of Worship
 Situating Intellect: Educating for Action
 Imagining the Kingdom

Part 1: Incarnate Significance: The Body as Background   29
 1. Erotic Comprehension   31
  Perceiving (by) Stories
  The Geography of Desire: Between Instinct and Intellect
  My Body, My Horizon
  Being-in-the-World with Schneider: A Case Study
  Erotic Comprehension: On Sex, Stories, and Silence
  The Primacy of Perception
 2. The Social Body   75
  The Critique of Theoretical Reason
  Habitus as Practical Sense
  Belief and the Body: The Logic of Practice
  Incorporation and Initiation: Writing on the Body

Part 2: Sanctified Perception   101

    3. **"We Tell Ourselves Stories in Order to Live": How Worship Works   103**
        Imaginative, Narrative Animals
        The Primacy of Metaphor and the Aesthetics of Human
           Understanding
        A General Poetics: Imagination, Metaphor, Narrative
        The iPhone-ization of Our World(view): Compressed Stories
           and Micropractices
    4. **Restor(y)ing the World: Christian Formation for Mission   151**
        Sanctifying Perception: Re-Narration Takes Practice
        Redeeming Ritual: Form Matters
        Redeeming Repetition: On Habituation
        Redeeming Reflection: On Liturgical Catechesis and
           Christian Education

    Name Index   193
    Subject Index   197

Sidebars

Picturing This

Picturing the End of Worship   1

Picturing the Limitations of Worldview: Reading Wendell Berry in Costco   8

Picturing Love and Worship in David Foster Wallace's *Infinite Jest*   22

Picturing a Feel for the World in *Bright Star*   46

Picturing Kinaesthetic Conversion in *The King's Speech*   66

Picturing the Pedagogy of Insignificance with Carson McCullers   98

Picturing Secular Liturgies in Nicholson Baker's *The Mezzanine*   103

Picturing the Sanctification of Perception in Jewish Morning Prayer   164

Picturing a Reflective, Sentimental Education   189

To Think About

Longing Leads to Action   7

Learning the Hard Way When It's the Only Way   14

Shaping a Worldview in *Downton Abbey*   21

Existential Maps of Our World   40

Chicken Sexing and Nonconscious Knowledge   52

Motor Intentionality in *Rise of the Planet of the Apes*   55

"Catching" Sleep   65

Newman on Faith *as* Love   88

Schooling as Ritual Performance   94

Slouching toward Ritual   96

Metaphor as Godfire   120
I Can't Say; Let Me Tell You a Story   130
War Games   138
Imagining the Reformation of Manners   158
Story and the Economy of Abundance   161
The Poetry of Prayer   175
Praying a World(view)   176
Love's Litany   183

Preface

Novelists often attest that their characters take on a life of their own. So while the writer begins with a plan—a story line, character sketches, a sense of the ending to which all of it is headed—the creative process is full of surprises. Not until the novelist is mired in the mess of production could she have known that the protagonist should go *there*, should meet *him*, should say *that*. Creators are not masters of the universe they create; they, too, are recipients of that world and need to follow the path on which they are taken, even if they might have invented it to begin with.

In my preface to *Desiring the Kingdom*, I sketched a program for the Cultural Liturgies trilogy in which volumes 2 and 3 would be scholarly monographs aimed at a narrower, more specialized audience of scholars. The idea was for volume 1 to provide an accessible overview of the model and argument, and then for volumes 2 and 3 to be narrow, deep explorations of particular aspects of the argument (philosophical anthropology in volume 2 and politics in volume 3). In the three years since I completed *Desiring the Kingdom*, during which I have had a number of opportunities to share and discuss my core argument with a wide range of audiences, I have decided to revise that original plan for a couple of related reasons.

First, as it turns out, *Desiring the Kingdom* was not as "accessible" as I thought it was! While that first volume may have seemed to me like a relatively popular sketch, as is often the case, scholars are not very good judges of what counts as accessibility. Many of the readers of *Desiring the Kingdom* perceived it as a challenging academic book, though obviously scholarly colleagues in philosophy and theology saw it differently—a bit whimsical in places, a little imprecise in others. Such is the fate of a hybrid book: too many footnotes and references to German philosophers to qualify as "popular"; not enough footnotes and too many creative asides to be properly "academic." Nonetheless, I've decided to live in that between space—to inhabit that hybridity—and ultimately to continue in that vein for all of the volumes of the Cultural Liturgies trilogy.

I recognize that there is a sense in which *Desiring the Kingdom* is a hypocritical book, or at least a book at risk of performative contradiction.[1] On the one hand, the book argues that we are, primarily and at root, *affective* animals whose worlds are made more by the imagination than by the intellect—that humans are those desiring creatures who live off of stories, narratives, images, and the stuff of *poiesis*. On the other hand, the book tries to make this case in a didactic way, on a theoretical register, articulating a philosophical anthropology. *Desiring the Kingdom* recognized the limits of such a project and tried to navigate its internal tensions by including a number of forays into the arts and literature, with long digressions in which all of this is "pictured" in novels, films, and poetry. But still.

While it might seem ludicrous to even breathe about this in the same sentence with Marcel Proust, I was intrigued to discover that the young Proust faced a similar challenge. In one of his earliest writing projects, before *À la recherche du temps perdu* (*In Search of Lost Time*), Proust was up against a similar challenge in terms of genre, working in the cracks between them. In his notebooks around the time he was working on the manuscript that we now know as *Contre Sainte-Beuve*, Proust would write: "Should I make it a novel, or a philosophical study—am I a novelist?" While it is hard for us to imagine him as anything *but* a novelist (indeed, Proust is perhaps the quintessential novelist), it's interesting to see Proust's vacillation in this regard. He was a writer in search of a *form*.

The themes of *Contre Sainte-Beuve* show us why, since the work opens with a jarring claim: "Every day I set less store on intellect."[2] Proust's particular concern is the limits of intellect with respect to memory (a theme that would dominate *In Search of Lost Time*): on this account, "intellectual" reconstructions of the past strip the past of its irreducible "poetry."[3] So honoring the past, and the uniqueness of memory, requires something different, something other than a didactic rehearsal of past "facts." But here Proust runs up against an irony and a tension:

1. That it is *not* a performative contradiction should be a signal to some critics of *Desiring the Kingdom*: obviously my argument and model do not denigrate intellectual or theoretical reflection in favor of some unthinking, uncritical practice. *Desiring the Kingdom* is itself a *theoretical* reflection on pretheoretical realities—it is an invitation to *reflect* on our embodied being-in-the-world as an impetus both to appreciate the power of affective formation and to re-enter practice differently, even with a new intentionality. I return to these matters in the final section of chap. 4, "Redeeming Reflection."

2. Marcel Proust, *On Art and Literature, 1896–1919*, trans. Sylvia Townsend Warner (New York: Carroll & Graf, 1997), 19.

3. Ibid., 22. "Compared with this past [i.e., the past evoked by the scent of a madeleine dipped in tea], this private essence of ourselves," Proust continues, "the truths of intellect seem scarcely real at all" (24).

> Perhaps it will cause surprise that I, who make light of the intellect, should
> have devoted the following few pages precisely to some of those consider-
> ations that intellect, in contradiction to the platitudes that we hear said or
> read in books, suggests to us. At a time when my days may be numbered
> (and besides, are we not all in the same case?) it is perhaps very frivolous
> of me to undertake an intellectual exercise. But if the truths of intellect are
> less precious than those secrets of feeling that I was talking about just now,
> yet in one way they too have their interest.[4]

Thus the reflective artist finds himself in this bind. "But perhaps in the
course of these pages we may be led," Proust hopes, "to realize that it
touches on very important intellectual problems, and on what is perhaps
for an artist the greatest of all: this relative inferiority of the intellect which
I spoke of at the beginning. *Yet* all the same, *it is intellect we must call on
to establish this inferiority.*"[5]

Desiring the Kingdom found itself in a similar jam, putting me in the
strange position of making a philosophical argument for relativizing the
importance of the intellect—a theoretical argument for delimiting the role
of the theoretical attitude. But again, Proust owns up to a productive
catch-22 in this regard: "If intellect does not deserve the crown of crowns,
only intellect is able to award it. And if intellect only ranks second in the
hierarchy of virtues, intellect alone is able to proclaim that the first place
must be given to instinct."[6]

Proust ultimately resolved this tension by writing a novel. While I hope
such a project might be in my future, it is not the task of this book. Nonetheless, I do feel compelled to write this volume and the next in a way that
is consistent with the central argument of Cultural Liturgies—and in a
form that at least somewhat attests to the centrality of the imagination in
my model and argument. As a small gesture in this direction, I have decided
to retain the voice and format of *Desiring the Kingdom* for volumes 2 and
3. Thus the reader will continue to find exercises that attempt to "picture"
the argument through engagements with literature, film, and poetry, and
I have tried generally to retain a voice that has a little more verve than one
usually hears in the dreaded scholarly monograph.

The second reason for revising the original plan—not consigning volumes 2 and 3 to the narrow irrelevance of scholarly monographs—is simply that there are wider audiences who are now looking for the sequel(s)

---

4. Ibid., 25. I should note that Proust is criticizing the literary critic Sainte-Beuve, whom
we might now describe anachronistically, following Charles Taylor, as an "intellectualist" critic
guilty of the "heresy of paraphrase." Much more on this in the chapters below. I discuss the
"heresy of paraphrase in more detail in chap. 4 below, in the section titled "Redeeming Ritual."
5. Ibid., 25 (emphasis added).
6. Ibid., 25–26.

to *Desiring the Kingdom*. So retooling the plan for this volume (and the subsequent third volume) is largely a matter of gratitude. *Desiring the Kingdom* found friends in places I wouldn't have anticipated: while it has been widely discussed in Christian higher education and regions of the theological academy, I am also grateful that my argument and model have been enthusiastically received by pastors, worship leaders, artists, and Christian educators at the K–12 level. Conversations with these audiences over the past few years have honed my instincts and helped me refine my argument in ways I otherwise would not have. These readers and conversation partners have also helped me to see just how and where the argument of *Desiring the Kingdom* hits the ground in ecclesial and pedagogical practice. Indeed, these practitioners are often able to concretize the argument in ways that I cannot. So out of gratitude, and in hopes of keeping them in the conversation, I have decided to retain the format and voice of volume 1 for the entire trilogy. Because of this, I've provided below a brief "how to" for readers from different audiences, with the hope of providing an angle of entry for each.

Acknowledgments

The long gestation of this book makes it impossible for me to properly acknowledge the myriad of debts I've accrued. The last few years have been an exhilarating whirlwind of conversations sparked by response to *Desiring the Kingdom*. I have found myself in places and conversations I would never have imagined and am profoundly grateful to a host of interlocutors who have helped me in further reflection on these matters.

I owe a significant debt to the Calvin Institute of Christian Worship, and especially to director John Witvliet, for constant encouragement, tangible support, and providing a community of practice that has both sustained and challenged me as I continue to think about these matters. My colleagues in the philosophy department at Calvin College are gracious in granting me a long leash to explore different areas and basically reinvent myself every few years. They have also affirmed my work as a philosopher speaking to wider audiences rather than just to the philosophical guild, and I'm grateful for their recognition of a diversity of gifts. I have also enjoyed teaching in Calvin College's new Department of Congregational and Ministry Studies, a fitting home for this line of research. All of this reflects the wider support of such work at Calvin College—a place in which I've nested, even as it has worked its way deep into my bones. I count my decade at Calvin College as one of the most tangible expressions of the fact that God loves me: I am profoundly grateful that a bumpkin like me has had the opportunity to inhabit a place so intellectually vibrant and deeply rooted. I'll never quite get over my wonder at the fact that I get to teach here. I'm especially grateful to a cadre of students over the years whose curiosity, passion, and earnest seeking have sustained my own. It is a pleasure to now count some of them as friends and a joy to see them pursue their callings.

In the years between the appearance of *Desiring the Kingdom* and this sequel, I had the joy of collaborating with my friend and colleague David

Smith on a multiyear research project on Christian practices and pedagogy that enabled me to extend reflection on these matters into a collegial community of friends. The volume that resulted from that collaboration—*Teaching and Christian Practices: Reshaping Faith and Learning*—is a kind of intervening sequel, a pedagogical volume 1.5 in the Cultural Liturgies project. More recently, I had opportunity in the summer of 2011 to field test much that follows in two seminars: a graduate seminar at Trinity College of the University of Toronto and a research seminar hosted by the Seminars in Christian Scholarship at Calvin College. Both were wonderful laboratories of thoughtful, interdisciplinary conversation from which I benefited immensely.

I'm grateful for a small circle of friends who read the manuscript in its penultimate form and offered helpful feedback, even if I didn't always listen. These included John Witvliet, David Smith, Michael Gulker, Kyle Bennett, Bob Covolo, and Clay Cooke.

I appreciate Tom Wright's willingness to let me share the title "Imagining the Kingdom" with him. We both hit upon this title, concurrently and independently (Tom used it as the title for his inaugural lecture at St. Andrew's), likely because, unbeknownst to each other, we'd both been reading Iain McGilchrist's generative book, *The Master and His Emissary*.

As always, I continue to be grateful for my long partnership with the folks at Baker Academic who have become friends and tireless champions for my work. Special thanks to Bob Hosack, Brian Bolger, Steve Ayers, Bobbi Jo Heyboer, Jeremy Wells, Bryan Dyer, and Trinity Graeser for all their support and encouragement—and patience and flexibility!

The soundtrack for this book is a mixed tape featuring the Avett Brothers, Mumford & Sons, Johnny Flynn's *A Larum*, and (fittingly) The Head and the Heart's self-titled album, with a regular loop of The National's *High Violet* in the background.

It is amazing to think how much our family has changed since I first began writing *Desiring the Kingdom*. I could never have imagined what it would be like to have four teenagers in the family, and I am constantly grateful for the mystery that parents can give birth to friends. This volume is dedicated to our youngest son, Jackson, who has become a young man with whom I can be myself. What more could a father hope for?

This book was completed at the end of a long, difficult year. In the midst of that time, when psalms of lament came easily to my tongue, I would berate God with the question: "*Where are you?*" In a quiet, patient, persistent whisper, he would invariably answer with a gracious reminder: the faithful presence of Deanna. Despite my Protestantism, marriage will always be a sacrament for me, because Deanna has been a means of grace beyond all I could have imagined.

How to Read This Book

Like *Desiring the Kingdom*, this book is something of a hybrid, pitched between the academy and the church, since its argument is aimed at both. That means, of course, that it's also doomed to fall between the cracks and end up disappointing both: too scholastic for practitioners and too colloquial for scholars. I've decided that I'm willing to risk the ire of both in order to not give up on either. But given that this will pose different challenges for different readers, permit me to offer a little instructional guide for different (though related) audiences.

For Practitioners

The ultimate *telos* of the Cultural Liturgies project is the renewal of practice, so in many ways practitioners are my ultimate audience. You are Christian educators, pastors, worship leaders, campus ministers, and those involved in worship arts. You are reflective about your ministry and teaching and are open to new models and metaphors and theories. But you are not looking for "theory for theory's sake." So in some ways, this book asks a lot of you. In particular, the first half of the book asks you to wade through expositions of French theorists (Merleau-Ponty and Bourdieu) while I lay the foundations for a liturgical anthropology. I can completely understand if you find yourself at times impatient in this section of the book. However, I do believe the heavy lifting in part 1 is essential for the more tangible discussion in part 2. You might look at part 1 as digging a theoretical well from which we'll then drink in part 2. Or think of part 1 as furnishing a theoretical toolbox for reconsidering and reappreciating the *how* and the *why* of worship and liturgical formation—and, more generally, the implications for Christian education and Christian formation. Both

Maurice Merleau-Ponty and Pierre Bourdieu offer theoretical models of habituation and formation that are suggestive, provocative, and at some points poetic. Rather than simply plunder them for juicy quotes, I have provided an exposition of their work that develops the context and "big picture" of their proposals, which should help you see just how and why I think their work has implications for a vision of Christian formation and education. But feel free to skip the footnotes.

I have tried to do a couple of things to help earn your patience in part 1. First, at various points I have paused to raise some questions about the implications of Merleau-Ponty and Bourdieu for how we think about the practices of Christian worship. I hope you'll find these to be little rest stops on a long road of theoretical reflection—contemplative pauses for thinking about how a phenomenology of embodiment begins to hit the ground for worship planning and liturgical formation. Consider them promissory notes that are then more fully explored in part 2. Second, I have continued to employ various creative asides to help illustrate their arguments and theories, drawing on film and literature. I hope these are interspersed such that just as your eyes begin to glaze over from absorbing the intricacies of phenomenology, you'll hit upon a reflection on *Rise of the Planet of the Apes* that refreshes your energy and attention.

Part 2 should then be "your" section of the book—the place where we'll explore the specific implications of a liturgical anthropology for an understanding of Christian worship and formation. Granted, part 2 is no how-to manual. While I hope it hews closer to practical concerns, it does so in a reflective mode and with big-picture concerns in mind. My goal in part 2 is to suggest how the philosophical analyses of "being-in-the-world" in part 1 reframes how we look at matters of formation and generate a new appreciation of how worship works. This should encourage a new kind of critical concern about the force and formative power of secular liturgies. But it should also encourage a new intentionality about Christian worship and worship planning. In turn, it should generate new intentionality about the shape of a distinctly Christian pedagogy in education. In both cases, I hope the argument and analyses of *Imagining the Kingdom* provide further depth and nuance to the central argument of *Desiring the Kingdom*.

For Scholars

This book is decidedly *not* a scholarly monograph—because of both its tone and its *telos* (which is ultimately the renewal of Christian practice). Nonetheless, I do think embedded in here are some original, constructive proposals that might advance conversations in philosophy of religion.

Indeed, implicit in my argument is a research agenda for both philosophy of religion and sociology of religion.

In particular, I would invite scholars to read my engagement with Merleau-Ponty as a foray into the continuing conversation between French phenomenology and philosophy of religion. That conversation, which has drawn on the work of Emmanuel Levinas, Jacques Derrida, Jean-Luc Marion, and others, has largely been a philosophy of God—concerned with themes of revelation, alterity, transcendence, "appearance," and so forth. This is a robust and important trajectory of research. However, it has not fostered a phenomenology of *religion*—a phenomenological analysis of religious *practice*. I hope the model sketched here contributes to a growing conversation at the intersection of philosophy and liturgy, perhaps even to the emergence of a philosophy *of* liturgy.[1] The liturgical anthropology sketched here also has implications for the social sciences, particularly social-scientific accounts of religion and religious phenomena.[2]

Some of the arguments and analyses here in *Imagining the Kingdom* could have been distilled in scholarly articles for relevant journals in the guild—and I may still pursue some trajectories of research in more

1. This is part of what Nicholas Wolterstorff sees as the "prospect" for philosophy of religion in "Analytic Philosophy of Religion: Retrospect and Prospect," in *Inquiring about God: Selected Essays*, ed. Terence Cuneo (Cambridge: Cambridge University Press, 2009), 1:17–34. Consider also Steven Kepnes, *Jewish Liturgical Reasoning* (New York: Oxford University Press, 2007), or Terence Cuneo's philosophical analysis of icons in worship in "If These Walls Could Only Speak," *Faith and Philosophy* 27 (2010): 123–41. For a consideration of trajectories in philosophy of religion that take liturgical practice seriously, see James K. A. Smith, "Philosophy of Religion Takes Practice: Liturgy as Source and Method in Philosophy of Religion," in *Contemporary Practice and Method in the Philosophy of Religion: New Essays*, ed. David Cheetham and Rolfe King (London: Continuum, 2008), 133–47. See also Jean-Yves Lacoste's parallel development of a kind of liturgical phenomenology as seen, for instance, in *Experience and the Absolute: Disputed Questions on the Humanity of Man*, trans. Mark Raftery-Skehan (Bronx, NY: Fordham University Press, 2004). Or consider Lacoste's phenomenology of prayer in "Liturgy and Coaffection," trans. Jeffrey L. Kosky, in *The Experience of God: A Postmodern Response*, ed. Kevin Hart and Barbara Wall (Bronx, NY: Fordham University Press, 2005), 93–103. For a helpful introduction to Lacoste's project, see Joseph Rivera, "Toward a Liturgical Existentialism," *New Blackfriars* (2012): 1–18.

2. For a sketch of the implications for sociology of religion, see James K. A. Smith, "Secular Liturgies and the Prospects for a 'Post-Secular' Sociology of Religion," in *The Post-Secular in Question*, ed. Philip Gorski, David Kyuman Kim, John Torpey, and Jonathan VanAntwerpen (New York: New York University Press, 2012), 159–84. I also think there is a conversation to be staged between my liturgical phenomenology—which includes an analysis of "secular liturgies"—and British discussions of "implicit religion" and "secular faith." See Edward Bailey, *Implicit Religion: An Introduction* (London: Middlesex University Press, 1998); Bailey, *Implicit Religion in Contemporary Society* (1996; repr., Leuven: Peeters, 2006), and Bailey, *The Secular Faith Controversy: Religion in Three Dimensions* (London: Continuum, 2001). On a more popular level, consider Alain de Botton, *Religion for Atheists: A Non-believer's Guide to the Uses of Religion* (London: Hamish Hamilton, 2012).

specialized conversations. But for now I have chosen to embed the scholarly proposals in this hybrid book. So to my scholarly colleagues, I ask for
your patience with some of the asides that follow. I would also appreciate
your attention to the footnotes: I've pushed down some matters of detail
into a sort of parallel conversation on the bottom of the page. I'd ask you
to remember that, at points, I have had to forgo some qualifications and
nuance for the sake of a wider audience. Significant literatures that I have
engaged do not appear in the footnotes below—including, no doubt, some
works you consider "essential." I'd like to invite you to read this book as
a phenomenological exercise in returning to "the things themselves" and
ask that you evaluate the argument on the basis of what it says rather than
what it leaves out.

Introduction

A Sentimental Education: On Christian Action

Following Calvin, then, Protestants may insist that ecclesial practices have nothing to do with effecting human justification, everything to do with human sanctification, and—most important—everything to do with divine agency and power.[1]

🌿 Picturing the End of Worship

As a child he couldn't *wait* for church to be over. The beginning of worship was, for Andrew, merely a T-minus-sixty countdown to the end. Indeed, more than once, Walter Mitty–like, he launched into his own reverie as the pastor summoned the congregation with the call to worship. The old, tired formulas of the pastor—"The psalmist reminds us of our purpose, calling us to worship . . ."—would be replaced in Andrew's imagination with the crackly static of rocket launch transmissions that seemed to be conducted inside tin cans:

Ccccuschk. "Apollo, we are all systems go, over?" *Ccccuschk.*

Tttschd. "Uh, roger that, Houston. All systems operational. We are go for launch, over." *Tttschd.*

Ccccuschk. "T minus three minutes to launch. Firing main engines, over?" *Ccccuschk.*

"Roger that, Houston. We are all systems go, over."

"T minus one minute to launch. Stand by for ignition."

---

1. Matthew Myer Boulton, *Life in God: John Calvin, Practical Formation, and the Future of Protestant Theology* (Grand Rapids: Eerdmans, 2011), 226.

"T minus ten, nine, eight, seven, six, five, four, three, two, one . . . we have ignition. We have lift off!"

If he was lucky, Andrew would emerge from his NASA fantasy around the time of the offering. All too often he came back to earth just before the moment of confession—which meant he was still T minus forty-five till the end. Ugh.

The bulletin would then become a checklist, a way to mark the droning passage of time. Confession? Check. Assurance of pardon? Check. Reading of the law? Check. Creed? Check. Pastoral prayer and prayers of the people? *Long* wait to be able to check that off, as an elder seems to be praying for the entire world. Bible reading? Check. Sermon? Wait for it . . . wait for it . . . still waiting. . . . Finally: check! We're getting close! Offering? Check! Wait—second offering for benevolence? Ugh, check (finally). Doxology (we're getting tantalizingly close now): check! Another prayer: check! Andrew can now taste it. A hymn (*seven* verses!?): finally, check. Here we are, the finish line, T minus thirty seconds, everyone stands, the end of worship is in sight. Benediction: yes! Freedom!

Andrew now smirks to himself as he recognizes that caged eagerness in his own eight-year-old daughter, Elizabeth, who practically catapults over him to reach the cookies and juice downstairs. But he himself sees the end of worship very differently now. Far from seeing it as the bursting moment of release into some unfettered freedom, Andrew now realizes that the end of worship is a *sending*, that the blessing at the conclusion of worship is also a commissioning, and that the "end" of worship, in terms of its *telos* and goal, is bound up with what they'll do next: head out the door into the world. We are not released at the conclusion of worship, Andrew thinks to himself; we are not merely "free to go," dismissed from some appointment or event. Having been drawn into the life of the triune God through our union with Christ, we are *sent*. The end of Christian worship comes with a responsibility. Like all those prophetic encounters with the living God, this encounter with the Triune God sends one away with a commission and a charge: "Go and *do*," in the power of the Spirit, as a witness to the risen Christ, inviting your neighbors to become citizens of the coming kingdom. What we've just done in worship is both a rehearsal of the entire history of the world and a rehearsal for kingdom come. The end of Christian worship brings us back to the beginning of creation, to our commissioning in the Garden and our deputizing as God's image-bearers, those responsible for tending and tilling God's good—but now broken—creation.

The end of worship, Andrew now realizes, is the *end* of worship. The culmination of Christian worship is its s/ending. In this time of already-not yet, the end and goal and *telos* of worship is being sent from this transformational encounter as God's witnesses and image-bearers. Christian worship is not some religious silo for our private refueling that replenishes our "inner" life. It is not merely some duty we observe in order to keep our eternal ducks in a row; nor is it some special sequestered "experience" that fills up a "religious" compartment in our souls, unhooked from what we do in the world Monday through Friday. Worship isn't a weekly retreat from reality into some escapist enclave; it is our induction into "the real world."[2] Worship is the space in which we learn to take the right things for granted[3] precisely so we can bear witness to the world that is to come and, in the power of the Spirit's transformation,[4] labor to make and remake God's world in accord with his desires for creation. We could never hope to entertain such a commission without the empowering work of the Spirit who tangibly meets us in worship.

This is why Andrew sees Elizabeth's eagerness for worship to end—and remembers his own youthful eagerness for the same—as an understandable naïveté about the burdens of this encounter. In contrast to Elizabeth's sense of sheer liberation from the doldrums, Andrew now experiences the end of worship with a certain sanctified ambivalence—a sort of holy ambiguity. On the one hand, he hungrily receives the gracious announcement of blessing; on the other hand, he senses the responsibility of the commission. This is no cheap grace. This is a space of Spirit-filled transformation for the sake of being sent: to go and make disciples; to be witnesses to Jerusalem and Samaria and to the ends of the earth; to take up once again our creational mandate to be God's image-bearers by being culture-makers. When worship ends on Sunday, it spills over into our cultural labor on Monday. And Andrew's only hope and prayer is that, by the grace of God and the power of the Spirit, everything that has preceded this sending has, over time, empowered him to be the witness he's sent to be.

The End of Christian Education and/as the End of Worship

The renewal of the church *and* the Christian university—a renewal of both Christian worship and Christian education—hinges on an understanding of human beings as "liturgical animals," creatures who can't *not* worship and who are fundamentally formed by worship practices. The reason such

2. As Rodney Clapp notes, "The grace of God is not something we naturally recognize. It is not a theory pieced together from naturally observed phenomena. It is instead the result of God's reaching out to us in mercy. It is through our acceptance and participation in that mercy that we are given the categories of creation, world, sin, reconciliation, and kingdom of God—the categories by which we claim to see 'reality' as it really is." "The Church as Worshiping Community: Welcome to the (Real) World," in *A Peculiar People: The Church as Culture in a Post-Christian Society* (Downers Grove, IL: InterVarsity, 1996), 97.

3. "Through worship God trains his people to take the right things for granted." Stanley Hauerwas and Samuel Wells, "The Gift of the Church and the Gifts God Gives It," in *The Blackwell Companion to Christian Ethics*, ed. Stanley Hauerwas and Samuel Wells (Oxford: Blackwell, 2006), 25.

4. See John D. Witvliet, "The Cumulative Power of Transformation in Public Worship: Cultivating Gratitude and Expectancy for the Holy Spirit's Work," in *Worship That Changes Lives: Multidisciplinary and Congregational Perspectives on Spiritual Transformation*, ed. Alexis Abernathy (Grand Rapids: Baker Academic, 2008), 41–58.

liturgies are so formative is precisely because it is these liturgies, whether Christian or "secular,"[5] that shape what we *love*. And we are what we love.[6]

The reason for articulating this model of the human person is ultimately to provide an adequate account of Christian *action*. This begins with grinding a new lens for cultural analysis: such a liturgical anthropology recalibrates cultural analysis and critique by recognizing the (de- and trans-) formative power of *practices*—communal, embodied rhythms, rituals, and routines that over time quietly and unconsciously prime and shape our desires and most fundamental longings. And it is recognition of this formative power of liturgical practices that then drives my constructive concern to encourage intentionality about Christian liturgical formation in two key institutions: the church and the Christian university—not because these are the only institutions that matter but because they are unique sites for intentional Christian formation and because they both exist for *sending*. Students leave a school via "commencement," and worshipers leave worship with a blessing and charge, sent into the world *for* the world. In both cases, we are sent from formation *for* mission. The focus on the church and the university is strategic, not exclusive: both are crucial institutions in the *missio Dei*.

A Christian university is a hybrid institution; it is simultaneously embedded in two quite different ecosystems. On the one hand, the Christian university is a *university*, an institution of higher education that is part of a network of colleges and universities engaged in teaching and research. Much of the shape and life of a Christian university reflects this wider sense of what higher education should look like (and accreditation agencies reinforce this aspect of our ecological situation). On the other hand, a Christian university is a *Christian* institution, which situates it in the ecosystem of the church and various other institutions of Christian mission. So the Christian university is located at the intersection of (at least) these two ecosystems, and it is precisely this hybridity that generates the unique mission and task of Christian higher education.

This is why, in *Desiring the Kingdom*, I argued that the mission of the Christian university should be conceived not just in terms of dissemination of *in*formation but also, and more fundamentally, as an exercise in *formation*. The Christian university does not simply deposit ideas into mind-receptacles, thereby providing just enough education to enable credentialing for a job. No, the Christian university offers an education that is *formative*—a holistic education that not only provides knowledge but

5. On the seemingly paradoxical notion of "secular liturgies," see James K. A. Smith, *Desiring the Kingdom: Worship, Worldview, and Cultural Formation* (Grand Rapids: Baker Academic, 2009), 88n20.

6. While I will very briefly rehearse the argument of *Desiring the Kingdom* in this introduction, for the most part this book assumes familiarity with that first volume.

also shapes our fundamental orientation to the world. It is what I'll call, in a slight tweak of Flaubert, a "sentimental education."

The alumni of Christian universities are sent into God's good (but broken) world equipped with new intellectual reservoirs and skills for thinking; but ideally they are also sent out from the Christian university with new habits and desires and virtues. They will have been habituated to love God and his kingdom—to love God and desire what he wants for creation—and thus engage the world. Indeed, if we are going to teach students rigorously and critically, we must also form them in what Augustine calls "the right order of love." In other words, the end (telos) of Christian education is action: the Christian university is a place from which students are sent as ambassadors of the coming kingdom of God. They are commissioned to undertake cultural labor that is redemptive and reconciling, reflecting Christ's work of reconciliation. It is in this way that Christian colleges are caught up in the missio Dei.[7] The alumni of Christian universities are primed and shaped to take up our task as God's image-bearers, cultivating God's good creation, working to renew a fallen world, bearing witness to how the world can be otherwise, bearing fresh olives to a world battered by the floodwaters of injustice.[8] We aren't just educating spectators or observers; we are educating actors—what Andy Crouch, echoing a long Reformed tradition, describes as "culture-makers."[9]

This end (telos) of Christian education in action is exactly the same as the end of Christian worship because both are expressions of mission. What happens at the end of historic Christian worship is a benediction—a blessing—which is also a commission: go in peace to love and serve the Lord. The blessing is also a charge, and it echoes the blessings and the commission originally given to humanity in the Garden: to be fruitful and fill the earth, to compassionately rule over creation, and to cultivate the garden of creation (Gen. 1:27–31; 2:15).

The ending of Christian worship, then, is a sending. Having encountered God in Word and sacrament, we are transformed and renewed and empowered by the Spirit to take up once again the original vocation of humanity: to be God's image-bearers by cultivating all the possibilities latent in God's creation, now renewing and restoring a broken, fallen world. Drawn into union with Christ, the "end" of Christian worship is bound up with our sending for Christian action, rightly ordered cultural

7. See Christopher J. H. Wright, *The Mission of God: Unlocking the Bible's Grand Narrative* (Downers Grove, IL: InterVarsity, 2006).

8. Cf. Calvin Seerveld, *Bearing Fresh Olive Leaves* (Toronto: Tuppence, 2000).

9. Andy Crouch, *Culture Making: Recovering Our Creative Calling* (Downers Grove, IL: InterVarsity Press, 2008). Of course, thinking is also a kind of doing, and reflection is crucial to intentional action. My point is not that we should do less thinking but rather that our action and "culture-making" is always already driven by *more* than what we "think."

labor, the creational task of making and remaking God's world.[10] We are (re)made to be *makers*.[11] This is why I believe the mission and task of the Christian university are bound up with the practices of Christian worship. While the Christian university and the church are different institutions, they have the same end, the same goal: to draw the people of God into union with Christ in order to thereby shape, form, equip, and prime actors—doers of the Word.[12]

So a robust account of Christian education and formation requires an adequate philosophy of action—something little thought about in contemporary discussions that are fixated on "the Christian mind." We have spent a generation thinking about thinking. But despite our "folk" accounts and (deluded) self-perception, we don't *think* our way through to action; much of our action is not the outcome of rational deliberation and conscious choice.[13] Much of our action is not "pushed" by ideas or conclusions; rather, it grows out of our character and is in a sense "pulled" out of us by our attraction to a *telos*. If we—and if the alumni of Christian universities—are going to be "prime citizens of the kingdom of God"[14] who *act* in the world as agents of renewal and redemptive culture-making, then it is not enough to equip our intellects to merely *think* rightly about the world. We also need to recruit our imaginations. Our hearts need to be captured by a vision of a *telos* that "pulls" out of us action that is directed toward the kingdom of God. That is why in *Desiring the Kingdom* I argued that providing people with a Christian

---

10. As J. Todd Billings well summarizes, "To act in communion with God—to obey the law—is to be truly and fully human." Billings, *Union with Christ: Reframing Theology and Ministry for the Church* (Grand Rapids: Baker Academic, 2011), 110.

11. See Smith, *Desiring the Kingdom*, 205–7.

12. Note the directionality here: Christian action is predicated on Christian communion. So Christian action is not "our" independent, heroic effort. Billings gets at this in the context of a discussion of Franciscus Junius's discussion of different "degrees, or dimensions, of divine grace in regeneration." Both justification and sanctification are "received as gifts in 'communion with Christ': it is not that justification is a gift and sanctification is an achievement. However, a distinct yet inseparable dimension of this union with Christ is 'the action emanating from the new creation,' the Spirit-empowered activation of our lives for love of God and neighbor" (ibid., 108, citing Franciscus Junius, *De libero hominis arbitrio, ante et post lapsum*, in W. J. van Asselt, J. M. Bac, and R. T. te Velde, eds., *Reformed Thought on Freedom* [Grand Rapids: Baker Academic, 2010], 106). My project in this book is to build on this claim by showing *how* the Spirit empowers us to so act, through an account of liturgically-formed habituation.

13. For an accessible overview of the issues here, see Daniel Kahneman, *Thinking, Fast and Slow* (New York: Farrar, Straus & Giroux, 2011). For a more detailed exploration, see John A. Bargh, "Bypassing the Will: Toward Demystifying the Nonconscious Control of Social Behavior," in *The New Unconscious*, ed. Ran R. Hassin, James S. Uleman, and John A. Bargh (New York: Oxford University Press, 2005), 37–58.

14. Cornelius Plantinga, *Engaging God's World: A Reformed Vision of Faith, Learning, and Living* (Grand Rapids: Eerdmans, 2002), 110.

To Think About: Longing Leads to Action

Action and creative cultural labor are generated more by visions than maxims, more by a *telos* than a rule. This intuition is captured in a saying attributed to Antoine de Saint-Exupéry, the author of *The Little Prince*: "If you want to build a ship, don't drum up people to collect wood and don't assign them tasks and work, but rather teach them to long for the endless immensity of the sea."

"worldview" is inadequate for the mission of both the church and the Christian university.[15]

The argument is not that worldview approaches and intellectual reflection are wrong but only that they are inadequate, and this inadequacy stems from the stunted anthropology they assume. Such a picture of education is insufficiently radical because it doesn't get to the root of our identity. By fixating on the intellectual aspect, such a model of the person—and its corresponding picture of education—undervalues and underestimates the importance of the affective; by focusing on what we think and believe, such a model misses the centrality and primacy of what we *love*; by focusing on education as the dissemination of *in*formation, we have missed the ways in which Christian education is really a project of *form*ation. In other words, at the heart of the argument is an antireductionism and the affirmation of a more holistic understanding of human persons and Christian education (and Christian formation more broadly).

Thus I make three intertwined proposals in *Desiring the Kingdom* that are at the heart of the Cultural Liturgies project and are all indebted to Saint Augustine, that patron saint of the Reformers: First, I sketch an alternative anthropology that emphasizes the primacy of love and the priority of the imagination in shaping our identity and governing our orientation to the world. Second, I emphasize that education is also about the formation ("aiming") of our love and desire, and that such formation happens through embodied, communal rituals we might call "liturgies"—including a range of "secular" liturgies that are pedagogies of desire. Third, given the formative priority of liturgical practices, I argue that the task of Christian education needs to be resituated within the ecclesial practices of Christian worship and liturgical formation. In other words, we need to reconnect worship and worldview, church and college.

15. For a more direct response to some concerns and criticisms of my argument in *Desiring the Kingdom*, see James K. A. Smith, "Worldview, Sphere Sovereignty, and *Desiring the Kingdom*: A Guide for (Perplexed) Reformed Folk," *Pro Rege* 39, no. 4 (June 2011): 15–24; Smith, "From Christian Scholarship to Christian Education [Response to a Review Symposium on *Desiring the Kingdom*]," *Christian Scholar's Review* 39 (2010): 229–32; and Smith, "Two Cheers for Worldview: A Response to Thiessen," *Journal of Education and Christian Belief* 14 (2010): 55–58.

To be very clear, this does not constitute a rejection of worldview per se.[16] Think of my argument as "two cheers" for this paradigm. However, I think there remain legitimate concerns with even the best rendition of worldview approaches insofar as these approaches tend to still conceive the task of Christian education as the dissemination of a *perspective*, a way to *see* the world. My criticism here is not that worldview is wrong but only that it is inadequate. It is an approach that imagines us (and our students) as primarily *spectators* of the world rather than as *actors* in the world. But if one of the goals of Christian education is to form what Neal Plantinga describes as "prime citizens of the kingdom," then we need to appreciate that our actions as citizens are based, not primarily on cognitive deliberation or even on our "perspectives," but for the most part on acquired habits, unconscious desires, and pre-intellectual dispositions. And so our education has to be attuned to how those desires and dispositions are formed. We might have a highly developed, articulate "worldview" and yet *act* in ways that are remarkably inconsistent with such a "perspective."

Picturing the Limitations of Worldview: Reading Wendell Berry in Costco

Let me try to make sense of this with an example. Over the past several years, through the steady evangelism of my wife, Deanna, I have become more and more convinced about the injustice and unhealthiness of our dominant systems of food production and consumption. For Deanna, this is expressed in a commitment to "good" eating—eating that is both healthy and just, enjoying foods that are the fruit of local gardens and farms, and eating foods that contribute to our flourishing. This finds expression both in her devotion to her gardens and her recruitment of the entire family in a kitchen that is always producing culinary delights (for which I'm incredibly grateful!). And through the influence of authors like Barbara Kingsolver, Michael Pollan, and especially Wendell Berry, I have become intellectually convinced that they offer the best perspective for thinking about these issues. Indeed, in many ways I've tried to own their perspective as my own.

But a funny thing happened on the way to the grocery store: I discovered a significant gap between my thought and my action. This hit home to me one day while I was immersed in reading Wendell Berry's delightful anthology, *Bringing It to the Table*. As I paused to reflect on a key point, and thus briefly took my nose out of the book, I was suddenly struck by an ugly irony: here I was reading Wendell Berry in the food court at Costco. There are so many things wrong with that sentence that I don't even know where to begin. Indeed, "the food court at Costco" might be a kind of shorthand for Berry's picture of the sixth circle of hell.

So how might one account for this gap between my thought and my action— between my passionate intellectual assent to these ideas and my status quo action?

16. I explicitly affirm the helpfulness of "worldview" in *Letters to a Young Calvinist: An Invitation to the Reformed Tradition* (Grand Rapids: Brazos, 2010).

Why do I *believe* Michael Pollan but still pull into the drive-through at McDonald's? This is exactly the intuition at the heart of this book. While Pollan and Berry may have successfully recruited my intellect, they have not been successful in converting my habits. Nor could they be, for so much of my action in and orientation to the world is governed by dispositions that are shaped by *practice*.

Implicit in the anthropology of *Desiring the Kingdom* is a philosophy of action—a tacit assumption about what drives or causes human behavior and action—and such a philosophy of action is germane to the goal and task of both Christian education and Christian formation more broadly. Such an account of the formative power of both "secular liturgies" and intentional Christian worship has a certain urgency precisely because it assumes that so much of our orientation to—and action in—the world is governed by preconscious habits and patterns of behavior, and those habits are formed by *environments* of practice. This stands in contrast to what Charles Taylor calls "intellectualist"[17] or "decisionist" models, which tend to overestimate "thinking" as the cause of action. This does not entail a crass determinism; nor does it exclude a role for reflective, deliberative, conscious "choice." However, such a model—shored up by recent research in cognitive science—does relativize the role of ratiocinative deliberation in action. More positively, it highlights the significant impact of environment (and attendant practices) in shaping our "adaptive unconscious," which then steers/drives action at a preconscious level. As such, we should be increasingly attentive to the formative role of environment and practice in shaping our desires while also recognizing our habitual orientation to the world that undergirds so much of our action.

The response to such a situation is not simply pressing people to *think more* about what they're doing. If I am intellectually convinced by Michael Pollan but still have the default disposition to pull into the drive-through at McDonald's, the solution is not to be constantly *thinking*—that approach is unsustainable and thus, ultimately, inadequate. It's not a matter of thinking trumping dispositions; it's a matter of acquiring new habits.

This can be illustrated with a related example from practices associated with food and eating.[18] In his book *Mindless Eating*, Cornell nutritionist Brian Wansink accounts for the American obesity epidemic in terms of the habits and practices that unconsciously shape our tastes and eating patterns.[19] We are trained to orient ourselves to food and food systems by practices and environments that shape our orientation at a preconscious level—and then we regularly act on the basis of those malformed desires and deep-seated habits. We eat "mindlessly" in the sense that we eat "without thinking

17. On such accounts, our action is thought to be the outcome of conscious, mental deliberation—the outcome of *thinking about it*. This is further explained in the next section.

18. While I am using practices of eating merely as a case study for a larger point about habituation, the specific concern with food is germane to the vision of the kingdom articulated in Scripture. For an incisive analysis, see Norman Wirzba, *Food and Faith: A Theology of Eating* (Cambridge: Cambridge University Press, 2011).

19. Brian Wansink, *Mindless Eating: Why We Eat More Than We Think* (New York: Bantam, 2007).

about it." So one might guess that the solution to this problem is to acquire knowledge—to encourage critical *thinking* so that reason trumps desire and so that critical reflection trumps unreflective habits. But that's not Wansink's antidote. In fact, he explicitly argues that the solution is not just a matter of mindful eating. "Thinking about it" will always be inadequate, like reading Wendell Berry in Costco, simply because so much of our action is not the outcome of a conscious, deliberative thought process. Drawing on extensive psychological research, Wansink demonstrates that we simply are not the sorts of animals who can be deliberatively "on" all the time. So the proper response to unhealthy mindless eating is not mind*ful* eating but rather *healthy* mindless eating, changing environments and practices in order to form different (unconscious) habits. This doesn't mean there is no role for critical reflection. Indeed, Wansink offers an *argument* to press people to change their practices, and that approach is only going to work if they are, to some degree, *convinced* by his argument. But the upshot or consequence is not that they will then *think* about every meal but rather that they will be propelled to change their environment and practices, thereby absorbing different habits and undoing old ones. As a result, even their "mindless" eating will be healthy; they will eat well (and justly) "without thinking about it"—though if you ask them, they can articulate why. Their new eating habits will have become "second nature."

A worldview approach would assume that the proper response to disordered mindless eating is mind*ful* eating, as if simply getting the right perspective on eating is sufficient. Similarly, an intellectualist model of education would assume that the proper response to the unconscious formation of "secular liturgies" would be critical reflection: thinking about it more, thinking about what we're doing. Of course such reflection and thinking are important and helpful; indeed, as Wansink would note, reflection is precisely what might lead us to immerse ourselves in different environments and commit ourselves to different practices, with the goal of ultimately acquiring different habits and dispositions. Similarly, the articulation of a Christian worldview is helpful, just as thinking about practices can be a reflective opportunity to take stock of our routines and rituals. Indeed, the entire Cultural Liturgies project is itself an invitation to reflect on our practices—to gain a Christian "perspective" on our immersion in cultural practices. The argument of *Desiring the Kingdom* is not that we need *less* than worldview, but *more*: Christian education will only be fully an education to the extent that it is also a formation of our habits. And such formation happens not only, or even primarily, by equipping the intellect but through the repetitive formation of embodied, communal practices. And the "core" of those formative practices is centered in the practices of Christian worship.

Situating Intellect: Educating for Action

The liturgical anthropology at the heart of my project entails a critique of worldview because it relativizes "thinking" and re-situates "intellect."

But the critique of worldview-talk is not a critique of worldview per se, nor is it a rejection of thinking per se. The point, rather, is that we have a tendency, in Christian higher education and even in the church, to overestimate the importance of thinking.[20] Now, many of those toiling in the not-so-ivory halls of Christian colleges and universities would be quite surprised to hear that thinking is being overvalued in North American Christianity. Indeed, quite the opposite seems to be true: evangelical piety tends to intensify a general anti-intellectual malaise that besets our culture. The response to such a situation would be to encourage more thinking, not less—to emphasize the importance of the mind rather than fall back into the soppy mushiness of "the heart" and its affections. In short, with its critique of rationalist or intellectualist models of the human person, it would seem that *Desiring the Kingdom* plays right into the hands of anti-intellectualism.[21] Indeed, some seem to worry that my model would simply have us spending all day in chapel or turning the Christian college into a glorified Sunday school. But such worries stem from a misunderstanding of my emphasis on worship with respect to worldview.[22] In particular, such a worry seems to read my claim that worship is a necessary and important condition for integral Christian education as if I were claiming that it is a *sufficient* condition for Christian education (and this includes Christian education in the wider sense of discipleship, even though my focus tends to be on Christian higher education). But I'm not suggesting we raze the physics labs and expand the chapel. I'm not suggesting we demolish the literature classroom and just stay in church all week. Nor do I anywhere suggest that a Christian university is not about the business of *ideas*! Of

20. I think this is exactly the import of Tom Wolfe's account of American higher education in his novel *I Am Charlotte Simmons*. See *Desiring the Kingdom*, 118–21, for discussion.

21. In this context, it's odd to be charged with some kind of anti-intellectualism, not only because I explicitly reject this on the first page of *Desiring the Kingdom* (17n2), but also because the book itself is not exactly a walk in the park. The entire argument of the book is a pretty rigorous engagement with a whole host of ideas, inviting the reader to think through complex theories from the likes of Heidegger, Augustine, Taylor, and Bourdieu, all in order to articulate a unique, integral Christian "perspective" on education. If the critic's reading of *Desiring the Kingdom* were correct, you'd wonder why I'd ever spend time on such a venture. Perhaps that's a clue that this is not the best way to read the book.

22. I grant that I'm making strong claims about primacy that might almost give the impression of a dichotomous relationship between worship and worldview; but I don't think I ever actually make the relation dichotomous, precisely for reasons I've already cited. In this respect, I see the (mis)impression as analogous to one that Iain McGilchrist notes in *The Master and His Emissary: The Divided Brain and the Making of the Western World* (New Haven: Yale University Press, 2010), 6–7: "Because I am involved in redressing a balance, I may at times seem to be sceptical of the tools of analytical discourse. I hope, however, it will be obvious from what I say that I hold absolutely no brief for those who wish to abandon reason or traduce language. . . . My quarrel is only with an excessive and misplaced rationalism which has never been subjected to the judgment of reason."

course it is. The issue is whether it is *just* trafficking in ideas. It's the latter that I'm rejecting.

Let's remember the heart of the argument here: because we are liturgical animals who are defined by what we love, and because our loves and desires are primed and shaped by formative practices, then a holistic model of Christian education—whether in the church, school, or university—needs to involve a *pedagogy of desire.* Such a pedagogy is not merely a conduit for disseminating *inform*ation; a pedagogy of desire is a strategy for *form*ation. Christian education, in this model, is not merely about dispensing Christian ideas or providing Christian "perspectives." It is more invasive than that, precisely because it is not just an education for observers or spectators—it should be an education for *actors*, for doers. A Christian education cannot be content to produce thinkers; it should aim to produce *agents*. Such formation not only offers content for minds; it also impinges on the nexus of habits and desires that functions as the activity center of the human person. The driving center of human action and behavior is a nexus of loves, longings, and habits that hums along under the hood, so to speak, *without needing to be thought about*.[23] These loves, longings, and habits orient and propel our being-in-the-world. The focus on formation is holistic because its end is Christian *action*: what's at stake here is not just how we think about the world but how we inhabit the world—how we *act*. We are what we love precisely because we *do* what we love.

It is this ultimate goal of shaping actors that creates misunderstandings. Reflecting the "thinking-thing"-ism of modernity, many models of Christian higher education (and many accounts of discipleship) are fixated on epistemic matters. Seeing Christianity as primarily a set of doctrines, beliefs, and ideas, they implicitly and functionally reduce Christian education to the acquisition of knowledge. They also tend to assume a stunted, misguided philosophy of action that mistakenly sees action as the outcome of rational deliberation. Hence most Christian accounts of education and pedagogy end up being covert epistemologies focused on what and how we know. But as I already sketched in *Desiring the Kingdom*, this is both a dated account of human action and a rationalistic reduction of Christian faith. Because my primary concern is not merely an epistemology but also a philosophy of action, critics react to the decentralization and relativization of knowing in my account as if this entailed a rejection of knowledge. But the goal is not to denigrate the intellect; rather, it is to situate theoretical reflection within the wider

---

23. But as we'll see in chap. 1 below, that doesn't mean they're not *intentional*. Nor are we merely talking about hardwired biological reflexes. Such habits are acquired and intentional; as Merleau-Ponty shows, they are "between" instinct and intellect.

purview of our fundamental pretheoretical orientation to the world.[24] On the basis of this, those who are fixated on an epistemic construal of Christian faith too hastily conclude that relativizing the intellect is somehow a rejection of the intellect, but that clearly doesn't follow. Rather, the project is to consider the significance of our non- and pre-intellectual orientation to the world; to appreciate all of the ways in which this shapes and governs our being in the world; and to therefore expand what we consider as falling within the purview of education. To situate (and relativize) the intellect is not anti-intellectual; it is to emphasize that even rationality needs to be *faithful*, needs to be disciplined and trained and habituated.[25]

Education operates on this pretheoretical register whether we recognize it or not. Pedagogies of desire form our habits, affections, and imaginations, thus shaping and priming our very orientation to the world. So if a Christian education is going to be holistic and formative, it needs to attend to much more than the intellect—which is why I emphasize that there is a unique "understanding" that is "carried" in Christian practices, particularly the practices of Christian worship. It is in such practices that our love is trained, disciplined, shaped, and formed. And it is, to some extent, *only* in such practices that this can happen. Attention to intellect is insufficient precisely because there is an irreducible, unique understanding that is only carried in practices and only absorbed through our immersion (over time) in those practices—and it is this nonconscious understanding that drives our action. My focus is on this "nonconscious understanding," not because I think "conscious" knowledge is unimportant but because I think we've spent most of our time focused on the latter and neglected attention to the former.

The focus of this second volume is to home in on these themes, further exploring the shape of a liturgical anthropology in order to articulate a Christian philosophy of action that (1) recognizes the nonconscious, pretheoretical "drivers" of our action and behavior, centered in what I'll call the imagination; (2) accounts for the bodily formation of our habituated orientation to the world; and thus (3) appreciates the centrality

24. Philosophically I locate my project in the vein of Charles Taylor's call to "overcome epistemology" and Hubert Dreyfus's critique of "the myth of the mental." See Charles Taylor, "Overcoming Epistemology," in *Philosophical Arguments* (Cambridge, MA: Harvard University Press, 1995), 1–19; Hubert L. Dreyfus, "Overcoming the Myth of the Mental: How Philosophers Can Profit from the Phenomenology of Everyday Expertise," *Proceedings and Addresses of the American Philosophical Association* 79 (2005): 47–65. We will return to these themes in more detail below.

25. Which is precisely why we can also speak of "intellectual virtues." For a relevant discussion, consider Ernest Sosa's account of what he calls "two levels of knowledge, the animal and the reflective," both of which are "a distinctive human accomplishment," in *A Virtue Epistemology: Apt Belief and Reflective Knowledge* (Oxford: Clarendon, 2007), 1.

To Think About: Learning the Hard Way When It's the Only Way

Mark Twain, that American master of the quip and homespun wisdom, provides a rather stark image that illustrates this point about the sort of irreducible understanding acquired only by practice, unable to be articulated otherwise: "A man who carries a cat by the tail learns something he can learn in no other way."[1]

1. Quoted in Garrison Keillor, review of *The Autobiography of Mark Twain*, vol. 1, ed. Harriet Elinor Smith (Berkeley, CA: University of California Press, 2010), in *New York Times*, December 19, 2010, Sunday Book Review, 6.

---

of story as rooted in this "bodily basis of meaning" and as a kind of pretheoretical compass that guides and generates human action. In short, the way to the heart is through the body, and the way into the body is through story.[26] And this is how worship works: Christian formation is a conversion of the imagination effected by the Spirit, who recruits our most fundamental desires by a kind of narrative enchantment—by inviting us narrative animals into a story that seeps into our bones and becomes the

26. It won't do to dismiss this claim as "narrative theology" and thus trot out epistemic worries about realism (per Francesca Murphy, *God Is Not a Story: Realism Revisited* [Oxford: Oxford University Press, 2007]). Such dismissals usually traffic in a false dichotomy: *either* story *or* "reality." My claim about the centrality of story here is not primarily an epistemic claim, nor is it an evasion of ontological import (when I talk about "story" I'm not identifying that with "fiction"). The point is not that what we know is sequestered in a story that may or may not touch upon "reality"; rather, the point is that we know reality *storiedly*—and that we are wired (created) to navigate our way through the world in this way. We need to resist being distracted by worries about "reference." Here (and, indeed, passim) I have been influenced by James Woods's account of the novel in *How Fiction Works* (New York: Farrar, Straus & Giroux, 2007). Discussing issues of "realism," he notes: "Brigid Lowe argues that the question of fiction's referentiality—does fiction make true statements about the world?—is the wrong one, because fiction does not ask us to *believe* things (in a philosophical sense) but to *imagine* them (in an artistic sense): 'Imagining the heat of the sun on your back is about as different an activity as can be from believing that tomorrow it will be sunny. One experience is all but sensual, the other wholly abstract. When we tell a story, although we may hope to teach a lesson, our primary objective is to produce an imaginative experience'" (237, citing Brigid Lowe, *Victorian Fiction and the Insights of Sympathy* [London: Anthem, 2007], emphasis original). What's at issue here is the shaping and activation of plausibility structures: "Hypothetical plausibility—probability—is the important and neglected idea here: probability involves the defense of the credible *imagination* against the incredible. . . . It is the artist's task to convince us that this could have happened" (238, emphasis original). Those fixated on the epistemic will worry about such language in connection with Christian worship; but my point is that Christian worship shapes our orientation to the world precisely by priming and calibrating our imagination. As Stanley Hauerwas and Sam Wells have put it, "It is in worship that we learn to take the right things for granted" ("The Gift of the Church"). Thus I might suggest, with Woods, that "'realism' and the technical or philosophical squabbles it has engendered seem like a school of bright red herrings" (*How Fiction Works*, 244).

orienting background of our being-in-the-world. Our incarnating God continues to meet us where we are: as imaginative creatures of habit. So we are invited into the life of the Triune God by being invited to inhabit concrete rituals and practices that are "habitations of the Spirit."[27] As the Son is incarnate—the Word made flesh meeting we who are flesh—so the Spirit meets us in tangible, embodied practices that are conduits of the Spirit's transformative power. The Spirit marshals our embodiment in order to rehabituate us to the kingdom of God. The material practices of Christian worship are not exercises in spiritual self-management but rather the creational means that our gracious God deigns to inhabit for our sanctification. So while liturgical formation sanctifies our perception for Christian action, Christian worship is primarily a site of divine action. As Matthew Boulton observes, commenting on John Calvin's vision of Christian formation, "the church's practices are fundamentally divine works of descent and accommodation, not human works of ascent and transcendence."[28] And yet our incarnating God descends to inhabit these practices precisely in order to lift us up into union with Christ.[29] This is *how* our hearts are lifted up to the Lord and recalibrated to be aimed at the kingdom of God: through material practices that shape the imaginative core of our being-in-the-world.

But we also need to recognize that this is how *secular* liturgies work: they, too, recruit our unconscious drives and desires through embodied stories that fuel our imagination and thus ultimately govern our action. And while Christian worship practices are distinguished by the presence of the Spirit and a very different story, not even secular liturgies are merely "natural"; they can be fueled by the "principalities and powers."[30] Precisely because of the need for *counter*-formation, it is crucial to see that intentional Christian formation—and hence intentional Christian worship—rests on both a kinaesthetics and a poetics because of the sorts of creatures we are.

It is this intertwining of embodiment, imagination, and story that shapes what follows. Drawing on work in French philosophy (Merleau-Ponty, Bourdieu), social psychology, and cognitive science of literature, my goal

27. Craig Dykstra, *Growing in the Life of Faith: Education and Christian Practices*, 2nd ed. (Louisville: Westminster John Knox, 2005), 63–64.

28. Boulton, *Life in God*, 227.

29. For further discussion of themes of ascension and union with Christ, see Laura Smit, "'The Depth Behind Things': Toward a Calvinist Sacramental Theology," in *Radical Orthodoxy and the Reformed Tradition: Creation, Covenant and Participation*, ed. James K. A. Smith and James H. Olthuis (Grand Rapids: Baker Academic, 2005), 205–28; Julie Canlis, *Calvin's Ladder: A Spiritual Theology of Ascent and Ascension* (Grand Rapids: Eerdmans, 2010); and J. Todd Billings, *Union with Christ: Reframing Theology and Ministry for the Church* (Grand Rapids: Baker Academic, 2011).

30. See *Desiring the Kingdom*, 93n5.

is to articulate a liturgical anthropology that accounts for the importance of the kinaesthetic and the poetic—that recognizes and explains the intertwinement of the body and story as the nexus of formation that ultimately generates *action*. To do so, we need to supplement *Desiring the Kingdom*'s account of desire with an account of the imagination.

Imagining the Kingdom

"How does a provincial farm boy become persuaded that he must travel as a soldier to another part of the world to kill people he knows nothing about?"[31] He is not merely *convinced*. He does not enlist for an idea, though he certainly signs up for an ideal—but the ideal to which he is devoted (the nation, freedom, a god) is not something he *knows*; it is something he *loves*. It is not a matter of having acquired some new bit of knowledge that tips the scale and makes it seem "rational" to become a soldier. No, the provincial farm boy is primed to be a soldier—fighting unknown enemies in distant lands for interests that are not his—because he has been conscripted into a mythology: he identifies himself within a story that has seeped into his bones at levels not even he is aware of. His being "persuaded" is not so much a conclusion he has reached as a sensibility he has imbibed.[32] He is the product of a sentimental education.[33]

William Cavanaugh raises this jarring question to get at something that is the focus of this book: the provincial farm boy is "persuaded," not in the regions of the intellect, but rather on the register of the imagination.[34] The dynamics of conscription—of our identities, our desires, our loves, our longings—operate more on the imagination than the intellect. By "imagination" here I don't mean something merely inventive or fantastic—the stuff of make-believe creativity—nor do I have in mind some romantic sense

31. William Cavanaugh, *Theopolitical Imagination* (London: T&T Clark, 2002), 1.

32. Which is precisely why we'll learn more about these dynamics from Jane Austen than from A. J. Ayer. On Austen, see Alasdair MacIntyre, *After Virtue*, 2nd ed. (Notre Dame: University of Notre Dame Press, 1984), 181–87, 239–43; and Peter Leithart, *Jane Austen* (Nashville: Thomas Nelson, 2010). Given the themes I'm pressing here, it is worth noting resonance with the titles of two Austen classics: *Persuasion* and *Sense and Sensibility*.

33. This does indeed seem to be the import of Flaubert's account of the young, impressionable Frederic Moreau, who has become someone quite different than he had intended, not because he was taught in *les grand écoles* but simply because he was immersed in all the sensual spaces of Parisian life. In this sense, Tom Wolfe's *I Am Charlotte Simmons* is a more contemporary *Sentimental Education*.

34. Cavanaugh, in ways similar to (but predating) Charles Taylor, appeals to Benedict Anderson's account of "social imaginaries" in *Imagined Communities: Reflections on the Origin and Spread of Nationalism* (London: Verso, 1991). For a discussion of social imaginaries drawing on Taylor's debt to Anderson, see *Desiring the Kingdom*, 63–71.

of Creator-like "invention"[35] or merely an act of "pretense,"[36] whereby we imagine something that is a fiction, something "pretend," as when we tell children, "Use your imagination!" I mean it more as a quasi-faculty whereby we construe the world on a precognitive level, on a register that is fundamentally *aesthetic* precisely because it is so closely tied to the *body*.[37] As embodied creatures, our orientation to the world begins from, and lives off of, the fuel of our bodies, including the "images" of the world that are absorbed by our bodies.[38] On this picture, the imagination is a kind

35. My concern here is that the imagination not be thought of primarily in terms of *our* autonomous abilities—an expression of what *we* can "come up with." In this regard William Desmond's critique of the modern conception of the imagination (vs. what he calls the "sacramental imagination") is instructive: "In both Enlightenment and Romanticism we find a culture of autonomy, granting that imaginative autonomy seems more ecstatic, rational autonomy more prosaic and domestic. Nevertheless, both autonomies have to do primarily with ourselves and our powers: *auto-nomos*—self-law. This situation is itself equivocal. There can be an aesthetic will to power in Romantic imagination, as there can be a rationalistic will to power in Enlightenment reason." William Desmond, *Is There a Sabbath for Thought? Between Religion and Philosophy* (Bronx, NY: Fordham University Press, 2005), 137. While I don't want to consider imagination as entirely "passive" or "receptive" (I do think it is crucial that we be able to imagine the world otherwise than how we "receive" it), I do think it is important to recognize a certain *responsive* character of the imagination. For an account of imagination as both "synthesizer" and "innovator," see Frank Schalow, "Methodological Elements in Heidegger's Employment of Imagination," *Journal of Philosophical Research* 23 (1998): 113–28.

36. I'm also rejecting the cognitivism that still plagues much of (especially analytic) philosophical accounts of the imagination as "pretense." In particular, I reject what Shaun Nichols describes as the "single code hypothesis," namely, the representationalist approach to imagination, which construes imagination as simply a different mode of propositional thinking. On this account, "propositional imagining involves 'pretense representations,'" and such representations "can have exactly the same content as a belief." The "crucial difference" between such pretense representations (of the imagination) and belief "is not given by the *content* of the representation. Rather, contemporary accounts of the imagination maintain that pretense representations differ from belief representations by their *function*" ("Just the Imagination: Why Imagining Doesn't Behave Like Believing," *Mind & Language* 21 [2006]: 460, emphasis original). On this model, imagination is still considered a primarily representational phenomenon, on the same order as "beliefs." For a classic statement, see Gregory Currie, "Pretence, Pretending, and Metarepresenting," *Mind & Language* 13 (1998): 35–55. More recently, see the studies collected in *The Architecture of the Imagination: New Essays on Pretence, Possibility, and Fiction*, ed. Shaun Nichols (New York: Oxford University Press, 2006). In contrast to such propositionalizing of the imagination (a cognitivist reductionism), I'm suggesting that the imagination is a primarily affective "faculty" or mode of intentionality.

37. In the sense that Mark Johnson uses the term in *The Meaning of the Body: Aesthetics of Human Understanding* (Chicago: University of Chicago Press, 2007); hereafter cited as *MB*. Johnson argues that "reason and logic grow out of our interactions in and with our environment," navigated by our bodies, and that the imagination is tied to that embodiment (13).

38. I grant that this picture is a kind of empiricism, basically rearticulating the empiricist maxim *nihil in intellectu nisi prius fuerit in sensu* (nothing is in the intellect unless it has first been in the senses). However, this axiom is at least as old as Aristotle (on the imagination in *De anima*). Perhaps most interesting is Augustine's allusion to this principle in *Sermo Dolbeau 25*: "Whatever has not entered through a sense of your body, also cannot be thought about by your

of midlevel organizing or synthesizing faculty that constitutes the world for us in a primarily affective mode—what Gaston Bachelard calls, in his "phenomenology of the imagination," "the poetic register."[39] There is a kind of precognitive perception that is to be distinguished from perception proper—that is, from perception as being cognizant of and attentive to an "object" in front of me. So if we are in a classroom and I direct your attention to the chair you are sitting in as an example of an aesthetic object, you're now perceiving the chair as an object. But up to that point, you had nonetheless construed this thing *as* a chair because you'd been sitting on it this whole time. As soon as you entered the room there was an automatic construal of the space that simply "happened" without your thinking about it, and at a level that was preconscious. Likewise, there is a difference between being *in* your bedroom and being conscious *of* your bedroom when you are having trouble falling asleep. In the latter instance, the room has sort of kicked into your conscious awareness in ways that it usually doesn't. Most of the time, it is "there," but in the background; your orientation to it is functioning at a different level. I'm suggesting that "the imagination" is a way to name this everyday capacity for such unconscious "understanding" of the world.[40]

In a similar way, John Kaag has tried to unhook the narrow association of imagination with the arts by defining the imagination more broadly as "the dynamic process by which organisms (and more particularly humans) negotiate their ever-changing circumstances by way of the creative powers of mind" and as "the creative and embodied processes of mind that are

---

mind" (glossing 1 Cor. 2:9). In *Sermons*, The Works of Saint Augustine, part 3, vol. 11, trans. Edmund Hill, ed. John E. Rotelle (Hyde Park, NY: New City Press, 1997), 367.

39. Gaston Bachelard, *The Poetics of Space*, trans. John R. Stigloe (Boston: Beacon Press, 1969): "The poetic register that corresponds to the soul must therefore remain open to our phenomenological investigations" (xx). What I'm calling "imagination" here seems most akin to what Bachelard describes as the "material imagination" (distinguished from "formal imagination").

40. For a related discussion, see Frank Schalow, "Imagination and Embodiment: The Task of Reincarnating the Self from a Heideggerian Perspective," *International Studies in Philosophy* 36 (2004): 161–75. I'm here trying to articulate something like Francisco Varela's notion of "enaction," which, I take it, rejects the narrow representationalism that still tends to "regard the cognitive life of an organism as a 'representational' coping, where perception is primary and the main source and drive for any valid cognition." Francisco Varela and Natalie Depraz, "Imagining: Embodiment, Phenomenology, and Transformation," in *Buddhism and Science: Breaking New Ground*, ed. B. Allan Wallace (New York: Columbia University Press, 2003), 200. Such a picture reduces us to information processors. In contrast, "enaction implies that sensorimotor coupling modulates but does not determine an ongoing endogenous activity that it configures into meaningful world items in an unceasing flow" (ibid.). This points to the *primacy* of the imagination: "Ordinary perception is, to an essential degree, sensorimotor constrained imagination. Imagination is central to life itself, not a marginal or epiphenomenal side-effect of perception" (202).

common to human beings on the whole and that are necessary to 'get on with our business' in our social and natural surroundings."[41]

So we'll heuristically employ "imagination" to name a kind of faculty by which we navigate and make sense of our world, but in ways and on a register that flies below the radar of conscious reflection, and specifically in ways that are fundamentally aesthetic in nature. As Phil Kenneson has described it, the imagination is "productive" rather than merely inventive: it is "that complex human social capacity to receive and construct an intelligible 'whole.'"[42] For the provincial farm boy, dying in a far-flung trench for the nation or freedom or the flag "makes sense," not because this is a valid conclusion to reach on the basis of the evidence, but rather because he has absorbed a fundamental orientation to the world that has a more visceral "logic" to it: he "knows" this is what he should do in the same way one "knows" that tears indicate sadness, or in the way one "knows" how to "make sense" of a poem or a painting.

We could say that the provincial farm boy's imagination has been conscripted by a secular liturgy.[43] Becoming a soldier—like being a Christian—takes practice. The formation of the imagination is a liturgical effect. The focus of this volume is to consider more carefully and deeply the dynamics of *how* that happens—to appreciate the dynamics of "persuasion" as an operation that works on the body by means of story, thereby affecting the whole person—including thinking and reflection. Any adequate account of liturgical formation—whether Christian or secular—will need to attend to the centrality of the imagination. That, I will show, requires attending to complex features of our embodiment. And it is precisely this embodiment, in turn, that makes us narrative animals.[44] So accounting for the dynamics

41. John Kaag, "The Neurological Dynamics of the Imagination," *Phenomenology and Cognitive Science* 8 (2009): 184–85.

42. Phil Kenneson, "Gathering: Worship, Formation, Imagination," in Hauerwas and Wells, *Blackwell Companion to Christian Ethics*, 56.

43. There is, of course, a Christian analogue to this: How does a provincial farm boy become persuaded to die as a martyr for the Christian faith? The answer is the same.

44. To speak of humans as liturgical or narrative "animals" is a philosophical shorthand for emphasizing our embodied, material nature (as in Aristotle's description of human beings as "rational animals"). In this respect, Alasdair MacIntyre's observation regarding the interpretation of Thomas Aquinas is germane to our project here. Some commentators, he notes, "have failed to ask the relevant questions about the relationship between our rationality and our animality. They have underestimated the importance of the fact that our bodies are animal bodies with the identity and continuities of animal bodies, and they have failed to recognize adequately that in this present life it is true of us that we do not merely have, but are our bodies" (*Dependent Rational Animals: Why Human Beings Need the Virtues* [Chicago: Open Court, 1999], 6). On the same page, MacIntyre extols Merleau-Ponty's phenomenology as a prompt to help philosophy remember our animality.

I am deeply appreciative of Eleonore Stump's brief on behalf of the irreducibility of narrative knowledge: "The Problem of Evil: Analytic Philosophy and Narrative," in *Analytic Theology:*

of liturgical formation—the dynamics implicit in Cavanaugh's account of the "theopolitical imagination"—requires recognizing and understanding this intertwinement of embodiment and story, of kinaesthetics and poetics.

We might formulate this as something of an axiom: an adequate liturgics must assume a kinaesthetics and a poetics, precisely because liturgies are compressed, performed narratives that recruit the imagination through the body. So if we are going to account for how the provincial farm boy is "persuaded," or how the martyr is "convinced," or how so many of us are quietly conscripted into the armies of consumerism and nationalism and narcissism—or how Christians are "made" by the banal, even boring, practices of being the body of Christ—then we need an account of how worship works. Such an account will need to appreciate the force and dynamics of the aesthetic and the narratival in shaping our imagination, which will require drilling down to the bodily basis of our narrativity. So a liturgical anthropology requires a Christian[45] phenomenology of our embodiment (a kinaesthetics), which will then be the platform for a Christian phenomenology of our aesthetic nature (a poetics).

But why is this important? How might it be helpful? What is the upshot of such an account of "how worship works"? Is this just an academic exercise, an attempt to explain what is a mystery? Or worse: Does such an account end up naturalizing the work of the Spirit and effectively marginalizing God? Does such a project really have implications for discipleship and the nitty-gritty realities of Christian formation? What do kinaesthetics and poetics have to do with the on-the-ground challenges of Christian education and spiritual formation?

There are very important practical implications of such philosophical reflection. Carefully thinking about how worship works has two concrete effects that constructively help the body of Christ. First, by displacing our naive "intellectualism" (whereby we mistakenly assume that we *think* our way into action) and recognizing how secular liturgies work, we will be able to appreciate the dynamics of *de*-formation and the subterranean mechanics of temptation—and thereby be better equipped to resist assimilation. Second, appreciating the bodily basis of worship and its entwinement with the

---

New Essays in Philosophical Theology, ed. Oliver Crisp and Michael Rea (New York: Oxford University Press, 2009), 251–64. However, I think her account can be deepened and assisted by making the sort of connection between narrative and embodiment that is noted by Merleau-Ponty, which is my task below.

45. Just because this is a philosophical account does not mean that it is a naturalistic account. We are simply attending to the features and conditions of our embodiment, which are the conditions of our creaturehood that are also gifts of the Creator. To speak of *creature*hood is to speak in categories of Christian theology and confession. However, this does mean that the conditions of creaturehood that make us liturgical animals are the same conditions that can make us idolatrous animals—which is precisely why Christian worship and secular liturgies both marshal the same "structure" of the human person while aiming in very different directions.

To Think About: Shaping a Worldview in *Downton Abbey*

The British drama *Downton Abbey* invokes two worlds foreign to many of us: the "upstairs" world of early twentieth-century British aristocracy and the "downstairs" world of the servants who attend to their every need. Each of these worlds has rigorous disciplines and rituals—one set of rituals bent on shaping "ladies" and "gentlemen" who are characterized by *noblesse oblige*; the other intended to mold docile servants who embody ideals of order and civility. These different worlds of formative ritual also have their own vestments and attire that both express and shape a mode of comportment to the world. A still-feudal vision of "England" is inscribed on their bodies. This link between vestments and social visions, between bodies and worldviews, was wryly noted by the actress Michelle Dockery, who plays Lady Mary Crawley. Noting that her posture had permanently changed because of the costumes for *Downton Abbey*, she commented: "It really helps you understand how a corset shapes your worldview—the way you breathe, and eat. I think it is the single reason that women are less accomplished historically than men. They couldn't actually breathe!"[1]

1. Rebecca Mead, "Downton Fever," *New Yorker*, January 16, 2012, 21. While this is offered as a witty aside, it should remind us that those same dynamics of formation that can shape us into who and what we're meant to be can also be marshaled to *de*-form and oppress. The antidote to such de-formation, however, is not a rejection of formation per se but the fostering of practices that form us well, practices that form us for flourishing.

---

aesthetic or narratival aspect of worship should foster a new intentionality about the shape of Christian worship. We should reappreciate the implicit (narrative) wisdom in historic Christian worship practices and approach the renewal of worship with an appreciation for the bodily basis of meaning and the fundamental aesthetics of human understanding. A significant implication of my argument is the importance of the arts for the witness of the church, the announcement of the gospel, and the formation of the body of Christ. While I will employ the work of Maurice Merleau-Ponty and Pierre Bourdieu as resources for articulating this phenomenology of embodiment, we shouldn't be surprised to find it even more vividly "pictured" for us in literature, given the intertwinement of embodiment and story. So before turning to an exposition of Merleau-Ponty's account of "erotic comprehension," let me provocatively prime the pump of our imaginations with a reflection on these themes in the work of novelist David Foster Wallace.[46]

46. Wallace himself describes the powerful effect of literature more colorfully. For example, in a conversation with David Lipsky about Wallace's early novel *The Broom of the System*, Wallace laments the novel's fixation on theory ("It was all about the *head*, you know?"), which leads to a broader critique of contemporary experimental fiction as "hellaciously unfun to read." David Lipsky, *Although of Course You End Up Becoming Yourself: A Road Trip with David Foster Wallace* (New York: Broadway Books, 2010), 36. But then he goes on to contrast such "heady" fiction with engaging novels that evince "that kind of stomach magic of, 'God *damn*, it's fun to

✿ Picturing Love and Worship
✿ in David Foster Wallace's *Infinite Jest*

David Foster Wallace, author of the sprawling *Infinite Jest*, is usually lumped with "post-modern" novelists such as Don DeLillo and Thomas Pynchon. The world of Wallace's fiction is remorselessly disenchanted: a drug-addled world of addiction and suicide backgrounded by the banality of American entertainment and consumer culture. And yet the author had this to say to a graduating class at Kenyon College in 2005:

> In the day-to-day trenches of adult life, there is no such thing as atheism. There is no such thing as not worshipping. Everybody worships. The only choice we get is what to worship. And an outstanding reason for choosing some sort of god or spiritual-type thing to worship—be it JC or Allah, be it Yahweh or the Wiccan mother-goddess or the Four Noble Truths or some infrangible set of ethical principles—is that pretty much anything else you worship will eat you alive. If you worship money and things—if they are where you tap real meaning in life—then you will never have enough. Never feel you have enough. It's the truth. Worship your own body and beauty and sexual allure and you will always feel ugly, and when time and age start showing, you will die a million deaths before they finally plant you. On one level, we all know this stuff already—it's been codified as myths, proverbs, clichés, bromides, epigrams, parables: the skeleton of every great story. The trick is keeping the truth up front in daily consciousness. Worship power—you will feel weak and afraid, and you will need ever more power over others to keep the fear at bay. Worship your intellect, being seen as smart—you will end up feeling stupid, a fraud, always on the verge of being found out.
>
> The insidious thing about these forms of worship is not that they're evil or sinful; it is that they are unconscious. They are default settings. They're the kind of worship you just gradually slip into, day after day, getting more and more selective about what you see and how you measure value without ever being fully aware that that's what you're doing.[47]

The "world" according to Wallace's novels is no sacramental universe; *Infinite Jest* is a long way from the enchanted, haunted worlds of Flannery O'Connor and Walker Percy. Indeed, the "immanentism" of Wallace's world is almost suffocating. And yet he suggests that not even our radical immanence escapes worship. Rather, we are immersed in rituals that shape us and determine, unconsciously, what we value. In *Infinite Jest*, this is constantly illustrated by the sort of formation that is effected at Enfield Tennis

---

read. I'd rather read right now than *eat*.'" To see the effect of literature as a kind of "stomach magic" attests to the visceral nature of how fiction works. In fact, later in the conversation the metaphor shifts a little lower: noting that "aesthetic experience" is ultimately "erotic," Wallace praises a Barthelme story because it gave him "an erection of the heart" (72).

47. "Plain Old Untrendy Troubles and Emotions," *The Guardian*, September 20, 2008, 2. A version of this has since been published as *This Is Water: Some Thoughts, Delivered on a Significant Occasion, about Living a Compassionate Life* (New York: Little, Brown, 2009).

Academy, through intense bodily regimens that shape adolescents into veritable tennis machines. Elite tennis players are made, not born, and they're created through ritual that automates a "feel for the game" that is nothing short of a sense of the world. Key to this is "repetition," as one of the upperclassmen, Troeltsch (!), tells the younger players:

> First last always. It's hearing the same motivational stuff over and over till sheer repetitive weight makes it sink down into the gut. It's making the same pivots and lunges and strokes over and over and over again. . . . It's repetitive movements and motions for their own sake, over and over until the accretive weight of the reps sinks the movements themselves down under your like consciousness into the more nether regions, through repetition they sink and soak into the hardware, the C.P.S. The machine-language. The autonomical part that makes you breathe and sweat. . . . Until you can do it without thinking about it, play.[48]

In fact Troeltsch compares this ritual, bodily automation to "age-of-manhood rituals in various cultures" (*IJ* 118). And Schtitt, one of the drill sergeant instructors, indicates that there's more than just tennis involved: "athletics was basically just training for citizenship" (*IJ* 82). This will be an important observation: tennis is not just about tennis.

The "secret" of this bodily formation is unveiled in a soliloquy given by an inebriated James Incandenza Sr. to his ten-year-old son, Jim Jr.:

> Son, you're ten, and this is hard news for somebody ten, even if you're almost five-eleven, a possible pituitary freak. Son, you're a body, son. That quick little scientific-prodigy's mind she's so proud of and won't quit twittering about: son, it's just neural spasms, those thoughts in your mind are just the sound of your head revving, and head is still just body, Jim. Commit this to memory. Head is body. (*IJ* 167)

After recounting his own failed attempts to inhabit his body well, his inability to bring it under the discipline of a tennis regimen, he recounts a final scene of failure on the court and can't refrain from invoking the religious:

> A rude whip-lashing shove square in the back and my promising body with all its webs of nerves pulsing and firing was in full airborne flight and came down on my knees . . . right down on my knees with all my weight and inertia on that scabrous hot sandpaper surface forced into what was an exact parody of an imitation of contemplative prayer, sliding forward. . . . My racquet had gone pinwheeling off Jim and my racquetless arms out before me sliding Jim in the attitude of a mortified monk in total prayer. . . . It was a religious moment. I learned what it

---

48. David Foster Wallace, *Infinite Jest* (1996; repr., New York: Back Bay Books, 2006), 117–18; hereafter cited as *IJ*. (Note that grammatical idiosyncracies are Wallace's.) Troeltsch goes on to note what psychologist Timothy Wilson would attribute to "automation": namely, once tasks are automated, this frees up space within consciousness (i.e., it counters "ego depletion") for more intentional acts: "Wait until it soaks into the hardware," he exhorts, "and then see the way this frees up your head. A whole shitload of head-space you don't need for the mechanics anymore, after they've sunk in" (ibid., 118).

means to be a body, Jim, just meat wrapped in a sort of flimsy nylon stocking. (*IJ* 168–69)

One might be tempted to think that this is the antithesis of the religious—a thoroughly disenchanted materialism without any hint of a "soul." And yet this picture of bodily discipline is, as James hints, almost monastic.[49] The liturgical formation of lived religion is not, generally, the sort of intellectualist gnosticism we associate with Enlightenment Protestantism (and its progeny, evangelical Protestantism): it exhibits none of the allergy to embodiment and materiality, nor does it reduce religion to the cognitive realm of beliefs and propositions. Indeed, the implicit wisdom of historic religious liturgies resonates with James Sr.'s "religious" epiphany that we *are* our bodies (even if we are also *more* than bodies).

The other site of ritual formation and transformation in the novel is the rehab center, Ennet House, home to various "Anonymous" programs: AA, NA, CA, and so on. Granted, this is also the place where an explicit spirituality emerges in the world of the novel.[50] As the narrator notes from experience: "In none of these Anonymous fellowships anywhere is it possible to avoid confronting the God stuff, eventually" (*IJ* 998n69). But what's of interest here is not just *that* "God" shows up, but *how*. The "religious impulse"[51] that Wallace is naming here is the fact that "we're absolutely dying to give ourselves away to something." In the world of the novel, that can either take the form of giving ourselves *up* to various addictions and diversions (drugs and various entertainments), or it can take the form of giving ourselves *over* to various disciplines (tennis, AA).[52]

It is in the disciplines of AA that God emerges in the story—which signals a kind of implicit liturgical anthropology at work in AA's practices and indirectly at work in *Infinite Jest* insofar as the "religious" appears in the novel in conjunction with embodied, incarnate practices. For instance, the narrator notes several times that "AA and NA and

49. The "almost" is important. While monastic formation, contrary to gnosticism, takes embodiment very seriously, it also resists the reductionistic materialism of James Incandenza Sr. ("just meat"). In the next chapter we'll see that Merleau-Ponty has similar concerns.

50. In a conversation about the book with David Lipsky, Wallace is explicit about AA functioning as a stand-in for religion: "A lot of the AA stuff in the book was mostly an excuse, was to try to have—it's very hard to talk about people's relationship with any kind of God, in any book later than like Dostoyevsky." But he concedes that *Infinite Jest* is trying to grapple with a "kind of distorted religious impulse." *Although of Course*, 82.

51. Ibid.

52. In his conversation with Lipsky we get some of Wallace's own commentary on this point: "So I think it's got something to do with, that we're just—we're absolutely dying to give ourselves away to something. To run, to escape, somehow." (Let's note that this is a pretty good paraphrase of the opening of Augustine's *Confessions*: "You have made us for yourself, and our hearts are restless until they rest in you.") But Wallace continues: "And there's some kinds of escape—in a sort of Flannery O'Connorish way—that end up, in a twist, making you confront yourself even more. And then there are *other* kinds that say, 'Give me seven dollars, and in return I will make you forget your name is David Wallace, that you have a pimple on your cheek, and that your gas bill is due" (Lipsky, *Although of Course*, 81). The former sorts of "giveaways" are *disciplines*; the latter are *diversions*. And interestingly enough, Wallace goes on to describe the latter as the "Turkish delight" of C. S. Lewis's *Chronicles of Narnia* (84).

CA's 'God' does not apparently require that you believe in Him/Her/It before He/She/It will help you" (*IJ* 201).[53] The quasi spirituality of AA, then, is not an intellectualist project; it's not so much a matter of knowledge (what one believes) as it is a matter of *practice* (what one *does*). In fact, it is precisely the non-intellectualist shape of the regimen that is a scandal to those addicts who think salvation is a matter of the right information. This scandal is exemplified by Geoffrey Day, an intellectual poser (reminiscent of Daniel Harding in *One Flew over the Cuckoo's Nest*) who is contemptuous about the rituals of AA. "So then at forty-six years of age I came here to learn to live by clichés," he whines. "To turn my will and life over to the care of clichés. Easy does it. First things first," etc. (*IJ* 270). What's most maddening for him is that his supposedly superior intellect is not prized in this environment, because the intellect isn't the primary site of (trans)forma-tion. Day wants this to be something he has to *figure out*, something he just needs to *comprehend*; he wants to be liberated from the addiction by *knowledge*. Just tell me what I need to know, he basically says. Let's drop the monotony of meetings and the daily regimen; just give me the information, the knowledge I need. "As if, I mean, what's supposedly going to be communicated at these *future* meetings I'm exhorted to trudge to that cannot simply be communicated *now*, at *this* meeting, instead of the glazed recitation of exhortations to attend these vague future revelatory meetings?" (*IJ* 1001). Day thinks the meetings are a means of dispensing the requisite information, a site of some propositional revelation; he misses the fact that what's redemptive is *the going*, not what he *gets*.

But when he goes, his intellectualism is further scandalized by the litany of clichés, and he protests that he just can't believe it, even if he wants to. However, this concern about the inability to *believe* still has a lingering intellectualism about it. Thus Don Gately, an Ennet House mentor, warns Day that the AA regimen eludes conceptual articulation:

> "The slogan I've heard that might work here is the slogan, *Analysis-Paralysis*," [Gately responds].
>
> "Oh lovely. Oh very nice. By all means don't *think* about the validity of what they're claiming your life hinges on. Oh do not ask what *is* it. Do not ask not whether it's not insane. Simply open wide for the spoon."
>
> "For me, the slogan means there's no set way to argue intellectual-type stuff about the Program. Surrender To Win, Give It Away to Keep It. God As You Under-stand Him. You can't think about it like an intellectual thing. Trust me because I been there, man. You can analyze it til you're breaking tables with your forehead

---

53. Cf. one of his later observations during his time in rehab: "That God might regard the issue of whether you believe there's a God or not as fairly low on his/her/its list of things s/he/it's interested in re you" (*IJ* 205). This can seem scandalous to Christian ears, and it is not unproblematic. However, one could also hear this as a way of saying that we "belong before we believe." In this respect, it's not so far from Pascal who, in his famous Wager, suggested that if you couldn't come to propositional assent about God's existence, then you could at least attend Mass to "grow" the belief in you. (I'm also reminded of the Peirce Pettis song, "God Believes in You": "[when] you swear you don't believe in him / God believes in you.")

and find a cause to walk away, back Out There, where the Disease is. Or you can stay and hang in and do the best you can." (*IJ* 1002)

The narrator even sympathizes with Day on this point, but has been through the ringer just enough to know otherwise:

Simple advice like this does seem like a lot of clichés—Day's right about how it seems. Yes, and if Geoffrey Day keeps on steering by the way things seem to him then he's a dead man for sure. Gately's already watched dozens come through here and leave early and go back Out There and then go to jail or die. If Day ever gets lucky and breaks down, finally, and comes to the front office at night to scream that he can't take it anymore and clutch at Gately's pantcuff and blubber and beg for help at any cost, Gately'll get to tell Day the thing is that the clichéd directives are a lot more deep and hard to actually *do*. To try and live by instead of just say" (*IJ* 273, emphasis original).[54]

Analysis does not effect a transformation in the person because the intellect is not the "driver" of human desire and action. Wallace's philosophical anthropology is much more affective than that. As noted in his Kenyon College address, it's not so much what we think as what we *worship*. And in *Infinite Jest*, worship is linked to love. In an early, surreal exchange between Steeply, a government agent, and Marathe, a member of the Wheelchair Assassins of southern Quebec, the two are wrangling about whether *love*—particularly love for a woman—was the source of recent warfare. In the course of the conversation, Steeply refers to the "fanatically patriotic Wheelchair Assassins." After a pause, Marathe responds to this remark:

"Your U.S.A. word for fanatic, 'fanatic,' do they teach you it comes from the Latin for 'temple'? It is meaning, literally, 'worshipper at the temple.'"

"Oh Jesus now here we go again," Steeply said.

"As, if you will give the permission, does this *love* you speak of, M. Tine's grand love. It means only the *attachment*. Tine is attached, fanatically. Our attachments are our temple, what we worship, no? What we give ourselves to, what we invest with faith. . . . Are we not all of us fanatics? . . . Choose your attachments carefully. Choose your temple of fanaticism with great care." (*IJ* 106–7)

On Marathe's accounting, it is not a question of *whether* we worship, but *what*; this is precisely because worship is bound up with love. The two terms are basically convertible. "You are what you love," he continues. And so this raises the question of formation, of the pedagogy of desire: "Who teaches your U.S.A. children how to choose their temple? What to love enough not to think two times? . . . For this choice determines all else. No? All other of our you say *free* choices follow from this: what is your temple?" (*IJ* 107).

---

54. From an interview Wallace gave *Salon*, we know that Day is, in fact, a character based on his own experience in a halfway house. And Wallace was particularly perplexed by the effectiveness of this clichéd regimen. See D. T. Max, "The Unfinished," *New Yorker*, March 9, 2009, 54.

Wallace's *Infinite Jest* affectively portrays several intuitions that resonate with my proposal: an anthropology that displaces "intellectualism," an attention to the formative power of embodied rituals, and the centrality of worship—particularly as linked to love. "We are what we love" amounts to "we are what we worship"—a thesis that has a long Augustinian pedigree.[55] And that love/worship shapes our so-called free choices; our "temple" determines all else. It is that intuition that I'm after when I claim that we are *liturgical* animals: in some fundamental way, we construct our world and act within it on the basis of what we worship.

55. One could do a bit of triangulation here to unpack my earlier suggestion that "worship" is akin to "care" in Heidegger's account. We know from his pre–*Being and Time* lectures that Heidegger's analysis of "care" owes much to Augustine's account of love or *caritas*. For Augustine, love and worship are intimately connected (see *City of God* 19.24–26). Thus it's not too much of a stretch to see a link between care and worship.

Incarnate Significance

THE BODY AS BACKGROUND

A liturgical anthropology is rooted in both a kinaesthetics and a poetics—an appreciation for the "bodily basis of meaning" (kinaesthetics) and a recognition that it is precisely this bodily comportment that primes us to be oriented by story, by the imagination (poetics). In part 1 we'll undertake introductory expositions of two key theorists of embodied intentionality: phenomenologist Maurice Merleau-Ponty and social theorist Pierre Bourdieu. Their work provides a theoretical toolbox and conceptual lexicon to help us name and describe the dynamics of habit formation, giving us insight into the nature of liturgical formation more specifically. By helping us to imagine human nature differently, they will also lead us to a theoretical appreciation for the primacy of the imagination.

1

Erotic Comprehension

Affect . . . is the name we give to those forces—visceral forces beneath, alongside, or generally *other than* conscious knowing, vital forces insisting beyond emotion—that can serve to drive us toward movement, toward thought and extension, that can likewise suspend us (as if in neutral) across a barely registering accretion of force-relations, or that can even leave us overwhelmed by the world's apparent intractability. Indeed, affect is persistent proof of a body's never less than ongoing immersion in and among the world's obstinacies and rhythms, its refusals as much as its invitations.[1]

Perceiving (by) Stories

Much of our action is not the fruit of conscious deliberation; instead, much of what we do grows out of our passional orientation to the world—affected by all the ways we've been primed to perceive the world.[2] In short,

---

1. Gregory J. Seigworth and Melissa Gregg, "An Inventory of Shimmers," in *The Affect Theory Reader*, ed. Melissa Gregg and Gregory J. Seigworth (Durham, NC: Duke University Press, 2010), 1.
2. Iain McGilchrist, *The Master and His Emissary: The Divided Brain and the Making of the Western World* (New Haven: Yale University Press, 2010), addresses those who would be concerned that this sounds like the loss of free will. To those who worry that this claim and all of the evidence that backs it up "seem to deny to consciousness any major role in the conduct of our day-to-day affairs," his response is blunt but encouraging: "Quite so. But as one of the contributors to this debate points out, this is only a problem if one imagines that, for me to decide something, I have to have willed it with the conscious part of my mind. Perhaps my unconscious is every bit as much 'me.' In fact it had better be because so little of life is conscious

31

our action emerges from how we *imagine* the world.[3] What we do is driven by who we are, by the kind of person we have become. And that shaping of our character is, to a great extent, the effect of stories that have captivated us, that have sunk into our bones—stories that "picture" what we think life is about, what constitutes "the good life." We live *into* the stories we've absorbed; we become characters in the drama that has captivated us. Thus, much of our action is acting out a kind of script that has unconsciously captured our imaginations. And such stories capture our imagination precisely because narrative trains our emotions, and those emotions actually condition our perception of the world. Here we need to appreciate the recent insights of cognitive science and neuroscience, which then help us see the importance of the imagination and story.

We are not disembodied choice machines who somehow end up in bodies that are embedded in a material milieu. No, we are actors, doers, engaged makers and muddlers in a material world that is our home, our environment, our milieu, our dwelling. A nuanced liturgical anthropology will need to displace the functional intellectualism that tends to dominate both philosophical accounts of agency and our everyday "folk" conceptions of choice and action. Even those Christian communities we usually criticize for their anti-intellectualism are, in fact, intellectualist in their implicit philosophies of action insofar as they believe that changing what we *think* will change what we *do*.[4] But what if we are actors before we are thinkers? What if our

---

at all" (186–87). To which I would add one further caution: we ought not to assume that the unconscious is a hardwired, merely biological reality. It is itself formed and acquired, and I can make *choices* to immerse myself in practices that will re-form my unconscious.

3. My proposal will implicitly push back on regnant paradigms in philosophy of action insofar as they uncritically assume an intellectualist account of action (or assume what Hubert Dreyfus calls "mentalism"); that is, most discussions in the field of philosophy of action have accepted something like Donald Davidson's restriction of what *counts* as "action" to those acts that are the outcome of conscious, deliberative choice guided by beliefs. All other behaviors or movements are attributed to involuntary instincts or reduced to mere reflexive responses. For a representative survey of this paradigm, see Alfred R. Mele, ed., *The Philosophy of Action* (Oxford: Oxford University Press, 1997); and Arthur Danto, *Analytical Philosophy of Action* (Cambridge: Cambridge University Press, 1973). In the Mele collection, Jaegwon Kim describes this as "the familiar 'belief-desire' pattern of action explanation" (*Philosophy of Action*, 257): an action is caused by a rational agent who has a belief about some state of affairs and a desire for some goal and thus executes an action on the basis of that belief and in order to achieve that goal. So every action has a "reason for which," and only movements that can be so explained count as "actions."

This paradigm, I will suggest, is working with a distinction that is too simple: *either* conscious, deliberate, chosen action *or* mere bodily reflex and instinct. As we'll see below, Merleau-Ponty (and Taylor and Dreyfus following him) identifies a kind of third space: a bodily know-how that guides and drives much that deserves to be called "action."

4. This was forthrightly pictured in an advertisement for a Bible memory verse program in a Christian magazine. Pictured in the ad was a man with a furrowed brow, across which was inscribed: "You are what you think." The ad went on to suggest that the regular input of Bible

action is driven and generated less by what we think and more by what we love? And what if those loves are formed on a register that hums along largely below the radar of consciousness—but are nonetheless acquired products of formation and not mere aspects of "hardwiring"? Then any adequate account of Christian formation and discipleship—and hence any holistic vision for Christian education—will need to appreciate the dynamics of habituation that make us the sorts of actors we are. This book aims to articulate a Christian philosophy of action that takes seriously the *creational*[5] conditions of human action: our embodiment, our finitude, our sociality, and the complexity of our being-in-the-world—the different ways that we "intend" our world. At the heart of my argument is the conviction that our incarnating, accommodating God meets us *in* and *through* these creaturely conditions. Just as God's revelation accommodates itself to the hermeneutical conditions of our finitude, so the transforming Spirit of God meets us as the finite creatures of habit we are. The sanctifying Spirit condescends to meet us as narrative, imaginative, ritual animals, giving us practices and liturgies for our sanctification.

In doing so, I'm pushing back against an "intellectualist" account of action that assumes that what I *do* is the outcome of what I *think*.[6] On this intellectualist account, I see a situation, consider my options, think through my obligations and the range of possible consequences, and then make a conscious choice to act as the outcome of that mental deliberation. Action, on this picture, is a conclusion to a deliberative, mental, rational process.

---

verses would transform behavior—that intellectual inputs would yield holiness outputs. Certainly memorization of Scripture is a good, but I will still argue that this assumes a naïve philosophy of action that underestimates—and therefore undervalues—the formative power of practices.

5. In this respect, I see this project as parallel to my project in *The Fall of Interpretation: Philosophical Foundations for a Creational Hermeneutic*, 2nd ed. (Grand Rapids: Baker Academic, 2012), where I outline the creational conditions of interpretation. Both are exercises in Christian *philosophy* rooted in a confessional understanding of creation and incarnation, attentive to the material conditions of our finitude and embodiment in light of that conviction. For a distinction of such a Christian philosophical project from "theology" proper, see ibid., 7–8. So to allay Barthian worries about any "natural theology" here, I would see my project as more akin to a "theology of nature" than a "natural theology"—per the distinction explored in David Moseley, "'Parables' and 'Polyphony': The Resonance of Music as Witness in the Theology of Karl Barth and Dietrich Bonhoeffer," in *Resonant Witness: Conversations between Music and Theology*, ed. Jeremy S. Begbie and Steven R. Guthrie (Grand Rapids: Eerdmans, 2011), 240–70, esp. 259–64.

6. I adopt this use of the term "intellectualist" following Charles Taylor's use of the term in "To Follow a Rule . . ." in *Bourdieu: Critical Perspectives*, ed. Craig Calhoun, Edward LiPuma, and Moishe Postone (Chicago: University of Chicago Press, 1993), 45–60, esp. 45–49. For a more technical philosophical discussion of the issues broached here, see James K. A. Smith, "Secular Liturgies and the Prospects for a 'Post-Secular' Sociology of Religion," in *The Post-Secular in Question*, ed. Philip Gorski, David Kyuman Kim, John Torpey, and Jonathan VanAntwerpen (New York: New York University Press, 2012), 159–84.

The problem is, we now know that very little of our action and behavior is generated in this way. A root problem of this intellectualist account of action is that it assumes that "seeing" and "evaluating" are two separate processes. In other words, it assumes that we first see the "facts" of the case, deliberate about the relevant "moral" principles that apply, and then make a choice, resulting in action. But in fact, perception and evaluation are inextricably intertwined: as soon as I take in a scene, before I "think" about it, I've already evaluated it on the basis of predispositions I bring to the situation. Perception is already an evaluation that then primes me to act in certain ways, depending on the formation of my character and my "passional orientation." In his important book *The Social Animal*, David Brooks summarizes it this way:

> Seeing and evaluating are not two separate processes, they are linked and basically simultaneous. The research of the past thirty years suggests that some people have taught themselves to perceive more skillfully than others. The person with good character has taught herself, or been taught by those around her, *to see situations in the right way*. When she sees something in the right way, she's rigged the game. She's triggered a whole network of unconscious judgments and responses in her mind, biasing her to act in a certain manner.[7]

Our intellectualist bias leads us to misunderstand the nature of action, including ethical action. We tend to assume that "educating for action" requires first uploading the relevant rules and axioms into our minds, then equipping agents with the critical thinking skills that will allow them to amass the relevant facts of a situation and then make the right decision—either for individual action or as a matter of policy. We then pose a question or quandary: for example, what should be done about the plight of poor urban schools? But what this intellectualist paradigm misses is the fact that we never simply perceive the so-called facts of the matter, nor do we act out principles and axioms in any straightforward, deductive way. It can't be a matter of first getting "the facts"; nor is it just a matter of knowing how to consciously apply relevant moral rules. As soon as the situation is *perceived*, there is already an evaluation that has occurred—a *priming* of our posture and stance toward the situation. As soon as I become acquainted with the situation of urban public education, I will have already been primed to see a whole world there. I "take in" a whole situation that is governed and shaped by affective dispositions I bring to the encounter. "One's feelings are not a reaction to, or a superposition on, one's cognitive assessment," McGilchrist notes, "but the reverse: the affect comes first,

7. Brooks, *The Social Animal: The Hidden Sources of Love, Character, and Achievement* (New York: Random House, 2011), 127 (emphasis added).

the thinking later. Some fascinating research confirms that affective judgment is not dependent on the outcome of a cognitive process."[8] Affect and
emotion are part of the "background" I bring with me that constitutes the
situation *as* a certain kind of situation. Thus McGilchrist defines affect
not merely as discrete emotions but as "a way of attending to the world (or
not attending to it), a way of relating to the world (or not relating to it), a
stance, a disposition, towards the world—ultimately a 'way of being' in the
world."[9] This is because of the primacy of bodily perception, what Mark
Johnson will call "the bodily basis of meaning": the fact that our bodies
mean the world in ways that are intentional without being intellectual.
"The essential core of being is subcortical," as McGilchrist provocatively
summarizes. "Emotion and the body are at the irreducible core of experience: they are not there merely to help out with cognition. Feeling is not
just an add-on, a flavoured coating for thought: it is at the heart of our
being, and reason emanates from that central core of the emotions, in an
attempt to limit and direct *them*, rather than the other way about."[10] The
whole person perceives and interprets the world, and the specific shape of
our material embodiment plays a significant role in that.

To "take it in" *as* a situation is to already feel and sense different sorts of
calls or obligations woven into the situation itself. In other words, what I
feel called to do in and about such a situation is not dictated by principles
that transcend the situation but rather by elicitations that are experienced
as immanent to the situation. The situation as perceived already comes
loaded (or not) with a call upon me. The call I feel in such a situation, even
if it is experienced as "obvious," can be radically different for someone
who has had different affective "training." So in the case of urban public
schools, one person will immediately and "obviously" see the situation as
calling for discipline—for policies that are meant to fight the laziness that
characterizes the "culture of poverty" while exercising "stewardship" of
public resources. Another person will "just see" the dynamics of disenfran-
chisement and the systemic oppression that generates such an oppression,
feeling a call to take up the work of individual empowerment and systemic
policy change. Any "facts" will already be seen in light of the affective
background each brings to the situation.[11]

One can begin to appreciate how this also plays out on a larger level:
What is this world we inhabit? *Whose* world is this? Who is my neighbor?

8. McGilchrist, *The Master and His Emissary*, 184.
9. Ibid.
10. Ibid., 185 (emphasis original).
11. That doesn't mean there are no "givens" or that there's no "there" *there*. It just means
that our selection of "givens" and data that count as "facts" is itself shaped and determined by
this affective priming. As McGilchrist puts it, "disposition towards the world comes first: any
cognitions are subsequent to and consequent upon that disposition" (ibid., 184).

Am I my brother's keeper? These are all questions that are implicitly answered in our affective take on the world—a construal of the world that is governed by our "emotional" training as much as (or really, more than, or at least *before*) it is governed by the information deposited in the intellect. Even to frame these as implicit "answers" to implicit "questions" is already to pose the matter too didactically. Instead, we should say that we have a "feel" for the world that is informed by stories that dispose us to inhabit the world as *either* a bounteous but broken gift of the gracious Creator *or* a closed system of scarcity and competition; and as a result, either I will just "naturally" be disposed to see others as neighbors, as image-bearers of God, whose very faces *call* to me in a way that is transcendent, or I will have a "take" on others as competitors, threats, impositions on my autonomy. That affective, emotional "background" is also part of the dispositions or tendencies that I bring to such a context. I'm not only primed to *see* the situation in a certain way, based on this emotional context; I'm also already inclined or disposed to *act* in a certain way—not as the result of a decision but as a sort of "natural" tendency given the inclinations that I've acquired, the habits that already prime me to "lean" in certain directions.

So generating good, just, virtuous action is not merely a matter of disseminating the relevant rules or principles;[12] it is more fundamentally dependent upon training affect—training people to "see situations in the right way." *That*, it turns out, requires training their *emotions* to be primed to take in and evaluate situations well. Our emotional perceptual apparatus (which I'm linking to "the imagination") is significantly "trained" by narrative. I will have implicitly and affectively absorbed stories and narratives and pictures about the situation of urban public education and will have learned to tell myself stories about poverty or race or secularity. I will have emotionally absorbed those stories from NPR or Fox News or (just maybe!) the testimonies of others or firsthand encounters. Even my firsthand encounters will be primed and positioned by the sorts of stories I've absorbed, so that I already enter this space and this conversation with a "take" that I've probably never articulated to myself. And such "storied" pedogogy, we'll see, is intimately linked to our embodiment.

This interplay is well described by Mark Johnson who emphasizes that the emotions are a mode of both internal assessment and external

---

12. Of course we can articulate rules and principles, but they will be a matter of making explicit what is implicit in the world; and they will not be as operative as we tend to assume when it comes down to generating action. As Hauerwas colorfully puts it, "No ethic, not even the most conservative, should be judged by its ability to influence the behavior of teenagers in the back seat of a car. What happens there will often happen irrespective of what 'ethic' has officially been taught." Stanley Hauerwas, "Sex in Public: How Adventurous Christians Are Doing It," in *The Hauerwas Reader*, ed. John Berkman and Michael Cartwright (Durham, NC: Duke University Press, 2001), 490.

appraisal.[13] So "the major neuroscientists agree that emotions play a central role in an organism's assessment of its internal milieu" (*MB* 54), which, in turn, is crucial for governing our bodily interaction with an environment. On the one hand, my body emotionally "knows" threats before I'm ever aware of them, for example; or I might actually be registering flirtation without ever being conscious of it. This is work carried out on an emotional register. On the other hand, emotions play a role in this "internal" monitoring because they also assess external situations. Emotions, in a way, make judgments for us: "*What* is meaningful to us, and *how* it is meaningful, depends fundamentally on our ongoing monitoring of our bodily states as we experience and act within our world" (*MB* 57). And since the emotions do that monitoring, our experience and action depend on the emotions. Emotion is one of the transcendental conditions of our experience. "Emotions are a primary means for our being in touch with our world. They are a crucial part of the meaning of what is happening" (*MB* 65). As David Brooks emphasizes, the emotions are a mode of appraisal that not only perceives a situation but also *evaluates* it. The way Johnson describes the interpretive work of the emotions sounds a lot like what we usually envision as the goal or outcome of education, particularly Christian education:

> By the time we feel an emotion, a mostly unconscious assessment has occurred of the situation we find ourselves in, and in cases where we are functioning optimally, we have frequently already taken steps to transform the situation in order to restore homeostasis and enrich the quality of our experience. We have *perceived and understood* our situation in a certain light, although with little or no conscious reflection. This is a way of saying that our world (our situation) stands forth meaningfully to us at every waking instant, due primarily to processes of emotion and feeling over which we have little [conscious] control. *And yet the situation is meaningful to us in the most important, primordial, and basic way that it can be meaningful—it shapes the basic contours of our experience. The situation specifies what will be significant to us and what objects, events, and persons mean to us at a pre-reflective level* (*MB* 66, emphasis original).[14]

13. We need to distinguish "feeling" from "emotion": "Emotional responses can occur long before we become aware that we are *feeling* an emotion," Mark Johnson, *The Meaning of the Body: Aesthetics of Human Understanding* (Chicago: University of Chicago Press, 2007), 59 (emphasis original); hereafter cited as *MB*. Feeling is conscious; emotion is unconscious; and "awareness" operates along a continuum.

14. Johnson helpfully invokes John Dewey's claim that emotions are not "in" us but rather find their locus in situations, realities that characterize a milieu of organism/environment interaction. So when I say "I am fearful," this really means "The *situation* is fearful" (*MB* 67, emphasis original). Emotions are "both *in us* and *in the world* at the same time. They are, in fact, one of the most pervasive ways that we are continually in touch with our environment" (*MB* 67, emphasis original).

We are always already immersed in a "situation" that is constituted *as* a situation on an emotional register: "we are living in and through a growing, changing situation that opens up toward new possibilities and that is transformed as it develops. That is the way human meaning works, and none of this happens without our bodies, or without our embodied interactions within environments that we inhabit and that change along with us" (*MB* 83). Our action is always *enaction*—part of a dance of embodiment and our environment, a mode of interaction that is governed and propelled as much (or more!) by our emotional appraisal of our situation as by our rational reflection on it. And that emotional appraisal is characterized by an irreducibility such that "we should not think that our embodied meaning, understanding, and reasoning could ever be adequately thought or grasped by our concepts, symbols, rules or patterns. Our situations, with all of their summing up, implying, and carrying forward, are *embodied situations*" (*MB* 83, emphasis original).

(The ultimate upshot of my argument is to suggest that educating for *Christian* action will require attending to the formation of our unconscious, to the priming and training of our emotions, which shape our perception of the world. And if such training happens through narratives, then educating for Christian action will require an education that is framed by participation in the Christian story. Our shorthand term for such a narrative practice is *worship*.)

Here my argument intersects with fascinating new work in literary criticism, specifically with research at the intersection of literature and cognitive science that has highlighted the importance of narrative for human consciousness—the centrality of story for how we navigate our way in the world.[15] Stories are means of "emotional prefocusing" that shape our tacit "take" on the world. And they do so because narrative operates on an affective register—what Merleau-Ponty calls "antepredicative" know-how, a knowing without thinking that is processed by the body, as it were. It's a take on the world that resides in our bones, as if the imagination is "closer" to our gut. The heart has reasons of which reason knows nothing—which is just to say that the heart has a story to tell and loves to hear one told. The heart drinks up narrative like it's mother's milk.

This is why our most basic, passional orientation to the world is primed and shaped by stories; it is stories that train and prime our emotions, which in turn condition our perception and hence our action. As Hogan summarizes,

15. See, for example, Brian Boyd, *On the Origin of Stories: Evolution, Cognition, and Fiction* (Cambridge, MA: Harvard University Press, 2009); Patrick Colm Hogan, *The Mind and Its Stories: Narrative Universals and Human Emotion* (Cambridge: Cambridge University Press, 2003); and Jenefer Robinson, *Deeper than Reason: Emotion and Its Role in Literature, Music, and Art* (Oxford: Oxford University Press, 2005).

Specific emotional experiences and outcomes are also, to some degree, shaped by our ideas about emotion, particularly by our emotion prototypes and our prototype narratives. Most obviously, we construe experiences in light of eliciting conditions for emotions and thus in light of stories, in a process that reacts back on those experiences. We do not merely see a particular event (for example, a spouse's behavior) in its own terms. We see it as approximating relevant prototypes and our emotional response is guided by this. Moreover, we place ourselves in standardized narrative sequences when we act on emotions.[16]

This helps us to appreciate the complex, unarticulated background of human action—including action that is morally relevant. "Behind" or "under" the action, as it were, is not necessarily a chain of deductive reasoning or reflective deliberation. Most often, and most fundamentally, there is an unarticulated (and inarticulable) set of dispositions and inclinations that are activated immediately upon perceiving a situation—because that perception is already an evaluation, a "take," a construal that is "seen" *emotionally*. The scene is colored with a certain affective hue that then inclines me to respond in certain ways. That emotional perception of a situation is not merely a hardwired, biological reflex; it is an acquired habit, a product of a passional orientation that has been learned in and through paradigmatic stories. And those stories and narratives that prime and orient my very perception of the world tap into deep wells of my embodied unconscious. I learn these stories with my body.

Having fallen prey to the intellectualism of modernity, both Christian worship and Christian pedagogy have underestimated the importance of this body/story nexus—this inextricable link between imagination, narrative, and embodiment—thereby forgetting the ancient Christian sacramental wisdom carried in the historic practices of Christian worship and the embodied legacies of spiritual and monastic disciplines. Failing to appreciate this, we have neglected formational resources that are indigenous to the Christian tradition, as it were; as a result, we have too often pursued flawed models of discipleship and Christian formation that have focused on convincing the intellect rather than recruiting the imagination. Moreover, because of this neglect and our stunted anthropology, we have failed to recognize the degree and extent to which secular liturgies *do* implicitly capitalize on our embodied penchant for storied formation. This becomes a way to account for Christian assimilation to consumerism, nationalism,

16. Hogan, *The Mind and Its Stories*, 242–43. Hogan considers Emma Bovary as a sort of "double-case": the character of Emma Bovary has her ideals of happiness shaped by romantic novels, while the novel *Madame Bovary* exercises its own "sentimental education" on the reader (245–46).

and various stripes of egoisms. These isms have had all the best embodied stories. The devil has had all the best liturgies.

A proper response to this situation is to change our *practice*—to reactivate and renew those liturgies, rituals, and disciplines that intentionally embody the story of the gospel and enact a vision of the coming kingdom of God in such a way that they'll seep into our bones and become the background for our perceptions, the baseline for our dispositions, and the basis for our (often unthought) action in the world. While the goal is renewed practice, we cannot simply return to a fabled past, nor can we simply impose foreign practices. In order to generate a *desire* to renew and reorient our practices, we do well to engage in reflection to help understand *why* this is needed. So while the goal is practical, the way there is theoretical. As Proust already reminded us, only the intellect can establish its own

---

To Think About: Existential Maps of Our World

In *The Web and the Rock*, Thomas Wolfe's autobiographical story mildly disguised as a novel, we follow the existential apprenticeship of George Webber, a globetrotting writer who returns to his small hometown only for it to feel even smaller. Throughout the novel is a concern with a sort of visceral geography, an understanding of place that is not objective or "map-like" but rather implicit and intuitive. In an opening description, Wolfe captures something of the embodied know-how by which we existentially map and make our worlds:

His was, in fact, a savagely divided childhood. Compelled to grow up in an environment and a household which he hated with every instinctive sense of loathing and repulsion of his being, he found himself longing constantly for another universe shaped in the colors of his own desire. And because he was told incessantly that the one he hated was good and admirable, and the one for which he secretly longed was evil and abominable, he came to have a feeling of personal guilt that was to torment him for many years. His sense of *place*, the feeling for specific locality that later became so strong in him, came, he thought, from all these associations of his youth—from his overwhelming conviction, or prejudice, that there were "good" places and "bad" ones. This feeling was developed so intensely in his childhood that there was hardly a street or a house, a hollow or a slope, a backyard or an alleyway in his own small world that did not bear the color of this prejudice. There were certain streets in town that he could scarely endure to walk along, and there were certain houses that he could not pass without a feeling of bleak repulsion and dislike. By the time he was twelve years old, he had constructed a kind of geography of his universe, composed of these powerful and instinctive affections and dislikes.[1]

1. Thomas Wolfe, *The Web and the Rock* (New York: Sun Dial, 1940), 10–11.

secondarity. By sketching the lineaments of a liturgical anthropology, we should come to a new appreciation of *why* historic Christian worship and spiritual formation had a specific embodied shape. In other words, doing some theoretical heavy lifting in philosophical anthropology should engender a new intentionality in worship planning, spiritual formation, and Christian pedagogy—a new intentionality about the *how* by helping us appreciate the *why*.

The kinaesthetic link between story, the body, and the imagination is implicit in historic Christian wisdom about spiritual formation and liturgical practice. However, rather than merely excavate that from historical sources, in this chapter I will engage Merleau-Ponty's phenomenology of embodiment as a catalyst for us to remember the incarnational, sacramental wisdom that is ours. No one has better mapped the interplay between imagination, perception, the body, and narrative.

The Geography of Desire: Between Instinct and Intellect

Maurice Merleau-Ponty's *Phenomenology of Perception* is a classic account of how the body "knows." This bodily knowing is what Merleau-Ponty calls "perception." But if we try to map this onto standard epistemologies and accounts of knowledge, we quickly realize that his notion of "perception" doesn't quite fit because our standard epistemologies provide maps to a world of our making, not the world we actually inhabit. Merleau-Ponty's project is motivated by Husserl's phenomenological maxim: to return to "the things themselves." The goal is to provide a phenomenological account of our being-in-the-world in all its messiness and complexity, rather than creating some neat and tidy world of "objects" and "subjects" and "ideas" and then confusing those with "the world." "To return to the things themselves," Merleau-Ponty advises, "is to return to that world which precedes knowledge, of which knowledge always *speaks*, and in relation to which every scientific schematization is an abstract and derivative sign-language, like geography in relation to the country-side in which we have learnt beforehand what a forest, a prairie or a river is."[17] To provide a phenomenology of perception, then, is to try to stand on our philosophical heads: offering a theoretical account that does justice to our pretheoretical navigation of the world.[18]

17. Maurice Merleau-Ponty, *Phenomenology of Perception*, trans. Colin Smith (London: Routledge, 1962), ix–x; hereafter cited as *PP*.
18. Merleau-Ponty will describe this in terms that resonate with the young Heidegger, describing his project as a phenomenology of the "natural attitude." I have discussed this methodological orientation in more detail in *Speech and Theology: Language and the Logic of Incarnation*, Radical Orthodoxy (London: Routledge, 2002), 82–112.

Our embedded and embodied perception of the world is nothing like the "knowledge" processed by "subjects" that perceive "objects." That traditional epistemological picture—which has now seeped into our "folk" conceptions of experience (*PP* 63–64)—is, Merleau-Ponty reminds us, *derivative*. It's like the difference between the coach's *x*'s and *o*'s on the chalkboard and what really happens on the football field. The *x* and *o* schematic is a useful fiction, a heuristic abstraction that doesn't begin to approach the complexity of what really happens when the offensive line stunt blocks to open up the three-hole for a counter run. Any newcomer to football who thought he would know what to do because he studied the playbook would be in for a rude awakening on the eighteen-yard line. What Merleau-Ponty is calling "perception" is the muddy, grizzled, bruising reality on the field in contrast to the deceptive simplicity of "knowledge"—the neat and tidy *x*'s and *o*'s in the playbook.[19] He goes on to describe this in a typically suggestive yet oblique way:

> The real is a closely woven fabric. It does not await our judgment before incorporating the most surprising phenomena, or before rejecting the most plausible figments of our imagination. Perception is not a science of the world, it is not even an act, a deliberate taking up of a position; it is the background from which all acts stand out, and is presupposed by them. The world is not an object such that I have in my possession the law of its making; it is the natural setting of, and field for, all my thoughts and all my explicit perceptions. Truth does not "inhabit" only the "inner man," or more accurately, there is no inner man, man is in the world, and only in the world does he know himself. (*PP* xi–xii)

Perception is not clumsy, unreflective judgment.[20] It is something different altogether and is the background that makes judgment, analysis, and

19. Merleau-Ponty notes Husserl's distinction between "intentionality of act, which is that of our judgments and of those occasions when we voluntarily take up a position . . . , and operative intentionality (*fungierende Intentionalität*), or that which produces the natural and antepredicative unity of the world and our life, being apparent in our desires, our evaluations and in the landscape we see, more clearly than in objective knowledge, and furnishing the text which our knowledge tries to translate into precise language" (*PP* xx). The *Phenomenology of Perception* (like this book) is seeking to provide a philosophical account of "operative" intentionality. But precisely for that reason, Merleau-Ponty points out the limits of *analysis*: "Our relationship to the world, as it is untiringly enunciated within us, is not a thing which can be any further clarified by analysis; philosophy can only place it once more before our eyes and present it for our ratification" (*PP* xx). Here we hit upon the methodological distinctiveness of phenomenology: its task is nuanced *description* in the face of "what gives," and its warrant is the extent to which such descriptions are compelling on the basis of our prephilosophical experience (cf. *PP* ix).

20. Here again Merleau-Ponty criticizes mere analysis for imposing foreign, simplistic categories on the rich complexity of embodied perception: "Analytical reflection becomes a purely

"knowledge" possible. "The world is not what I think," Merleau-Ponty cautions, "but what I live through" (*PP* xviii).

Merleau-Ponty is attentive to what we might call our "hybridity," our sort of incarnational suspension between angelhood and animality—as mind *and* body.[21] He is trying to describe our comportment to the world as neither intellectualist[22] nor merely a reflexive biological response to stimuli. Our being-in-the-world is *between* instinct and intellect. Such an account of embodied perception pushes back against Cartesian "thinking-thing"-ism that would reduce us to minds merely carried in the vehicles of our bodies as well as a reductionistic animalism that would reduce all of our action and perception to mere biological response to stimuli. I don't just abstractly *think* my way through the world, but neither am I merely a passive victim of impressions, bounced around by instinctual reflexes.[23] I'm not an angel, but neither am I an insect (*PP* 90); I am not merely a mind trucking around in a body, but neither am I just a bundle of biological mechanisms passively responding to my environment.

So what we need, Merleau-Ponty argues, is a model of the human person that does not fall prey to the dichotomies of mind *or* body but rather does

regressive doctrine, according to which every perception is a muddled form of intellection" (*PP* 44). Embodied perception is not just rudimentary knowledge; it is something different altogether: "there is a significance of the percept which has no equivalent in the universe of the understanding" (*PP* 54). Indeed, "a complete reform of understanding is called for if we are to translate phenomena accurately" (*PP* 56).

21. These are the reductionisms that Tom More, a medical doctor, seeks to evade in Walker Percy's novel *Love in the Ruins: The Adventures of a Bad Catholic at a Time Near the End of the World* (New York: Farrar, Straus & Giroux, 1971). Armed with his Ontological Lapsometer, More can measure the degrees of "angelism" or "animalism" (or "bestialism"). "I have learned," he says, "that a reading over 6 generally means that a person has so abstracted himself from himself and from the world around him, seeing things as theories and himself as a shadow, that he cannot, so to speak, reenter the lovely ordinary world" (34). But he also feels that medical science easily falls into animalism, since "there still persists in the medical profession the quaint superstition that only that which is visible is real" (29).

22. Merleau-Ponty is a catalyst for Taylor's critique of intellectualism. The opening chapters of *Phenomenology of Perception* constitute a deconstruction of both an empiricist reductionism and a rationalist intellectualism. "Intellectualism is unequal to dealing with this perceptual life, either falling short of it [or] overshooting it" (*PP* 45). In fact, Merleau-Ponty takes intellectualism and empiricism to be sort of mirror images of each other, beset by common "prejudices" and a common failure to honor the hybridity of perception.

23. Actually, Merleau-Ponty highlights that not even our reflexive responses are merely passive, "blind" processes: "they adjust themselves to a 'direction' of the situation, and express our orientation towards a 'behavioural setting' just as much as the action of the 'geographical setting' upon us" (*PP* 91). So even our reflexes are "intentional" in the sense that they are a way we "aim" at the world: "The reflex does not arise from objective stimuli, but moves back towards them, and invests them with a meaning which they do not possess taken singly as psychological agents, but only when taken as a situation" (*PP* 91–92).

justice to our "betweenness"[24] and its peculiar preconscious knowledge: We are not just "subjects"; neither are we mere "objects."[25] We are incarnate inhabitants of our world. Thus Merleau-Ponty adopts the Heideggerian neologism "being-in-the-world" to honor this richness and complexity. We don't *have* being-in-the-world; we *are* being-in-the-world—embedded, embodied actors at home in an environment that we navigate with a kind of intentionality that precedes knowledge and whose locus is in the body. Struggling to name this, Merleau-Ponty describes it as "preconcious knowledge." It is an appreciation for such preconscious knowledge that is required if we are going to develop an adequate, nuanced philosophy of action.

As Merleau-Ponty describes it, we build up a habitual way of being-in-the-world that is carried in our body, one that is "known" on a level that precedes and eludes conscious reflection and objectification.[26] "The body is the vehicle of being in the world, and to have a body is, for a living creature, to be *inter*volved in a definite environment, to identify oneself with certain projects and be continually committed to them" (*PP* 94, emphasis added). My body is not just an object that moves through otherwise neutral space; rather, my body is surrounded by this "practical field" that shapes and constitutes its world. The cup is pick-up-able because I have hands and it has a handle. It's not even that I "see" the cup "as" pick-up-able; that is too objectifying. It *is* pick-up-able for me, for my body. The stairs or rocks *are* climbable because my practical field already constitutes them as such. So we can no longer separate the body as physiological mechanism from the "habit-body" that has built up over time (*PP* 95).

It is this "habitual body" that "knows" with a "preconscious knowledge." It is the locus for a way of life. This is illustrated by those cases where a physiological change in the body does not change the habitual body with its acquired orientation to the world: "Some subjects can come near to blindness without changing their 'world': they can be seen colliding with objects everywhere, but they are not aware of no longer being open to visual qualities, and the structure of their conduct remains unmodified. Other patients, on the other hand, lose their world as soon as its contents

24. Iain McGilchrist invokes the same notion: the world generated by "right brain" understanding is characterized by a "betweenness" that is not true of the "left brain" analysis and ratiocination (*The Master and His Emissary*, 31).

25. He clarifies this vis-à-vis the Cartesian philosophical lexicon that has bequeathed us these dichotomies: the human person is neither merely *res cogitans* nor merely *res extensa*; "being-in-the-world" is "distinguished from every third person process [and] from every first person form or knowledge" (*PP* 92).

26. Merleau-Ponty actually gets at this with a long consideration of the phenomenon of "phantom limbs," which testifies to just how significantly we become habituated to a bodily mode of being-in-the-world: "To have a phantom arm is to remain open to all the actions of which the arm alone is capable; it is to retain the *practical field* which one enjoyed before the mutilation" (*PP* 94, emphasis original).

are removed; they abandon their habitual way of life even before it has become impossible, making themselves into premature invalids and breaking
their vital contact with the world before losing sensory contact with it"(*PP*
92). When the latter patients "decide" that they can't see, they no longer
know how to make their way in the world: their preconscious, habituated
knowledge is no longer drawn upon; they shrink from the world. The
former patients' orientation to their environment is so habituated that
they don't realize they no longer have the body to pull it off. From both
cases Merleau-Ponty draws the conclusion that our "world" is not just
an external source of stimuli. To the contrary, "There is, then, a certain
consistency in our 'world,' relatively independent of stimuli, which refuses
to allow us to treat being-in-the-world as a collection of reflexes—[and]
a certain energy in the pulsation of existence, relatively independent of
our voluntary thoughts, which prevents us from treating it as an *act* of
consciousness" (*PP* 92, emphasis original). Indeed, "my body is the pivot
of the world" (*PP* 94).

So the body carries a kind of acquired, habituated knowledge or know-
how that is irreducible and inarticulable, and yet fundamentally *orienting*
for our being-in-the-world. Merleau-Ponty invokes a painful example of
this: "We do not understand the absence or death of a friend until the time
comes when we expect a reply from him and when we realize that we shall
never again receive one; so at first we avoid asking in order not to have to
notice this silence; we turn aside from those areas of our life in which we
might meet this nothingness, but this very fact necessitates that we intuit
them" (*PP* 93). Just what or who "knows" that? I'm not thinking about it;
indeed, I'm working at not thinking about it and don't even realize that
I'm doing so. Nonetheless I continue to carry this embodied knowledge
and expectation of a "phantom" friend. On some register of habit, I'm
still expecting my friend to be home or to answer the phone; I haven't quite
given up the expectation that I'll bump into him walking up the stairs at
church as I've encountered him hundreds of times. I don't "realize" his
absence until I'm stopped short when my habitual orientation to the world
runs up against his absence: when I thoughtlessly begin to text him about
the Packers game only to realize, in horror, as if for the first time, that he's
not on the other end of the line. And never will be again. Only then does
my knowledge become conscious.

What sort of knowledge is this? How does a body know? How does my
body *learn*? And what if Christian faith was also this sort of "way of life"
that is inscribed in our "habit-body"? What if being a disciple of Jesus
meant that we were characterized by a sort of "momentum that throws
us into our tasks" (*PP* 94)? What if the work of the Spirit was to form and
reform and transform that "certain energy in the pulsation of existence"
that orients our being-in-the-world? What would it look like for Christ

to leverage this body that is the pivot of my world? Merleau-Ponty's phenomenology of embodiment provides resources for us to begin to answer these questions and to have a new appreciation for how worship works.

🌿 Picturing a Feel for the World in *Bright Star*

As I noted in *Desiring the Kingdom*, the liturgical anthropology I'm articulating here is "romantic" in the sense that it counters the rationalism born of the Enlightenment legacy.[27] There is a resonance between the holistic affirmations of a liturgical anthropology and Romanticism's revaluing of emotion and the aesthetic. Both affirm the priority of intuition to reason and the primacy of the aesthetic to the rational.[28] And like Merleau-Ponty, both affirm an irreducibility to our bodily, sensuous relation to the world.

The intuitions of Romanticism are powerfully embodied in Jane Campion's film *Bright Star*—not least because the film is focused on one of the great Romantic poets, John Keats. In some ways, the film *performs* what I've been trying to expound from Merleau-Ponty's theorizing, and critical reflection on the film might help us to appreciate elements of Merleau-Ponty's philosophical anthropology. In particular, reflecting on the interplay between Keats's poetry and Campion's film—between his words and her pictures—will be an occasion to appreciate something of the irreducibility of that knowledge which is a "feel for the world."

The narrative engine that drives the film is the interplay of Keats's two loves: poetry and Fanny Brawne. (The push-and-shove match between the two is refereed by Keats's friend, Charles Brown, whose own devotion to poetry—and appreciation of Keats's gift—makes him a defensive corner of this love triangle.) Keats's poetry is a rhapsodic blend of diction and devotion to nature that sets language alight with new fires and a new honesty about not just the beauty but also the brokenness of the world. Indeed, Keats feels so modern to us that a contemporary reader might easily forget that his words were penned in the early 1800s. Consider just one stanza from "Ode to a Nightingale":

> Fade far away, dissolve, and quite forget
>   What thou among the leaves hast never known,
> The weariness, the fever, and the fret
>   Here, where men sit and hear each other groan;

---

27. See James K. A. Smith, *Desiring the Kingdom: Worship, Worldview, and Cultural Formation* (Grand Rapids: Baker Academic, 2009), 77–80, 123–24. For a relevant discussion of "Romantic" theology, see John Milbank, "The New Divide: Romantic versus Classical Orthodoxy," *Modern Theology* 26 (2010): 26–38.

28. There are also important differences. Romanticism retains the Enlightenment's affirmation of the individual and autonomy—it's just that in Romanticism this manifests itself as an expressivism. A Christian liturgical anthropology, because of its Augustinian debts, will reject *both* "autonomisms."

Where palsy shakes a few, sad, last grey hairs,
   Where youth grows ale, and spectre-thin, and dies;
Where but to think is to be full of sorrow
   And leaden-eyed despairs,
Where Beauty cannot keep her lustrous eyes,
   Or new Love pine at them beyond to-morrow.[29]

These are words to be read aloud, words that need to be instantiated in the air, touched with the tongue. Evoking—yea, *producing*—a world was at the heart of Keats's art, and his poetry evokes a tangibility that is unmistakable. Indeed, for Keats, poetry is not merely an instrumental way to convey ideas. Poetry is its own end—its own irreducible understanding of the world in which one *dwells*, not merely through which one travels. This is unfolded in an important exchange between Keats and Fanny Brawne in *Bright Star*:

"I still don't know how to work out a poem," Fanny confesses.
   Keats quietly replies with a halting soliloquy. "A poem needs understanding through the senses," he begins. "The point of diving in a lake is not immediately to swim to the shore but to be *in* the lake, to luxuriate in the sensation of water. You do not work the lake out. It is an experience beyond thought. Poetry soothes and emboldens the soul to accept mystery."
   "I love mystery," Fanny replies meekly, back on her heels after this outpouring.

The poem is both called forth by the world and *is* its own world—and one inhabits it on its own terms. It is something in which one "luxuriates"—something in which one dwells, ruminates. A poem is something you soak up, spend time with, rest in. This is not an escape from the "real" world; it is a different way of inhabiting *this* world, a space in which you learn something about the world that you could have never known otherwise. It is an "experience beyond thought," a unique "understanding through the senses."

Keats's aesthetic vision and project is well captured by Christopher Ricks, in a critical review of Campion's film, a critique that I think is instructive precisely because of *how* it is wrong. As Ricks summarizes, "In Keats's art (his letters quite as much as his poems), even the word 'description' falls short of his astonishing achievement, in that his imagination never limits itself to describing; rather, thanks to a whole range of corporeal imaginings, it realizes."[30] It is clearly this aesthetic project that has captivated the director Jane Campion. She, too, is interested in realizing a world. But her medium is film, not poetry—she traffics in images, not words. And yet her film is an homage to Keats's art, not by trying to merely represent it but rather by a parallel aesthetic effort that also

29. John Keats, "Ode to a Nightingale," st. 3, in *Essential Keats*, ed. Philip Levine (New York: Ecco, 1987), 101–2.
30. Christopher Ricks, "Undermining Keats," *New York Review of Books* 56, no. 20 (December 17, 2009): 46.

means to create an understanding through the senses, an experience beyond thought (which is precisely why any plot summary of the film would be quite beside the point).[31]

Interestingly, Ricks misses just this point in his criticism. Indeed, he chastises Campion for "undermining" Keats by deigning to add pictures to his already graphic words. In response to the film, Ricks thunders a commandment:

> It is imperative that the pictures within such a film as *Bright Star* practice one simply unremitting act of self-abnegation: of never being pictures of the very things that a great writer has superbly—by means of the chosen medium of words alone—enabled us to imagine, to picture. A film that proceeds to furnish competing pictures of its own will render pointless the previous acts of imagination that it purports to respect or to honor. For among the accomplishments of the poets is that he or she brings it about that we see with the mind's eye, as against the eye of the flesh.[32]

In other words, what Keats has already painted with poetry shouldn't be photographed with Campion's camera, as if Keats's poetry needed graphic images to help it somehow—turning his odes into picture books with captions. On Ricks's viewing, Campion has undermined Keats by trying to supplement his poems as if the film was trying to make up for something lacking in Keats's poetry—Campion's art assisting, even rescuing, the art of the poet.

But Ricks is exactly wrong, and he's wrong because he both underestimates Keats and misunderstands Campion. Ricks's problem is that he remains trapped within a representationalist model of the arts—both poetry and film. Thus he still construes Keats's goal as primarily *picturing*—"seeing"—whereas Keats himself has a more fulsome hope: to understand by (all) the senses, to pen words that evoke a *feel* for the world, a sensibility and sensuousness in which one luxuriates and dwells. And Campion's aesthetic vision is exactly the same, though her medium is different. Campion is not merely trying to "represent" the story of John Keats or "illustrate" his poetry, providing a graphic supplement to make up for some supposed deficiency in Keats's words. No, what we have here are two different, parallel forms both trying to achieve the Romantic aesthetic ideal, which recognizes the irreducibility of the aesthetic as its own "understanding" of the world. Campion is not inviting viewers merely to "see" John and Fanny; she is inviting them to indwell their world, their experience, to feel with them. Thus *Bright Star* is a sumptuous experience in its own right: it is its own rhapsody of color and sound, light and shadow, movement and rest. Campion has directed the actors to comport themselves in ways that don't merely "express" some emotion but rather embody a comportment to the world that we immediately "know" and "understand" without being able to articulate a word about it. The lush physicality of the environment captured in panned-out, sweeping cinematography is complemented by microattention to the tremors of a hand, light glancing off an alabaster breast, the ever-so-slight downward turn of the

---

31. It seems to me a similar aesthetic is at work in the *oeuvre* of director Wes Anderson.
32. Ibid.

corner of a mouth. The frame of the lens *makes* the world in ways that we've never seen it before, yet immediately understand. Even the sound in this film is crucial: a minimalist stringed sound track complemented by the creaks of ancient chairs; the scrape of horses' hooves on cobblestone; and long, charged silences, all together creating an ambience of sound that now envelops the world we inhabit. One should never ask of any scene in this movie, "What does it mean?" The movie doesn't mean something *else*—it isn't trying to "express" an idea or convey a "message"; it *means* itself. It *means* in its showing. And once you accept the invitation to inhabit it, you "understand" something you couldn't have known otherwise.[33] Ricks's criticism misses the fact that Campion's visual poetics has its own irreduciblity and stands as a "Romantic" work of art by its own right.

My Body, My Horizon

My body is not an "object" for me—it is not a thing among things, something I "see" or "touch" like I do a tool or an instrument or even the body of another person. My body is not something I have, but something I *am*; it is the "me" that dwells in the world. This means that my body, for the most part, is not something of which I am conscious; rather, it is the condition of possibility for my consciousness. It is my constant *background*. Indeed, Mark Johnson has noted that the very composition of our body functionally encourages us to forget it. Strangely enough, it is our bodies that sort of encourage us to be dualists: "Our lived experience itself reinforces an apparently inescapable dualistic view of mind versus body. We don't have to work to ignore the working of our bodies. On the contrary, our bodies hide themselves from us in their very acts of making meaning and experience possible" (*MB* 4). The "successful functioning of our bodies requires that our bodily organs and operations recede and even hide in our acts of experiencing things in the world." Indeed, this is necessary precisely in order to afford us a range of possibilities, making possible our fluid, automated experience of the world. Thus Johnson invokes an axiom from Leder: "Insofar as I perceive through an organ, it necessarily recedes from the perceptual field it discloses. I do not smell my nasal tissue, hear my ear, or taste my taste buds but perceive with and through such organs." The body is thus that background that can never be fully put in front of us—the "bodily schema" that is our frame of reference and condition for experience (*MB* 5). This explains "the bodily basis of our latent Cartesianism" (*MB* 6).

33. That also means, of course, that the "truth" of Campion's film is not reducible to my description or summary. My prosaic account can only hope to invite the reader to see the film and thereby experience what Campion has created.

In a similar way, Merleau-Ponty emphasizes that the body's "permanence is not a permanence in the world, but a permanence on my part. To
say that it is always near me, always there for me, is to say that it is never
really in front of me, that I cannot array it before my eyes, that it remains
marginal to all my perceptions, that it is *with* me" (PP 104).[34] The body is
not an object among a world of objects; it is the background and horizon
of possibility that makes it possible for me to encounter a world of objects. "In so far as it sees or touches the world, my body can therefore be
neither seen nor touched. What prevents its ever being an object, ever being
'completely constituted' is that *it is that by which there are objects*. It is
neither tangible nor visible in so far as it is that which sees and touches"
(PP 105, emphasis added). Our bodies are not just vehicles for our minds
but "our means of communication" with the world: the "horizon latent in
all our experience and itself ever-present and anterior to every determining
thought" (PP 106).

Merleau-Ponty's description here assumes a phenomenological account
of experience whereby our experience is "constituted" against a "background" that primes us to construe the world in certain ways, to configure
the dizzying array of sense impressions into a "world." The influx of intuitional data that is "given," that comes at me in my immersion in experience,
is "put together" (constituted) *as* something precisely within the context
of my "horizons." In a way, there is an almost overwhelming amount of
"givenness" (intuition) that is coming at me right now—a wash of sense
data impressing itself upon my entire body. It is only because I have some
"background" presuppositions and habits, acquired over time, that I can
instantly "constitute" this influx of intuitions into a manageable world:
the cup here, the barista there, the door over there, the music overhead,
the chattery din of conversation, the smell of fresh-brewed Sumatran coffee infusing the whole experience. These phenomena "are" insofar as I
constitute them *as* something—and that constitution (putting-together)
requires "horizons" that frame the whole experience, give it a context that
then facilitates constitution.[35]

But I didn't *think* about an ounce of this when I walked in here, and
haven't *thought* about it for a second until I just wrote the sentences above.
Constitution happens on a register that precedes occurent consciousness. It

34. As Merleau-Ponty continues: "In other words, I observe external objects with my body,
I handle them, examine them, walk round them, but my body itself is a thing which I do not
observe: in order to be able to do so, I should need the use of a second body which itself would
be unobservable" (PP 104).

35. The role of constitution comes to light if you can recall an experience where you encountered some "givenness" that you could *not* constitute because you couldn't make sense of
it against the repertoire available in your "background." Think of the Coke bottle that drops
into the experience of the African natives in the opening of the film *The Gods Must Be Crazy*.

is not an "act"; it is not a decision; it requires no deliberation. As Martin Heidegger already pointed out, much of the work of constitution happens *in situ*, while I'm engaged in *doing* something, trying to accomplish something, such that constitution is more pragmatic than intellectual. Indeed, for the most part, I don't constitute "objects" as something to merely observe; rather, I constitute things as *pragmata*—things to be *used* as I make my way in the world as an engaged *actor* rather than some sort of disengaged spectator. So when I walked into this coffee shop, I didn't "see" a chair and a table; I came here *to* write, and so *sat* on the chair and *put* my laptop on the table. The sitting and putting are exercises in constitution that did not engage my ratiocinative capacities for a second. The "horizons" of experience (my background expectations) are not something I have to consciously invoke or "think about" in order to constitute my world; they are operative without thinking. I am regularly "making sense" of my world on a register that has nothing to do with logic or even "knowledge" as usually defined. In this way, Merleau-Ponty surmises, I navigate my world with an "intelligence" that has nothing to do with intellectualism (*PP* 147).

However, these horizons and this background are not hardwired givens. While there is a certain givenness to the biological platform of the body that makes such constitution possible, my background horizons are acquired over time. My horizons have a history and represent a buildup of habituations and dispositions and inclinations to construe my world in certain ways. While my horizons are ineluctably social and shared—indeed, I acquire them *from others*—they are not a priori or universal. The same influx of intuitional data can be constituted in very different ways, and this is true with everything from the mundane to the moral. The givenness that I construe as a urinal can be construed by Duchamps as a work of art; the homeless person on the sidewalk can, in an instant, without thinking, be construed as a lazy leech on society or a sad testimony to the failure of mental health systems. My "background" is precisely that buildup of possible ways of construing the world that I have inherited and imbibed from others. Actually, even more strongly, my "background" is the buildup of habits and inclinations that dispose me to regularly construe my world in certain ways. And as I'll suggest below, Christian worship is, in some sense, construal training: it is a divine encounter that should, over time, effect "background" transformation by reshaping my horizons of constitution.

What Merleau-Ponty brings to this conversation is an even deeper appreciation for how the constitution of our experience is something that is carried out in and by the body. It's not just that constitution is carried out by a kind of mental unconscious; it's that the body itself is always already constituting my world precisely because the body is at home in the world. "To be a consciousness or rather *to be an experience*," Merleau-Ponty concludes, "is to hold inner communication with the world, the body, and other people, to be *with* them instead of being beside them" (*PP* 111, emphasis original). When we attend to our experience and take seriously our embodiment, we encounter, "beneath objective thought which moves among ready-made things, a first opening upon things without which there would be no objective knowledge" (*PP* 111). That "opening upon things" is the "pivot of the world" we encountered earlier: it is the lived body that *knows* without thinking (*PP* 149).

Merleau-Ponty highlights this distinct bodily comportment—this non-objective "knowing"—through a consideration of how we relate to *place*. "There is," he says, "a knowledge of place which is reducible to a sort of co-existence with that place, and which is not simply nothing, even though it cannot be conveyed by a description" (*PP* 121). He describes his own experience of place as an example: "When I move about my house, *I know without thinking about it* that walking towards the bathrooms means passing near the bedroom, that looking at the window means having the fireplace on my left, and in this small world each gesture, each perception is immediately located in relation to a great number of possible co-ordinates" (*PP* 149, emphasis added). I know place "antepredicatively" (*PP* 149)—prior to and without predication. "My flat is, for me, not a set of closely associated images [or representations]. It remains a familiar domain round about me only as long as I still have 'in my hands' or 'in

---

To Think About: Chicken Sexing and Nonconscious Knowledge

David Brooks's *The Social Animal* is a masterful encapsulation of recent research in cognitive science and psychology that has, in many ways, corroborated Merleau-Ponty's account of being-in-the-world—particularly the extent to which we "know" our world at a nonconscious level. While the cognitive unconscious is by no means infallible, it certainly enacts its own wisdom, its own "know-how." In fact, many of our conscious processes are nestled upon a functional confidence in the unconscious. Brooks cites a striking, memorable example of this:

> These perceptual skills can be astonishingly subtle. Many chicken farms employ professional chicken sexers. They look at newly hatched chicks and tell whether the chicks are male or female even though, to the untrained eye, the chicks all look the same. Experienced sexers can look at eight hundred to one thousand chicks an hour and determine their gender with 99 percent accuracy. How do they figure it out? They couldn't tell you. There is just something different about the males and females, and they know it when they see it.[1]

1. David Brooks, *The Social Animal: The Hidden Sources of Love, Character, and Achievement* (New York: Random House, 2011), 241.

my legs' the main distances and directions involved, and as long as from my body intentional threads run out towards it" (*PP* 150).

What if inhabiting the world *as* God's creation requires a similar "antepredicative" knowledge of place? How would we absorb such an understanding, such a "feel" for the world? Knowing the doctrine of creation will be insufficient; our inhabitation of the world *as* creation will require a deeper rehabituation. And that happens, I'll suggest, in the embodied practices of Christian worship.

Being-in-the-World with Schneider: A Case Study

In order to unpack this notion of bodily intelligence, let's follow Merleau-Ponty's close attention to a particular case—that of Schneider, a war veteran who has experienced brain damage that has transformed his orientation to the world. The *ab*normality of Schneider's bodily comportment is meant to highlight the *normal* being-in-the-world that we otherwise take for granted and fail to notice. Of interest here is the fact that Schneider navigates the world in ways that conform to the "intellectualist" model of the human person: he *thinks* his way through *everything*; he objectifies even his own body; he makes his way in the world as an information processor. Schneider is the poster child of intellectualism, a living, breathing Cartesian subject. But of course Merleau-Ponty will show that this is *not* how we normally navigate experience, hence pointing up the errors and limitations of the intellectualist model of the person.

For Schneider, something is missing in the *between*; something of his hybridity has gone awry. "In looking to his body to perform the movement for him he is like a speaker who cannot utter a word without following a text written beforehand" (*PP* 126). He can think, and he can move, but the normal "know-how" between the two is nonfunctional for him. "What he lacks," Merleau-Ponty concludes, "is neither motility nor thought, and we are brought to the recognition of something between movement as a third person process and thought as a representation of movement" (*PP* 126–27). This "something between" he calls "motor intentionality"—a way in which the body "aims" at the world, "means" the world, without deliberative processing. "When I motion my friend to come nearer," for example,

> my intention is not a thought prepared within me and I do not perceive the signal in my body. I beckon across the world, I beckon over there, where my friend is; the distance between us, his consent or refusal are immediately read in my gesture; there is not a perception followed by a movement, for both form a system which varies as a whole. If, for example, realizing that I am not going to be obeyed, I vary my gesture, we have here, not two distinct acts of consciousness. What happens is that I see my partner's unwillingness,

and my gesture of impatience emerges from this situation without any intervening thought. (*PP* 127)

Lacking this motor intentionality—this embodied intelligence between instinct and intellect—*all* of Schneider's experience has the distance and abstraction of scientific observation, which only highlights that this is *not* how we usually make our way in the world. For example,

> If a fountain pen is shown to the patient, in such a way that the clip is not seen, the phases of recognition are as follows: "It is black, blue and shiny," says the patient. "There is a white patch on it, and it is rather long; it has the shape of a stick. It may be some sort of instrument. It shines and reflects light. It could also be a coloured glass." The pen is then brought closer and the clip is turned towards the patient. He goes on: "It must be a pencil or a fountain pen." (He touches his breast pocket.) "It is put there, to make notes with." (*PP* 151)

What should be noted is that intellectualist models of the human person effectively suggest that we all process our experience in this way, if only at lightning speed. But Merleau-Ponty's point is not that Schneider is just *slow* in his intellectual processing of experience; rather, it is that we don't normally process our experience "intellectually" in this way. "Motor intentionality" is a shorthand to describe a different and irreducible mode of worldly "intelligence" that is characteristic of being-in-the-world. What's missing for Schneider is precisely what is operative in our everyday experience: an "intentional arc" that's operative under the hood of consciousness. "The life of consciousness—cognitive life, the life of desire or perceptual life—is subtended by an 'intentional arc' which projects round about us our past, our future, our human setting, our physical, ideological and moral situation, or rather which results in our being situated in all these respects" (*PP* 157). This intentional arc that subtends consciousness is not a merely passive receptivity to stimuli. It is a kind of *intentionality*—it aims at the world, it projects a "world" and gives significance to our experience such that we can find ourselves "in a situation." It's in this sense that Merleau-Ponty claims this motor intentionality makes things exist. This "motility" he even describes as our most basic form of intentionality. "Consciousness is in the first place not a matter of 'I think that' but of 'I can.'" So "movement is not thought about movement, and bodily space is not space thought of or represented" (*PP* 159). Rather, I move in a setting that is already "made sense of" on this order of motor intentionality.

We now begin to see how a different model of consciousness yields a very different approach to action. Action is intentional, but *not* because I have posited conscious "intentions" for myself through a process of intellectual deliberation; rather, my action is intentional because it is undertaken with

To Think About: Motor Intentionality in *Rise of the Planet of the Apes*

Merleau-Ponty's account of motor intentionality is a critique of "intellectualism"—a view of the human person that sees human beings as "thinkers" who make their way in the world by a kind of rational processing. Intellectualism sees only one kind of "intelligence" and sees all of our action as the outcome of deliberative thought processes. For the intellectualist, we *think* our way into action. Merleau-Ponty's argument is that intellectualism fails to recognize other modes by which we make sense of our world—other modes of "intelligence" that intend the world on a more visceral register. The body "knows" in its own way, and all the factors of my embodiment are part of the background against which I constitute my world. If my eyes were located at waist level, for example, I would inhabit an entirely different world. The bodily conditions of perception frame what counts as "intelligence."

But intellectualism is a hard habit to break, even for Hollywood. The recent blockbuster *Rise of the Planet of the Apes* purveys just this sort of intellectualism in its portrayal of the "rise" of a colony of simians capable of speech, eventually able to dominate humans. The story line ignores the bodily conditions of "intelligence" and construes rationality as a disembodied, brain-based capability. So a drug that merely boosts brain functioning is sufficient to make the apes "intelligent" *as humans are intelligent*: able to manipulate tools, to read social cues, to exhibit compassion, and ultimately even to speak. It is suggested that the apes are able to achieve human-like "intelligence" simply because the drug makes them *smarter*, and that they become able to speak because they *want* to.

But this is intellectualism at its best (or worst), assuming that intelligence is centered in "mind" and has a trickle-down effect on our action—as if being "smarter" is sufficient to transform our being-in-the-world. What's forgotten in this portrayal are the bodily conditions of our being-in-the-world: humans "intelligently" navigate their world because they have binocular vision, an upright posture, and (famously) opposable thumbs, all of which are then habituated to walking. They also have jaws and teeth and tongues that are conducive to speech. No amount of "smarts" can overcome the constraints of jaws and tongues that do not afford speech. So, ironically, a movie that illustrates the rise of apes to human intelligence forgets the bodily (animal)[1] basis of *human* being-in-the-world.

1. The term *animal* (as in "liturgical animal" or "imaginative animal") is just a philosophical way of naming our embodiment, of saying that we are not essentially souls or only minds but embodied thinkers that Aristotle called "rational animals." We aren't angels. Merleau-Ponty and Johnson press us to situate the rationality *in* our animality, in our embodiment. Alasdair MacIntyre makes the same point: "our whole initial bodily comportment towards the world is originally an animal comportment" (*Dependent Rational Animals*, 49). And we do not transcend that animality or embodiment: "when, through having become language-users, we under the guidance of parents and others restructure that comportment, elaborate and in new ways correct our beliefs and redirect our activities, *we never make ourselves independent of our animal nature and inheritance*. . . . Our second culturally formed language-using nature is a set of partial, but only partial, transformations of our first animal nature" (ibid., emphasis added).

a goal and project to which I am aimed—but that "aim" and directionality is fundamentally carried in my embodied comportment to the world.
My actions "make sense," not as conclusions to little syllogistic processes
I've carried out in my head, but as expressions of motor intentionality.[36]
"Consciousness," he argues, "is being-towards-the-thing through the intermediary[37] of the body. A movement is learned when the body has understood it, that is, when it has incorporated it into its 'world,' and to move
one's body is to aim at things through it; it is to allow oneself to respond
to their call, which is made upon it independently of any representation"
(PP 159–61). Our bodies both make and respond to the world—and do so
in ways that are independent of representations or deliberative processing,
yet still "intelligent," still with a "sense" about them. So our action is not
the outcome of ratiocination: "motility," Merleau-Ponty emphasizes, "is
not, as it were, a handmaid of consciousness." The body is not waiting for
a directive from the control center of the intellect. In many ways it already
"knows" where to go and what to do because it has absorbed a habitual
orientation to an environment.

What I have described above as "the imagination" is at this same juncture
of embodiment and habit, intentionality and construal. Merleau-Ponty
labels it with a more technical name, *praktognosia*, a "know-*how*": "Our
bodily experience of movement is not a particular case of knowledge; it
provides us with a way of access to the world and the object, with a 'praktognosia,' which has to be recognized as original and perhaps as primary.
My body has its world, or understands its world, without having to make
use of my 'symbolic' or 'objectifying function'" (PP 162). *Praktognosia*
names this *original* and *primary* "access to the world" by which I "understand" the world without recourse to discursive, propositional processing.
My movement and navigation of an environment is not an application of
what I know or a practical deduction from what I know. It is its own kind of
peculiar knowledge or understanding that is original (i.e., unique, irreducible) and primary (i.e., it undergirds and makes possible what we usually
count as "knowledge"). So motility, or motor intentionality, "possesses
the basic power of giving a meaning (*Sinngebung*[38]). Even if subsequently,
thought and perception of space are freed from motility and spatial being,

36. I should note that, for Merleau-Ponty, motor intentionality is more than just "motor
memory" (PP 161–62).
37. Even Merleau-Ponty struggles with available terms here. Of course given his argument
above, the body can't be just an "intermediary," an instrument of something *other* than the
body. As he suggests in the next sentence, the body "understands." His whole point is that we
are our bodies—while also *more* than our bodies. The use of "intermediary" language here I
chalk up to lexical limitations. This also explains the regular use of scare quotes as he tries to
talk of the "understanding" of the body, and so forth.
38. Husserl's term, translated as "constitution" above.

for us to be able to conceive space, it is in the first place necessary that we should have been thrust into it by our body" (PP 164, emphasis added).

Only an appreciation of this embodied know-how, this visceral knowledge, can enable us to understand how *habits* are acquired. And such habits are central to a liturgical anthropology. As we've just noted, our inclinations to construe and constitute the world are themselves habits—dispositional inclinations to perceive the world in a certain way, against the background of a specific horizon. Furthermore, at the heart of a liturgical anthropology is an appreciation for the centrality of habit in guiding and generating our *action*. Insofar as virtue (and vice) is at the center of a Christian account of action, we are on the terrain of *habits*. If we truly absorb the implications of Merleau-Ponty's embodied anthropology, then we'll need to challenge some of our (false) assumptions about habit acquisition. Indeed, "the acquisition of habit as a rearrangement and renewal of the corporeal schema presents great difficulties to traditional philosophies, which are always inclined to conceive synthesis as intellectual synthesis" (*PP* 164). In other words, if human persons are conceived as fundamentally thinking things, then "habit" will always be some sort of intellectual accomplishment—the outcome of thinking. Habit will be thought to originate as an act of the intellect. But this regularly proves itself both wrong and inadequate. For example, I don't acquire the habits of a dancer by analysis and reflection—though "theory" can serve my practice. But the *praktognosia* of the dancer is caught, not taught.[39] And this is not just true of motor functions: "we may extend to all habits what we have said about motor ones. In fact every habit is both motor and perceptual, because it lies, as we have said, between explicit perception and actual movement" (*PP* 175). The acquisition of habit happens on a register that eludes and exceeds the intellect. Nonetheless, it is still an acquisition, an embodied orientation that is acquired, that we *learn*.

As Merleau-Ponty provocatively puts it, "Habit expresses our power of dilating our being-in-the-world" (*PP* 166).[40] Such habit "is neither a form of knowledge nor an involuntary action" (PP 166). This insight is crucial. Once again Merleau-Ponty is prompting us to recognize the *between*, this

39. As Merleau-Ponty himself notes, "Before the formula of a new dance can incorporate certain elements of general motility, it must first have had, as it were, the stamp of movement set upon it. As has often been said, it is the body which 'catches' and 'comprehends' movement. The acquisition of a habit is indeed the grasping of a significance, but it is the motor grasping of a motor significance" (*PP* 165).

40. Merleau-Ponty suggests examples of such habituated "dilation": "A woman may, without any calculation, keep a safe distance between the feather in her hat and things which might break it off. She feels where the feather is just as we feel where our hand is." Similarly, "if I am in the habit of driving a car, I enter a narrow opening and see that I can 'get through' without comparing the width of the opening with that of the wings [*PP* was published in 1945!], just as I go through a doorway without checking the width of the doorway against that of my body" (*PP* 165).

middle space of our being-in-the-world—between instinct and intellect, between reflex and reflexivity. So habit is not "knowledge" in the usual sense; but neither is it just the *re*action of some unthinking, passive piece of meat. Habit "is knowledge in the hands, which is forthcoming only when bodily effort is made, and cannot be formulated in detachment from that effort" (*PP* 166). Of course this makes little sense given what we generally think of when we think of "knowledge." Merleau-Ponty is well aware of the cognitive dissonance here:

> We said earlier that it is the body which "understands" in the acquisition of habit. This way of putting it will appear absurd, if understanding is subsuming a sense-datum under an idea [the traditional "intellectualist" account of understanding], and if the body is an object. *But the phenomenon of habit is just what prompts us to revise our notion of "understand" and our notion of the body.* To understand is to experience the harmony between what we aim at and what is given, between the intention and the performance—and the body is our anchorage in the world. (*PP* 167, emphasis original)

The phenomenon of habit requires a more nuanced, layered anthropology that pushes back against the reductionisms of both intellectualism and materialism. If we are going to make sense of the centrality of habit in our orientation to the world, we'll have to both revise our notion of "understanding" to include the bodily know-how of *praktognosia* and reject the Cartesian view of the body as mere *res extensa*, as nonrational substance. I understand in ways I don't know, and it is my body that understands. If we're going to make sense of that, what we need is "a new meaning of the word 'meaning'" (*PP* 170). And if we are going to appreciate Christian faith as a kind of "know-*how*" that generates action oriented to the kingdom, we will need to grapple with Merleau-Ponty's account of the materiality of habit formation. We'll need to do the same if we are going to adequately appreciate just how secular liturgies inscribe in us their own *praktognosia*.

Erotic Comprehension: On Sex, Stories, and Silence

We can now appreciate just what's missing for poor Schneider: he lacks *praktognosia*, that hybrid know-how, that understanding of the world that we carry in our bodies and by which we viscerally intend—and thus give meaning to—our world. Two particular instances of Schneider's inability to "mean" the world in this way are both illuminating and suggestive.

The first is Schneider's inability to understand stories. He is able to receive, process, and recite facts, but he is unable to catch the gist of a narrative with all of its ups and downs, crises and climaxes, characters and emotions. "Indeed, if a story is told to the patient, it is observed that instead of grasping it as a melodic whole with down and up beats, with its characteristic rhythm or flow, he remembers it only as a succession of facts to be noted one by one" (*PP* 153). The absence of *praktognosia* means that Schneider also lacks an aesthetic sense that "understands" the truth that is carried, not just in a story's content, but in its style and narrative rhythms. For Schneider the words of a story "are devoid, *not*, it is true, of that intellectual meaning arrived at through analysis, but [of] that primary meaning reached through co-existence" (*PP* 154, emphasis added). He is unable to understand the "sense" of a story because he is *only* able to analyze it and process it intellectually. He lacks the narrative sense that affectively "understands" a story, and thus is unable to appreciate the distinctive force and truth of a story that exceeds and eludes the analysis of content. Schneider is unable to understand the *truth* of a story because stories are understood with a motor intentionality, on the register of *praktognosia*. There is an irreducibility to stories that can only be grasped by the imagination—but that is precisely what Schneider lacks.[41]

Schneider's strange inability highlights how we normally understand stories: "There is, then, in the normal subject, an essence of the story which emerges as it is told, without any express analysis, and this subsequently guides along any reproduction of the narrative. The story for [the normal subject] is a certain human event, recognizable by its style, and here the subject 'understands' because he has the power to live, beyond his immediate experience, through the events described." Whereas for Schneider the words of a story are just discrete signs to be deciphered for information, for those of us with the imagination to understand, the words of the story become "the transparent envelope of meaning *within* which [we] might live" (*PP* 153). The sense and force of the story is something we "catch" without analysis (indeed, analysis of the story will sometimes undercut our antepredicative grasp of it). Schneider filters a story through the intellect because he lacks the imagination to grasp its more holistic truth. He is processing with the mind something that he should feel in his bones. And

41. Schneider, in other words, actually processes the world as a "cognitivist" (where "cognitivism" represents a paradigm for "intelligence" that sees all intelligence as the logical manipulation of formal, symbolic representations). On this specific point, Hubert Dreyfus's critique of cognitivism in "Overcoming the Myth of the Mental: How Philosophers Can Profit from the Phenomenology of Everyday Expertise," *Proceedings and Addresses of the American Philosophical Association* 79 (2005), is directly relevant. Dreyfus points out that the cognitivist paradigm that governed research into artificial intelligence exhibits the paucity of this narrow construal of intelligence. Leaders in the field of AI, such as Marvin Minsky at MIT, thought that reproducing human intelligence in computers required the development of machines that could process millions of facts and thus "understand" the world. "In the early seventies, however, Minsky's AI lab ran into an unexpected problem. Computers couldn't comprehend the simple stories understood by four-year-olds" (48). Comprehending a story is something more and other than processing facts.

this is because he lacks that "between"—that know-how of *praktognosia*, the intentional arc that is embedded in our embodiment.

There is a synergy between stories and bodies, between poems and our physiology. There is an irreducible materiality to both that makes a difference. Materiality matters. So the poem is not just a disembodied idea or a distilled content.

> The poem is not independent of every material aid, and it would be irrecoverably lost if its text were not preserved down to the last detail. Its meaning is not arbitrary and does not dwell in the firmament of ideas: it is locked in the words printed on some perishable page. In that sense, like every work of art, the poem exists as a thing and does not eternally survive as does a[n ideal] truth. A novel, poem, painting or musical work are individuals, that is, beings in which the expression is indistinguishable from the thing expressed—their meaning, accessible only through direct contact. (*PP* 174–75)

The meaning of the work of art cannot be distinguished from its material form because such meaning is not just an ideal intellectual content that could be indiscriminately transposed from container to container. The material meaning of the work of art is bound up with its material form and is resonant with our own materiality, made sense of by our bodies. "It is in this sense," Merleau-Ponty concludes, "that our body is comparable to a work of art. It is a nexus of living meanings" (*PP* 175).[42] There is an incarnate significance at work here: the material meaning of the poem "means" uniquely because it is "meant" on the register of motor intentionality. The kinaesthetic and the poetic are linked.

A similar link exists between the kinaesthetic and the erotic. And given that a liturgical anthropology sees human persons as *desiring* creatures—as "erotic"[43] animals—we can also find suggestive analyses in Merleau-Ponty's account of sexuality. As with poetry and art, he is interested in sexuality because it is one of those "between" aspects of our being-in-the-world—a

---

42. Compare Nathan D. Mitchell's discussion of the body as "narrative" in Christian liturgy, in *Meeting Mystery: Liturgy, Worship, Sacraments* (Maryknoll, NY: Orbis Books, 2006), 182–83. As Mitchell provocatively suggests, "*our bodies make our prayers*. . . . After all, the mind will say anything one wants to hear; the body never lies. Liturgy speaks a language whose primary story—whose native narrative or *text*—is the *body itself*" (224, emphasis original). My thanks to John Witvliet for pointing me to this rich discussion which, in many ways, is a complement to my project here. Whereas Mitchell is in conversation with Derrida and Marion, I'm engaging Merleau-Ponty and Bourdieu (both absent from his work).

43. As I noted in *Desiring the Kingdom*, 52–55, Augustine's account of *agape* sees it as rightly ordered *eros*, so there is no inherent antithesis between *agape* and *eros*, though *eros* is obviously susceptible to all kinds of *dis*ordering. Indeed, one could suggest that contemporary culture is dominated by an ethos of disordered *eros*—which, in a sad, backhanded way, still testifies to our hunger and longing as desiring creatures. Sin does not shut down desire; it misdirects and disorders it.

"vital zone" that is operative "somewhere between automatic response [instinct] and representation [intellect]" (*PP* 180). And once again, Schneider's deficiencies offer insights about normal functioning in this regard. Schneider's world is sexually flat: there is no attraction, no arousal, no temptation, no flirtation. Touch does not stimulate him, nor do images awaken any libidinal drive. So what's wrong? Is this just a physiological problem? No, because it was his brain that was injured (specifically, a limited area of the occipital region). Sexuality, then, is not just some animal response to stimuli embedded in biological organs; sexuality is a product of *meaning*. "If sexuality in man were an autonomous reflex apparatus," Merleau-Ponty observes, "if the object of sexual desire affected some organ of pleasurable sensation anatomically defined, then the effect of the cerebral injury would be to free these automatic responses and take the form of accentuated sexual behavior" (*PP* 180). But that's not what happens. So the pathology suggests that sexuality is a realm of meaning *between* instinct and intellect. As such, an understanding of sexual meaning will, in turn, provide insight into "erotic perception" more broadly.

A woman's body doesn't mean anything sexually for Schneider because his own bodily complex is unable to *mean* the world sexually. "Perception has lost its erotic structure," Merleau-Ponty comments, "both spatially and temporally. What has disappeared from the patient is his power of projecting before himself a sexual world, of putting himself in an erotic situation." The spaces in which Schneider moves are never charged with sexual energy or tension or meaning because he is unable to constitute the world in that way. Tactile stimuli that he otherwise senses have "ceased to speak to his body." As one of my students commented, Schneider could do his homework in a strip club because "sexuality" is a meaning given to an environment—a "take" on a situation—and Schneider, lacking the "between" *praktognosia* to "get" this, simply fails to experience a situation as sexually charged. In other words, "the patient no longer asks, of his environment, this mute and permanent question which constitutes normal sexuality." This isn't because he can't see what's in front of him or somehow lacks the appropriate sense organs; in fact, he can calmly and coolly describe what's in front of him. But it is precisely this calm and cool detachment that confirms that his being-in-the-world is no longer sexually constituted: he is able to coolly perceive the situation "because he does not live it and is not caught up in it" (*PP* 181).

So it's not that Schneider lacks representations; nor is it that his body doesn't register sight or touch. The issue is something *between* the two. "At this stage one begins to suspect a mode of perception distinct from objective perception, a kind of significance distinct from intellectual significance which is not pure 'awareness of something.' Erotic perception is not a *cogitation* which aims at a *cogitatum*; through one body it aims at another body, and takes place in the world, not in a consciousness" (*PP* 181, emphasis original). Erotic perception is still a mode of intentionality insofar as it is a way of "meaning" the world, a way of intending the world *as* something. Such perception isn't just animal reflex or response to stimuli.[44] Merleau-Ponty is trying to account for a mode and register of meaning that is not intellectual or propositional or ratiocinative—a mode of perception that is distinct from thinking. When I perceive a situation as sexually charged or as having a kind of sexual significance, such perception is not the result of some deductive, rational process. For example, if I have been adequately socialized to pick up on certain cues, I will "know" when someone is flirting with me. Now, the sort of "training" that equips me to "know" such a sexual situation is rarely if ever didactic and explicit; it's rather a kind of know-how one "picks up." Furthermore, if someone were to ask me to articulate *how* I "knew" so-and-so was flirting with me, I might not be able to propositionally articulate the criteria by which I made such a judgment. Nonetheless, the inability to articulate such sexual "understanding" does not thereby prove the perception wrong or false—it can also indicate that "there is an erotic 'comprehension' not on the order of understanding" (*PP* 181). In fact, Merleau-Ponty hints that this is a comprehension *of* desire, a comprehension *by* desire.

An "erotic 'comprehension' not on the order of [intellectual] understanding": this encapsulates what I want to draw from Merleau-Ponty. In the second part of this book I will extend and extrapolate from this notion to suggest that a *Christian* "perception" of the world is also a kind of erotic comprehension—a visceral "between" way of meaning the world that constitutes our environment as God's good-but-broken creation that, in turn, calls to us and beckons for a response (cf. *PP* 160–61).[45] Such a constitution of the world is governed more by the imagination than by the intellect, which is why it is crucial to consider how we fuel and form the imagination. Cool, "objective" perception of the world will fail to properly *understand* the world and its call upon us—as the garden we are called to cultivate; as the tragic arena in which we are called to embody compassion and forgiveness; as the field of the Lord in which we are to both play and work, proclaim and praise. If we only learn to *think* "Christianly," we run the risk of becoming Schneiders: calmly and coolly seeing what's in front of us without really *perceiving* what's at stake.

This bodily constitution of the world is illustrated in a third case study that Merleau-Ponty analyzes: the rather Shakespearean case of a young

44. Nor is such erotic perception hardwired; while it is "automated," it has been acquired and is relative to cultural contexts and hence has to be *learned*.

45. Cf. Jean-Louis Chrétien, *The Call and the Response*, trans. Aaron Davenport (Bronx, NY: Fordham University Press, 2004).

woman whose mother has forbidden her from seeing again the young man with whom she is in love. At first she cannot sleep; then she loses her appetite; and finally, she loses her speech. This loss of speech also happened after an earlier trauma in the girl's life—an earthquake that induced fright (*PP* 185–86). Refusing the simplistic, dualistic account offered by Freudian analysis, Merleau-Ponty once again sees in this case a backhanded attestation to a kind of emotional constitution of our world. Specifically, he notes that speech is fundamentally a means of relationality, "those relations with others having the spoken word as their vehicle" (*PP* 186). Her silence, then, is a refusal of relationality given the loss of the relation so precious to her. But note how Merleau-Ponty describes the situation: "In so far as the emotion elects to find its expression in loss of speech, this is because of all bodily functions speech is the most intimately linked with communal existence, or, as we shall put it, with co-existence. Loss of speech, then, stands for the refusal of co-existence" (*PP* 186). It is the *emotion* that finds expression, not a thought or an idea.

In other words, her silence is not a *choice* she has deliberately made. She is not refusing to talk, giving her family the silent treatment (like Dwayne in *Little Miss Sunshine*). She is unable to talk—and hence relate—because another part of her, as it were, is refusing this relation. So her silence is somewhere *between* a conscious choice and a physiological lack. In fact, Merleau-Ponty reconsiders the notion that the silence "expresses" something other than itself, since that might mistakenly convey an intellectualist account of what's going on, as if the young woman is "trying to say something" that she has in her head. Interestingly, he avails himself of language traditionally associated with the sacraments in order to avoid an intellectualist account.

> The body does not constantly express the modalities of existence in the way that stripes indicate rank, or a house-number a house: the sign here does not only convey its significance, it is filled with it; it is, in a way, what it signifies. . . . The sick girl does not mime with her body a drama played out "in her consciousness." By losing her voice she does not present a public version of an "inner state," she does not make a "gesture" like that of the head of a state shaking hands with the engine driver and embracing a peasant, or that of a friend who takes offence and stops speaking to me. To have lost one's voice is not to keep silence: one keeps silence only when one can speak. (*PP* 186–87)

The young woman is not simply trying to convey or express something she knows or thinks; her silence is not a sign that merely points to some interior meaning. Her silence *means* something in itself, and that meaning is not intended by her intellect but rather is meant by her whole person, even in ways that elude her intellect and faculty of choice. Her loss of voice is not "voluntary," but neither is it an injury that befalls her nor a disease that afflicts her. The case complicates and challenges all of our intellectualist habits of mind about the will and "intentional" action.[46] There is a mode of intentionality here that is not on the order of deliberation or articulation; and there is a kind of "action" here that is not the outcome of intentional deliberation. But her loss of speech is nonetheless still intentional—still meaningful and meaning-making.

This is why the "solution" to her problem is not a matter of knowledge. "In treating this condition," Merleau-Ponty observes, "psychological medicine[47] does not act on the patient by making [her] *know* the origin of [her] illness: sometimes a touch of the hand puts a stop to the spasms and restores to the patient [her] speech and the same procedure, having acquired a ritual significance, will subsequently be enough to deal with fresh attacks" (*PP* 189). Even if the patient could intellectually understand and process her loss of speech, this would not adequately reach the visceral level on which her silence "means" something. "Neither the symptom nor cure is worked out at the level of objective or positing consciousness, but below that level" (*PP* 189).[48] Instead, any response needs to meet her in her embodiment. And such a tactile response is what Merleau-Ponty rightly calls "ritual."

Any adequate response to the young woman's loss of speech will need to be kinaesthetic—it will need to address her being-in-the-world by connecting with the body. When Merleau-Ponty invokes ritual, he means just this kind of tactile, bodily regimen that reorients our being-in-the-world.

> Precisely because my body can shut itself off from the world, it is also what opens me out upon the world and places me in a situation there. The momentum of existence towards others, towards the future, towards the world can be restored as a river unfreezes. The girl will recover her voice, not by an intellectual effort or by an abstract decree of the will, but through a conversion in which the whole of her body makes a concentrated effort in the form of a genuine gesture. . . . The memory or the voice is recovered when the body once more opens itself to others or to the past, when it opens the

46. "Will presupposes a field of possibilities among which I choose: here is Peter, I can speak to him or not. But if I lose my power of speech, Peter no longer exists for me as an interlocutor, sought after or rejected; what collapses is the whole field of possibilities" (*PP* 188).

47. While I am not able to explore them here, Merleau-Ponty's account—and a liturgical anthropology—clearly has implications for how we think about counseling and psychology. "Nouthetic" or "biblical" counseling would be a stark example of an intellectualist model of the human person. See Jay E. Adams, *Competent to Counsel* (Grand Rapids: Zondervan, 1986).

48. I'm encouraged that even Merleau-Ponty has to resort to the clunky picture of "levels" of consciousness. We are always working with inadequate metaphors here (cf. Kahneman's admission regarding the inadequacy but heuristic value of "System 1" and "System 2" in *Thinking, Fast and Slow*, 20–21).

To Think About: "Catching" Sleep

In the context of discussing this mode of intentionality between intellect and instinct, and a kind of action that is neither voluntary nor involuntary, Merleau-Ponty points to an intriguing analogy: *sleep*. I cannot "choose" to *fall* asleep. The best I can do is choose to put myself in a posture and rhythm that *welcomes* sleep. "I lie down in bed, on my left side, with my knees drawn up; I close my eyes and breathe slowly, putting my plans out of my mind. But the power of my will or consciousness stops there" (*PP* 189). I *want* to go to sleep, and I've chosen to climb into bed—but in another sense sleep is not something under my control or at my beckoned call. "I call up the visitation of sleep by imitating the breathing and posture of the sleeper. . . . There is a moment when sleep 'comes,' settling on this imitation of itself which I have been offering to it, and *I succeed in becoming what I was trying to be*" (*PP* 189–90, emphasis added). Sleep is a gift to be received, not a decision to be made. And yet it is a gift that requires a *posture* of reception—a kind of active welcome. What if being filled with the Spirit had the same dynamic? What if Christian practices are what Craig Dykstra calls "habitations of the Spirit" precisely because they *posture* us to be filled and sanctified? What if we need to first adopt a bodily posture in order to become what we are trying to be?

---

way to co-existence and once more (in the active sense) acquires significance beyond itself. (*PP* 191)

Her reorientation is a reconfiguration of her being-in-the-world; but this is not effected by acquiring new knowledge. It is a rehabituation that is effected in and with the body. Intellectual effort and rational deliberation will not save her; she will be transformed by "genuine gesture"—by the sort of tactile, gut-level ritual already described above. If her world is going to mean differently—and *call* differently—then her being-in-the-world will require a kinaesthetic conversion because it is the body that "establishes our first consonance with the world." The "body expresses its existence at every moment"—but Merleau-Ponty immediately cautions that this is not some interior "mind" choosing to externally express something merely through a medium. At work in the body is a "primary process of signification in which the thing expressed does not exist apart from the expression, and in which the signs themselves induce their significance externally." Perhaps unwittingly (though I doubt it),[49] Merleau-Ponty has

---

49. Since Merleau-Ponty pursues the analogy in more detail later: "Just as the sacrament not only symbolizes, in sensible species, an operation of Grace, but is also the real presence of God, which it causes to occupy a fragment of space and communicates to those who eat of the consecrated bread, in the same way the sensible not only has a motor and vital significance, but is nothing other than a certain way of being in the world suggested to us from some point in space, and seized and acted upon by our body, provided that it is capable of doing so" (*PP* 246).

just rearticulated the classic Augustinian understanding of the sacraments as not just symbols of some other reality but as the very presence and effectual power of that which they signify. So if the body is like a poem or work of art, we might also suggest that the body is like a sacrament. Which perhaps explains why Merleau-Ponty describes this meaning of the body as "incarnate significance": "In this way the body expresses total existence, not because it is an external accompaniment to that existence, but because existence realizes itself in the body." So "the relation of expression to thing expressed, or of sign to meaning is not a one-way relationship like that between original text and translation. Neither body *nor existence* can be regarded as the original of the human being, since they presuppose each other, and because the body is solidified or generalized existence, and existence a perpetual incarnation" (*PP* 192, emphasis original). Before (and as) we think about the world we already *mean* it at gut level.

Picturing Kinaesthetic Conversion in *The King's Speech*

To reconfigure our very comportment to the world requires a rehabituation of motor intentionality. And because we are not merely intellectual beings, such rehabituation requires a kinaesthetic conversion that touches on the "between" of our incarnate significance. It won't be enough to change our minds; we need to somehow convert our bodies, recalibrate our being-in-the-world at the nexus of body and mind. Conceptual or intellectual changes will be insufficient to effect real change; similarly, merely mechanical approaches will be inadequate. Merleau-Ponty's holistic account emphasizes the quintessential of the both/and, of the "between."

Such a kinaesthetic conversion is pictured quite powerfully in the Academy Award–winning film *The King's Speech*. The story, you might recall, centers around the relationship of George VI, the Duke of York, and Lionel Logue, an Australian colonial who has set himself up as a speech therapist. George VI is beset by a debilitating stammer, which is proving a challenge given that his royal vocation requires public speaking of the highest order. And the specter of inheriting the crown looms over him because of the illness of his father and the embarrassing and compromising shenanigans of his older brother, Edward. So George's faithful cheerleader, his wife Elizabeth, has been searching for therapists and speech pathologists who can help her husband. But to no avail: all of them treat the problem reductionistically. Some are "mechanists" who think the problem is merely biological, something to be cured by tongue exercises or other bodily gymnastics (or, ridiculously, by smoking to relax the throat). Others, most notably George's father, King George V, are decided "intellectualists" in their approach to the problem. For these intellectualists, young George, known as "Bertie" to his family, simply needs to muster the will to speak properly, as if he lacked the courage or fortitude, as if his stuttering was a kind of verbal laziness, as if it came down to a matter of simply *choosing* to speak properly. Thus King George V regularly berates his son. "Enunciate!" he shouts.

This comes to a head after one of the king's Christmas broadcasts over the new "wireless" technology. Upon finishing his speech, a model of eloquence, he turns to Bertie and mocks him with what might mistakenly appear to be encouragement: "Easy when you *know* how." (Note the emphasis.)

So the king sets up Bertie for some practice. "Have a go yourself," he exhorts, admonishing him to face the microphone. "Sit up, straight back, face boldly up to the bloody thing and stare it square in the eye as you would any Englishman. Show who's in command!"

Bertie's efforts are pointless and hopeless. But his father tries to impress upon him the urgency of his being able to command his tongue. The king will soon be dead, and Edward's indiscretions will lead to his implosion. All of this while Hitler and Stalin are marching across the continent. "Who will stand between us, the jackboots, and the proletarian abyss?" his father asks. "You." Bertie has to face the fact that he will be doing a lot more of this. And so once again, King George barks at his stammering son: "Get it out, boy! Just take your time. Form your words carefully. Relax! Just *try* it! DO IT!"

As one might imagine, neither mechanism nor intellectualism affects Bertie's stammer, and it is the failure of every other strategy that brings Elizabeth to the rather seedy environs of Mr. Logue's office. Logue's "antipodean" methods are considered unorthodox, but at the end of her rope, Her Royal Highness has ventured outside the fold to working-class London in search of a cure.

The first encounter between Elizabeth and Lionel is fraught with a physicality that we can feel without realizing it. Each of them exhibits a very different bodily comportment to the world, each of which carries its own worldview. Elizabeth is circumspect, tight, clipped, and distant—touching anything seems to be an invasion of her authority. Lionel is gangly and fluid, gregarious and familiar. He is comfortable in his own skin, until he realizes that the "Mrs. Johnson" with whom he is speaking is, in fact, Her Royal Highness, the Duchess of York. Nonetheless, the rules for treatment cannot be compromised: if the Duke of York is to be treated by Mr. Logue, it will have to be in his office, in an air of familiarity and equality. "My castle, my rules," Lionel stipulates. Elizabeth agrees.

Lionel, while trying to show appropriate deference to His Royal Highness, nonetheless quickly establishes a space of equality by insisting on calling George by his familiar name, "Bertie"—to Bertie's chagrin. But Bertie becomes even more uncomfortable as this first appointment takes what seems to be a strange turn when Lionel deigns to ask him personal questions.

"What was your earliest memory?" Lionel asks.

"I'm not here to discuss personal matters," Bertie replies tersely, then insists with a temper. But Lionel won't be dissuaded from this line of questioning.

"When did the defect begin?" Though Bertie suggests he's always spoken with a stutter, Lionel assures him that no infant starts to speak with a stammer. "So when did yours start?" Bertie can't remember not doing it.

Suffice it to say that the first appointment does not go well. Indeed, Lionel's unorthodox procedures irritate the Duke of York and seem like quackery compared to the
"mechanists" he's seen in the past. What Bertie doesn't realize, of course, is that Lionel is
trying to dig down to his *story*. Lionel, we might say, is something of a phenomenologist, a pre-incarnation of Merleau-Ponty who discerns that Bertie's stammer is *both*
bodily *and* psychological. It is a part of his being-in-the-world, arising at the intersection of body and mind, rooted in the "between-ness" of his incarnate existence. And if
there's going to be a change for Bertie, it's going to be a kinaesthetic conversion at the
intersection of his body and his story. When Bertie eventually returns to Lionel seeking help, we can see Lionel's regimen working at this same intersection. So, on the one
hand, Lionel addresses the body. Here we see a humorous montage of physical exercises and material regimens to which Bertie is subjected. We see His Royal Highness
shaking his jowls, hopping up and down, swaying his arms in looping arcs while humming "Jack and Jill," even lying on the floor doing diaphragm exercises with the Duchess
of York on his belly (which she quite enjoys!). The scenes of these visceral disciplines are
spliced with scenes of his public speaking, which are showing some signs of improvement. But he's in no danger of being described as eloquent.

Which is why, on the other hand, Lionel is fundamentally interested in getting to
the bottom of Bertie's story, drilling down to the narrative that he now carries in his
body, the tale that has tied his tongue. There seems to be a new openness and vulnerability when Bertie visits Lionel after the death of his father. King George V's passing
has stirred relational depths in his son, pried loose something that had congealed in his
unconscious. In the distraction of handling Lionel's son's model planes, Bertie begins
to open up: "I always wanted to build models." The wistful way he says this gives us the
impression that it never happened—either because it wasn't allowed or because his
father was never available to help. In the course of the conversation, he admits that his
father encouraged David, his older brother, to tease Bertie about his stuttering, as if he
could be shamed out of his stammer. As Bertie continues to recount aspects of his family history, his stammer returns and halts the conversation. Lionel encourages him to
sing his way through the stammer.

But Lionel notices something else as Bertie is applying glue to a wing on the model
plane: "Are you naturally right handed?" he asks.

"Left," Bertie replies. "I was punished. Now I use the right."

"Any other corrections?" Lionel inquires.

"Knock knees," Bertie admits. He was forced to wear metal splints to correct the
problem, a "solution" that was agonizing for him. But "straight legs now," he notes.

As Lionel tentatively explores Bertie's story and family dynamics, he wonders who
Bertie felt closest to. His closest relationships, it turns out, are with nannies. "Not my
first nanny, though," Bertie remembers, painfully. "She loved David . . . hated me. When I
was presented to my parents for the daily viewing, she'd . . ."

The stammering produced by the memory halts him. Lionel encourages him to sing
through the story. And so to the tune of "Swanee River," Bertie recounts the painful
pattern:

"She pinch me so I'd cry, and be sent away at once, then she wouldn't feed me, *far far away* . . ." He then resumes the story in his regular voice: "Took three years for my parents to notice. As you can imagine, it caused some stomach problems. Still."

This brief testimony—the recounting of this personal *story*—will be a turning point for Bertie. For Lionel realizes that the only adequate prescription for Bertie's stammer is re-narration. The stutter burbles up from a submerged story that Bertie carries in his gut. If he is going to speak differently, speak *well*, then he needs to tell himself a different story—at that unconscious level at which we all tell ourselves stories we never hear. Any hope for Bertie's eloquence is bound up with a reconfiguration of his very bodily comportment to the world. But that is bound up with a story that is submerged in his body. If Bertie is going to find his voice he needs to first be re-narrated into a different story.

The urgency of this has become amplified because now, to his horror, Bertie has become King George VI. As his father predicted, he must speak up. Indeed, he must now give the speech of his life as Britain enters a war with Germany, doing battle with the jackboots that have been marching across Europe and thus confronting that demonic orator, Adolf Hitler. So after a hurtful episode, the new king returns apologetically to Lionel for help as he prepares to deliver a Christmas speech.

"Like your dad used to," Lionel observes. "But he's not here anymore."

"Yes he is," Bertie retorts. "He's on that shilling I just gave you."

Lionel gets at something deeper here, sees an opening for re-narration: "Easy enough to give away. You don't have to carry him around in your pocket. Or your brother. You don't need to be afraid of the things that scared you when you were five. You're very much your own man, Bertie. Your face is next."

Lionel is inviting Bertie into a different story, but that invitation to re-narrate his being-in-the-world is not unconnected to the bodily regimen that recalibrates his "habit-body," as Merleau-Ponty calls it. Indeed, both of these intersect: it is because we carry a story in our bones that we comport ourselves to the world in certain ways. Lionel is trying to retrain Bertie's body and soul with a story that will sound familiar to us: "Be not afraid." When Lionel finally coaxes from Bertie, on the eve of his coronation, the shouted claim, "I have a voice!" Lionel's quiet reply reiterates this new story: "You're the bravest man I know. And you'll make a bloody good king."

The Primacy of Perception

"Our own body is in the world as the heart is in the organism." Reflection on this analogy is expansive: my body, the embodied "I," is what nourishes and pumps life into my world. "It keeps the visible spectacle constantly alive, it breathes life into it and sustains it inwardly, and with it forms a system" (*PP* 233). In an important sense, there is no "world"

without my body—no environment unless and until my incarnate significance constitutes what gives itself *as* a world. This is why the "theory of
the body schema is, implicitly, a theory of perception." In other words,
the phenomenology of perception is fundamentally a phenomenology of
incarnate significance, of bodily being-in-the-world. "We have relearned
to feel our body; we have found underneath the objective and detached
knowledge of the body that other knowledge we have of it in virtue of
its always being with us and of the fact that we are our body." Precisely
because "we perceive the world with our body," we are now in a position
to appreciate that "the body is a natural self and, as it were, the subject of
perception" (*PP* 239). This is not a rejection of intellection or "objective
thought" per se; neither does Merleau-Ponty mean to consign us to mere
biological responses to stimuli. Indeed, his appreciation of the centrality
of the body in the constitution of meaning is decidedly antireductionist,
resisting both materialism and intellectualism.[50] In fact, in a sense, perception *precedes* stimuli; before anything *counts* as a stimulus my world must
first be constituted in such a way that what's given stimulates. We saw this
above in the case of Schneider: various inputs, while "objectively" present,
simply didn't *count* as stimuli because he couldn't *perceive* the world sexually. Without perception, there are no stimuli; instead, "the world cease-
lessly assails and beleaguers subjectivity as waves wash round a wreck on
the shore" (*PP* 241). What I respond to as a stimulus has been constituted
as such by horizons of perception that are pre-intellectual. "Apart from
the probing of my eye or my hand, and before my body synchronizes
with it, the sensible is nothing but a vague beckoning" (*PP* 248). So "all
knowledge takes its place within the horizons opened up by perception"
(*PP* 241). There are many modes of knowing, and "objective" knowledge
is certainly one of them—but objective knowledge is made possible by a
primary perception that is not on the order of thinking.

   This perception is a kind of attunement that is prior to knowledge as we
generally think of it. But it is still an understanding of the world insofar
as it is a way of intending the world. Our perception of the world is not
a kind of detached observation—the world is not a specimen that we put
under the microscope of our detached gaze; rather, perception—that experience of the world that is shot through with incarnate significance—is
"literally a form of communion" (*PP* 246). It is our most fundamental way
of being-in-the-world as being-*with*-the-world. The picture of perception

---

50. While I have highlighted Merleau-Ponty's constant critique of intellectualism, he also
pushes back on empiricism: "Perception owes nothing to what we know in other ways about
the world, about *stimuli* as physics describes them and about the sense organs as described by
biology" (*PP* 240). In other words, perception is not just impressions that hit bodily receptors.
To avoid such reductionism, Merleau-Ponty will even sometimes avail himself of the language
of "soul" (*PP* 99, 102).

here is fundamentally relational, and *not* because Merleau-Ponty is primarily concerned with how I perceive other persons. Rather, he is suggesting that my perception is a kind of "communion" because I am not just *in* the world; I am *with* the world. This world to which I'm attuned is my home, my dwelling. There is a primordial embededness that characterizes incarnate significance—an "opening upon" things in virtue of "a kind of primordial contract and through a gift of nature, with no effort made on my part" (*PP* 251). I am not some foreign visitor to the world of experience; I don't need to "gain access"; I'm at home in the world, *made* to perceive the world. Such perception and sensation, he concludes, is "coexistence or communion. The sensation of blue is not the knowledge or positing of a certain identifiable *quale* throughout all the experiences of it which I have, as the geometer's circle is the same in Paris and Tokyo" (*PP* 249). My experience and perception of the blue in the postcard above my desk is nothing like my relation to the calendar beside it. The calendar is a shorthand way to objectively organize my time; it conveys to me at a glance information that I process in ways that are largely detached and uninvolved. But the blue in that postcard will always bring me back to the sliver of blue sky that cracked through for just a moment above Lake Coniston as I peered from Ruskin's turret at Brantwood. That same blue is then infused with the poetry of Wordsworth and the charged world of the Romantics and not for a moment would I think I could ever explain or account for what I perceive in that blue. But that doesn't mean it doesn't count as meaningful or even as truth. My perception of that blue is still *intentional*, Merleau-Ponty would emphasize, but in such a way that I *relate* to it rather than just observe it. It is this *involvement* that he tries to capture when he describes perception as communion and co-existence: "If the qualities radiate around them a certain mode of existence, if they have the power to cast a spell and what we called just now a sacramental value, this is because the sentient subject does not posit them as objects, but enters into a sympathetic relation with them" (*PP* 248).

There is a wholeness to our experience that is the work of consciousness—an "act" of constitution—but neither the consciousness nor the act are deliberate. They are not something we "think about." Perception, as Merleau-Ponty puts it, is not "an incipient science"; that is, we don't "put together" our experience by deduction. "Though perception brings together our sensory experiences into a single world, it does not do so in the way that scientific colligation gathers together objects or phenomena, but in the way that binocular vision grasps one sole object" (*PP* 268). This isn't something we think through or occurently process. It is, in other words, a "notional" unity: "We pass from double vision to the single object, not through an inspection of the mind, but when the two eyes cease to function each on its own account and are used as a single organ by one single gaze. It is not the epistemological subject who brings about the synthesis, but the body, when it escapes from dispersion, pulls itself together and tends by all means in its power towards one single goal of its activity, and when one single intention is formed in it through the phenomenon of synergy." There is a certain "work" being done in so constituting—and thus experiencing—the world, but it's as if it is carried out by operatives who don't report to our intellectual awareness and whom we have trusted (and trained!) without ever consciously employing. What's at work here is a mode of intentionality that "is not a thought"; it is an intentionality— and hence a meaning-making—that "does not come into being through the transparency of any consciousness, but takes for granted all the latent knowledge of itself that my body possesses" (*PP* 270). Here is a knowledge or understanding of the world that is carried in my body. "My body is the fabric into which all objects are woven" (*PP* 273). So "in perception we do not think the object and we do not think ourselves thinking it, we are given over to the object and we merge into this body which is better informed than we are about the world" (*PP* 277).[51]

And it is just this bodily attunement and perception that underwrites "objective" knowledge and intellectual reflection. It is not *either* perception *or* knowledge. It's not a question of choosing to settle for some crude, unthinking kinaesthetic perception of the world and thus forgoing intellectual reflection; rather, I perceive in order to understand. Merleau-Ponty has emphasized that perception is not just some kind of crude, ham-fisted theorizing of the world; rather, perception is a fundamentally different (and primary) way of intending the world, of *meaning* the world *with* the body. Perception does not just provide the raw materials to be processed by intellection. However, that doesn't mean there is no relation between perception and objective knowledge. In fact, the latter is rooted in the former as its condition of possibility. Reflection is embedded in "primary perception" that is "non-thetic [i.e., non-positing], pre-objective and pre-conscious experience" (*PP* 281). Merleau-Ponty's account does not denigrate reflection or devalue objective knowledge. He simply *situates* it and emphasizes its dependence on the primacy of perception. So it's not a matter of valorizing perception *over* reflection but of reconceiving the nature and task of reflection. What Merleau-Ponty offers, then, is a new account of what we're doing when we "know" the world objectively in a reflective mode. "The task of a radical reflection," he concludes, "the kind that aims at self-comprehension, consists, paradoxically enough, in recovering the unreflective experience of the world, and subsequently reassigning to it the

---

51. Here Merleau-Ponty falls into that regrettable habit of clumsily distinguishing "we" from "our bodies," when previously he has clearly emphasized that we don't *have* bodies, but we *are* our bodies (and more).

verificatory attitude and reflective operations, and displaying reflection as one possibility of my being" (*PP* 280). So it's a matter of coming up with a *theory* of perception that does justice to the fact that we don't, first and foremost, *think* about the world. "Hence reflection does not itself grasp its full significance unless it refers to the unreflective fund of experience *which it presupposes*, upon which it draws, and which constitutes for it a kind of original past, a past which has never been a present" (*PP* 281–82, emphasis original). And so we are back to Proust: the intellect is called upon to establish its own inferiority or secondarity.

If Merleau-Ponty is right, and obviously I think he is, then we need to constantly ask ourselves the question, How do we *teach* the body? If "my body and my senses are precisely that familiarity with the world born of habit, that implicit or sedimentary body of knowledge" (*PP* 277), then we need to ask, How is the body habituated? How do we recruit the imagination that is embedded and carried in our bodily comportment to the world? How is the body trained to *perceive* the world? Enter Pierre Bourdieu.

2

The Social Body

I don't think concepts have any relevance in religion. Analogy is not concept. It is community. It is resonance. . . . I think of Jasper, Bergson, and Buber as very inferior conceptualist types, quite out of touch with the immediate analogical awareness that begins in the senses and is derailed by concepts or ideas.[1]

The Critique of Theoretical Reason

A liturgical anthropology is a strange beast: it offers a theoretical model of the human person that emphasizes that we are not primarily theorizers. It is an intellectual project that argues for the relativization of the intellect. A liturgical anthropology is a theoretical attempt to appreciate our pretheoretical navigation of the world—a *theory* about the primacy and irreducibility of *practice*.

As such, the development of a liturgical anthropology parallels Pierre Bourdieu's project in the social sciences. In particular, Bourdieu's fieldwork led him to a realization of the limits of anthropology as a science: while the anthropologist is ultimately trying to understand a (foreign) world of practice, his methods involve a distance and objectification that effectively

---

1. Marshall McLuhan, in a letter to Fr. John W. Mole, OMI, in *The Medium and the Light: Reflections on Religion*, ed. Eric McLuhan and Jacek Szklarek (Toronto: Stoddart, 1999), 69. McLuhan puts this quite starkly—more contrastively than I would. But the very contrast is provocative.

75

erase the integrity of that "world." "It took me a long time to understand," Bourdieu confesses, "that the logic of practice can only be grasped through constructs which destroy it as such, so long as one fails to consider the nature, or rather the effects, of instruments of objectification."[2] This is because the theoretical stance of the social scientist is characterized by an "epistemological break"—a stepping back from involvement in a community of practice to reflect on and "understand" the practice from outside, in a sense. This epistemological break introduces a distance that is foreign to those immersed in the community of practice—an "objectifying" distance not characteristic of practitioners. This is why the epistemological break is also "a social discontinuity" (LP 26, 33): theoretical observers, by their very distance and objectivity, have effectively excused themselves from the community of practice, even if they might be present for the ritual or involved in the ceremony. So the very project of a "scientific" understanding of practice seems to be doomed from the start.

But Bourdieu wasn't willing to give up on science itself or castigate theoretical reflection as inherently problematic (LP 11). There is a virtue to theoretical reflection on practice and the attempt to understand what's at stake in communities of practice. So it's not a matter of choosing between theory or practice. Instead, what Bourdieu is after is an adequate theory of practice that is a sort of two-edged sword: on the one hand, this calls for an adequate understanding of the nature of practice as its own irreducible know-how; on the other hand, an adequate theory of practice requires a theoretical account of what we're doing when we scientifically reflect on practice.[3] What social scientists had failed to do, he argues, is objectively consider their own objectifying relation to what they study (LP 14–15); they had never made the *practice* of study a matter of study. Recognizing the limits of a science of practice is not reason to abandon science but rather an occasion to reconsider the assumptions that science brings to its consideration of practice.[4]

Thus Bourdieu describes his task, with a Kantian echo, as a "critique of theoretical reason." A critique of theoretical reason is not a rejection

2. Pierre Bourdieu, *The Logic of Practice*, trans. Richard Nice (Stanford, CA: Stanford University Press, 1990), 11; hereafter cited as *LP*.

3. "Social science must not only, as objectivism would have it, break with native experience and the native representation of that experience, but also, by a second break, call into question the presuppositions inherent in the position of the 'objective' observer who, seeking to interpret practices, tends to bring into the object the principles of his relation to the object, as is shown for example by the privileged status he gives to communicative and epistemic functions" (*LP* 27).

4. As Bourdieu himself later suggests, we might consider this relationship between theory and practice an analogue to the relation between theology and worship. So what Bourdieu recognizes as the unique challenges of social science and reflection *on* social practice would be analogous to theological reflection on liturgical practice. It might help some readers to keep this analogy in mind as we work through Bourdieu's analysis.

of theoretical reason but rather, per Kant, a consideration of its limits and conditions. Such "critical reflexion on the limits of theoretical understanding is not intended to discredit theoretical knowledge." Rather, the point is to give theoretical interpretation of practice "a solid basis by freeing it from the distortions arising from the epistemological and social conditions of its production"; that is, "it aims simply to bring to light the theory of practice which theoretical knowledge implicitly applies and so to make possible a truly scientific knowledge of practice and of the practical mode of knowledge" (*LP* 27). The problem isn't theoretical reflection on practice; the question is whether our theoretical analysis of practice is working with assumptions that honor the unique nature of "practical knowledge"—the irreducible "logic of practice." For example, interpretations of practice too often smuggle in assumptions that effectively construe practitioners as thinkers, constituting the world of practice in the image of the scientist. Bourdieu describes this as "intellectualocentrism" but emphasizes that science need not be inherently intellectualist (*LP* 29). One can imagine theory otherwise; one can engage in constructive, theoretical interpretations *of* practice informed by assumptions that do justice to the irreducible logic of practice. It is just such a theory of practice that Bourdieu is after, and it is directly germane to the task of a liturgical anthropology.

At one point Bourdieu describes his goal as "a theory . . . of what it is to be 'native'": "One has quite simply to bring into scientific work and into the theory of practices that it seeks to produce, a theory—which cannot be found through theoretical experience alone—of what it is to be 'native,' that is, to be in that relationship of 'learned ignorance,' of immediate but unselfconscious understanding which defines the practical relationship to the world" (*LP* 18–19). Natives—that is, practitioners "unselfconsciously" embedded in a community of practice—are not primarily theorists. They are not "thinking" their way through the world; they are not reflecting on what they're doing—which is precisely why any adequate interpretation of what's going on *in* such a community of practice will need to resist the temptation to construe practitioners as implicit theorizers. Instead, a theory of what it is to be "native" will need to honor and appreciate a "pre-logical logic of practice" (*LP* 19).[5]

Bourdieu's "critique of theoretical reason" has two different targets in view: what he describes as "objectivism" and "subjectivism," or what we might call intellectualism and voluntarism. Against intellectualist accounts of practice, Bourdieu aims to articulate a nuanced theory of practice that

5. The "pre-logical logic of practice" is to be distinguished from "logical logic," the logic of objectification. "And this difference, which is inherent in intellectual activity and the intellectual condition, is no doubt what intellectual discourse has least chance of accurately expressing" (*LP* 19). Welcome to the tensions of the Cultural Liturgies project!

does justice to the irreducibility of practical knowledge—that sort of know-how that is "carried" in practice. As such, he will be constantly critical of what we might call a theoret*ism*[6] that remakes practitioners in the image of the theorist.[7] Such theorists "adopt the viewpoint of an 'impartial spectator' who seeks to understand for the sake of understanding and who tends to assign this hermeneutic intention to the agents' practice"—as if practitioners were really just anonymous academics. In other words, the "theoreticizing" theorist studies a community of practitioners "as if they were asking themselves the questions *he* asks himself about them"—as if they were curious Western spectators rather than embedded practitioners (*LP* 31, emphasis original).[8] Bourdieu illustrates this with the case of linguists who construe language as if it were some impartial means of trading symbols rather than a relational network for getting something done[9]—who imagine language in the hands of spectators rather than employed by *users*, as if we were primarily grammarians rather than orators. "Unlike the orator, the grammarian has nothing to do with language except to study it in order to codify it. By the very treatment he applies to it, taking it as an object of analysis instead of using it to think and speak, he constitutes it as a *logos* opposed to *praxis*" (LP 31).[10] The intellectualist theorist unwittingly substitutes "the observer's relation to practice for the practical

6. Bourdieu describes "theoreticist triumphalism" as "the very air breathed by all those who claim the status of an intellectual" (*LP* 288n6).

7. "The 'thinker' betrays his secret conviction that action is fully performed only when it is understood, interpreted, expressed, by identifying the implicit with the unthought and by denying the status of authentic thought to the tacit and practical thought that is inherent in all 'sensible' action" (*LP* 36). Thus action becomes "something to be deciphered, when it leads one to say, for example, that a gesture or ritual act *expresses* something, rather than saying, quite simply, that it is 'sensible' (*sensé*) or, as in English, that it 'makes sense.' No doubt because they know and recognize no other thought than the thought of the 'thinker,' and cannot grant human dignity without granting what seems to be constitutive of that dignity, anthropologists have never known how to rescue the people they were studying from the barbarism of pre-logic except by identifying them with the most prestigious of their colleagues—logicians or philosophers (I am thinking of the famous title, 'The primitive as philosopher')" (*LP* 37, emphasis original). One could compare the common claim that "every believer is a theologian," which reflects a similar bias.

8. Or as he'll put this later, "the theoretical error" consists "in presenting the theoretical view of practice as the practical relation to practice" (*LP* 81). This is one of the errors "that flow from the tendency to confuse the actor's point of view with the spectator's point of view, for example looking for answers to a spectator's questions that practice never asks because it has no need to ask them, instead of wondering if the essence of practice is not precisely that it excludes such questions" (*LP* 82–83). This reminds me of an offhand remark David Burrell once made in conversation: "Neo-Thomism is that system which answers all of the questions you never thought to ask."

9. Objectivism "proceeds as if it were intended solely for knowledge and as if all the interactions within it were purely symbolic exchanges" (*LP* 52).

10. How much work in philosophy of religion and theology is the work of (and for) grammarians rather than orators?

relation to practice" (*LP* 34). Bourdieu is out to resist this by articulating a methodology that recognizes the unique and irreducible nature of the practitioner's relation to practice, which will require articulating the unique "logic of practice" at work for practitioners. This will be the focus of our exposition below.

On a second front, and in ways directly germane to our concern with a philosophy of action, Bourdieu will also challenge a "subjectivism" that fails to properly understand practice because it assumes a flawed picture of freedom. While Bourdieu's poster child for subjectivism is Sartre, this voluntarist model of the human person is widely assumed in "rational choice" theory and other social science paradigms. Such a model is a kind of "decisionism" that paints a picture of the subject as radically autonomous, each action the fruit of an unencumbered decision. Such a human being borders on being a kind of god.[11] "Refusing to recognize anything resembling durable dispositions or probable eventualities, Sartre makes each action a kind of antecedent-less confrontation between the subject and the world" (*LP* 42). In sum, the subject is seen as a "consciousness without inertia," without an environment or a past impinging on its autonomy.

Bourdieu is concerned that when interpretations of practice work with this assumption about autonomy they fail to truly understand what drives action in a community of practice. Once again, the theorist ends up re-making the world of practitioners in his own image: "Just as objectivism universalizes the theorist's relation to the object of science, so subjectivism universalizes the experience that the subject of theoretical discourse has of himself as a subject. A professional exponent of consciousness committed to the illusion of 'consciousness without inertia,' without a past and without an exterior, he endows all the subjects with whom he decides to identify . . . with his own experience as a pure, free-floating subject" (*LP* 45–46). Herein lies one of the "anthropological fictions" that Bourdieu is out to debunk (*LP* 47). We simply are not autonomous animals who float in the world unencumbered except by our own freedom. The autonomous "rational actor" is without dispositions or inclinations—without *habits*—and that is precisely the problem: such a theory of human persons will never truly understand human action because it fails to recognize the "inertia" of *habitus*, the complex of inclinations and dispositions that make us lean into the world with a habituated momentum in certain directions. We don't "decide" our way into every action. Our being-in-the-world is characterized by inclinations that propel us to all sorts of action

11. "Like Descartes' God, whose freedom is limited only by a free decision, such as the one which is the source of the continuity of creation, and in particular of the constancy of truths and values, the Sartrian subject, whether an individual or collective subject, can break out of the absolute discontinuity of choices without past or future only by the free resolution of a pledge and self-loyalty or by the free abdication of bad faith" (*LP* 43, cf. 45).

"without thinking."[12] Thus one of the core contributions of Bourdieu's "theory of practice *as* practice" (*LP* 52) is to recognize the centrality of *habitus*, of habituated inclinations that spawn meaningful action. In fact, for Bourdieu, the "logic of practice" and the centrality of *habitus* are inextricably linked: habit *is* the embodied know-how (the "practical sense") that is "carried" in a community of practice. The remainder of this chapter will further explicate these central concepts in Bourdieu with a view to marshaling them to reframe *liturgical* practice—both Christian and "secular."

Habitus as Practical Sense

In trying to (theoretically) understand the "logic of practice," we need a properly calibrated theoretical radar. If we approach practice with a theoretical radar set by "intellectualist" assumptions, Bourdieu worries we will end up missing what is unique and irreducible about "practical sense"—that visceral knowledge that is carried in a community of practice even if it is not (and cannot be) articulated in propositions. So if we're going to do justice to practice in our scientific and theoretical reflection *on* practice—that is, if we are going to get a handle on "a reason immanent in practices, whose 'origin' lies neither in the 'decisions' of reason understood as rational calculation nor in the determinations of mechanisms external to and superior to agents" (*LP* 50)—then we need a "theory of practice *as* practice" (*LP* 52, emphasis added) rather than a theory of practice as if it were just some mode of "expressing" what we *think*. We need to try to understand practitioners *as* practitioners, as fundamentally "doers" who are *acting* in and upon their world, not just "thinkers" who happen to be "doing" stuff.

So Bourdieu's project is to develop a "theory of practice as practice" that evades intellectualism without falling prey to a mechanistic determinism—an account of practice that avoids the twin reductionisms of seeing human action as either "rational action or mechanical reaction" (*LP* 50). It is with this concern in mind that he introduces a concept central to his account, the notion of *habitus*: "The theory of practice as practice insists, contrary to positivist materialism, that the objects of knowledge are constructed, not passively recorded, and, contrary to intellectualist idealism, that the principle of this construction is the system of structured, structuring dispositions, the *habitus*, which is constituted in practice and is always oriented

12. "How can one fail to see that decision, if decision there is, and the 'system of preferences' which underlies it, depend not only on all the previous choices of the decider but also on the condition in which his 'choices' have been made, which include all the choices of those who have chosen for him, in his place, pre-judging his judgments and so shaping his judgment" (*LP* 49–50).

toward practical functions" (*LP* 52). This dense introduction of the term requires some unpacking. The language of *habitus* has a philosophical echo that reverberates from Aristotle's account of virtue, in which habits are those dispositions that incline us to a certain end. Bourdieu's invocation of the term activates that echo, but also stretches it in new directions. Note that *habitus* is shorthand for what he calls a "system of structured, structuring dispositions." But dispositions toward what? Well, dispositions to *construct* (or constitute) our world in certain ways. We aren't just blank slates that passively "record" the world, as empiricism and materialism would have us believe; we constitute and construct our world. But contrary to intellectualism, that constitution happens "in practice" and is oriented toward action (a "practical function"),[13] not mere observation. *Habitus*, then, is shorthand to refer to those "dispositions" we have to constitute the world in certain ways—the habitual way that we construct our world. And those dispositions and habits are not primarily intellectual or rational; they are certainly not something we "think about."

Thus Bourdieu glosses *habitus* to emphasize this point that a *habitus* is always sort of bigger than me—it is a communal, collective disposition that gets inscribed in me. It is always both personal and political. Thus he describes *habitus* as "systems of durable, transposable dispositions, structured structures predisposed to function as structuring structures, that is, as principles which generate and organize practices and representations that can be objectively adapted to their outcomes without presupposing conscious aiming at ends or an express mastery of the operations necessary to attain them" (*LP* 53). Here we see some new features of *habitus*. First, a *habitus* is both durable and transposable—something that endures over time and is communicable, able to be shared and passed on. In this sense, a *habitus* is a kind of embodied tradition, not as some external "deposit" of data or content but as a handed-down way of being. It is in this sense that a *habitus* is a "structured" structure—it is something that comes *to* me, from outside me, conditioning and enabling my constitution of the world. And it functions as a structur*ing* structure because it inclines me to constitute the world in certain ways, conditioning my construction of meaning.

This is why *habitus* is intertwined with institutions. On the one hand, "the *habitus*, which is constituted in the course of an individual history" is "what makes it possible to inhabit institutions, to appropriate them practically" (*LP* 57). I will be "at home" in a community of practice just to the extent that the shared *habitus* of the community has become inscribed in me, absorbed into my "individual history." I learn how to be *in* community

---

13. We need to keep in mind that whenever Bourdieu talks about something being "practical," he means that it is a matter of *praxis*, of *action*.

by acquiring *from* the community and its institutions a *habitus*.[14] On the other hand, that *habitus* inscribed in me "is what enables the institution to attain full realization: it is through the capacity for incorporation,[15] which exploits the body's readiness to take seriously the performative magic of the social, that the king, the banker, or the priest are hereditary monarchy, financial capitalism or the Church made flesh" (*LP* 57). In other words, "an institution, even an economy, is complete and fully viable only if it is durably objectified not only in things, that is, in the logic, transcending individual agents, of a particular field, but also in bodies, in durable dispositions to recognize and comply with the demands immanent in the field" (*LP* 58). I need the community and social body to enable me to perceive the world; however, the social body needs *my* body to instantiate its vision and practice.[16]

Second, this handed-down disposition to constitute the world in certain ways functions without "conscious aiming"; the constituting engine of *habitus* can run quietly under the hood without me ever thinking of it, sort of like the silent engine of a Prius that takes you to the market even if you forget it's running. You don't need to hear the engine running in order for it to do its work. *Habitus* is that nexus of dispositions by which we constitute our world without rational deliberation or conscious awareness. This doesn't mean that *habitus* excludes deliberation or is somehow opposed to "strategic calculation."[17] Bourdieu notes that it is possible to

14. One could wonder whether Bourdieu, as an anthropologist used to studying largely homogenous societies, is sufficiently attentive to what Charles Taylor calls the "fragilization" and "cross-pressures" of modern societies—our insertion in multiple, competing *habitus*.

15. We must hear *corpus*, "body," in this "in*corpor*ation": to be in*corpor*ated is to be knit into the social body and to have the community's *habitus* inscribed in my body. It doesn't take too much imagination to see that the dynamics being described by Bourdieu are directly relevant to concerns about evangelism, discipleship, and Christian initiation, which are also about in*corpor*ation and union with Christ. For relevant discussion, see Tory K. Baucum, *Evangelical Hospitality: Catechetical Evangelism in the Early Church and Its Recovery Today* (Metuchen, NJ: Scarecrow, 2008).

16. "The habitus is precisely this immanent law, *lex insita*, inscribed in bodies by identical histories, which is the precondition not only for the co-ordination of practices but also for practices of co-ordination" (*LP* 59).

17. In a similar way, Mark Johnson emphasizes that thinking and conceptualization are *emergent* from our bodily interaction with the world: logic is kind of the "grammar" of our *felt* orientation. So concepts are not discrete metaphysical entities, and logic is not an inferential system that drops down from heaven or the mind of God: both are emergent from, and dependent upon, our embodied being-in-the-world. "Concepts are not themselves things or quasi-things. They are not mysterious abstract entities with a special ontological significance that sets them over against sensations or percepts. Our language of 'concepts' is just our way of saying that we are able to mark various meaningful qualities and patterns within our experience, and we are able to mark these distinctions in a way that permits us to recognize something that is *the same* over and over across different experiences and thoughts" (*MB* 88, emphasis original). So instead of speaking of concepts as something we "have" or use, we should speak of conceptual*izing* as something we (embodied beings) *do*.

"perform in a conscious mode the operation that the *habitus* performs quite differently" (*LP* 53). I can now "consciously" pick up the cup beside me, whereas up to this point I simply did so "without thinking about it." Bourdieu's only point is that the unconscious direction of *habitus* is primary. It is because I always already navigate the world by *habitus* that I can step back to deliberate and calculate.[18] I "think about" the world second; first I'm engaged in it as an actor whose motivations and ends are practical and largely "unconscious." It is *habitus* that is "the basis of perception" and all subsequent experiences (*LP* 54). Indeed, in some significant sense, experience is only possible because of *habitus*.

But because *habitus* is doing all of this work under the hood, it can be forgotten and "taken for granted" (*LP* 56, 58). Indeed, the constitutive operation of *habitus* can be so seamless and "automatic" (*LP* 58) that one could mistakenly think it is natural, some kind of hardwiring accrued through evolutionary adaptation and now rooted not just in our bones but in our genes. But that would be the materialist reduction that fails to recognize that *habitus* is *acquired*, that it has a history that is both collective and individual.

> The *habitus*—embodied history, internalized as a second nature and so forgotten as history—is the active presence of the whole past of which it is the product. As such, it is what gives practices their relative autonomy with respect to external determinations of the immediate present. This autonomy is that of the past, enacted and acting, which, functioning as accumulated capital, produces history on the basis of history and so ensures the permanence in change that makes the individual agent a world within the world. The *habitus* is a spontaneity without consciousness or will, opposed as much to the mechanical necessity of things without history in mechanistic theories as it is to the reflexive freedom of subjects "without inertia" in rationalist theories. (*LP* 56)

So *habitus* is very much like an Aristotelian habit: it is acquired, and therefore has a history; it carries an entire past with it (*LP* 54). But it has been appropriated and incorporated to such an extent that it is as if it were natural—it becomes "second nature." So it's *not* natural, and therefore not just instinctual reaction; but neither is it conscious or deliberative. Once again, like Merleau-Ponty's *praktognosia*, Bourdieu's *habitus* is a "between."

18. "Stimuli do not exist for practice in their objective truth, as conditional, conventional triggers, acting only on condition that they encounter agents conditioned to recognize them [which would be an 'intellectualist' picture]. The practical world that is constituted in the relationship with the *habitus*, acting as a system of cognitive and motivating structures, is a world of already realized ends—procedures to follow, paths to take—and of objects endowed with a 'permanent teleological character,' in Husserl's phrase, tools or institutions" (*LP* 53).

For just this reason, Bourdieu sees the concept of *habitus* as a way to break out of false dichotomies between freedom and determinism, intellect and instinct. "As an acquired system of generative schemes, the *habitus* makes possible the free production of all the thoughts, perceptions and actions inherent in the particular conditions of its production—and only those" (*LP* 55). A *habitus* is a *condition* of possibility: like horizons of expectation, a *habitus* circumscribes just how we'll be inclined to constitute the world. However, a *habitus* is also a condition *of possibility*: rather than being some limit on my range of possible experiences, it's what makes *any* experience possible. The *habitus* both governs and enables perception.

> This infinite yet strictly limited generative capacity is difficult to understand only so long as one remains locked in the usual antinomies—which the concept of the *habitus* aims to transcend—of determinism and freedom, conditioning and creativity, consciousness and the unconscious, or the individual and society. Because the *habitus* is an infinite capacity for generating products—thoughts, perceptions, expressions and actions—whose limits are set by the historically and socially situated conditions of production, the conditioned and conditional freedom it provides is as remote from creation of unpredictable novelty as it is from simple mechanical reproduction of the original conditioning. (*LP* 55)

Habitus, then, is a kind of compatibilism. As a social being acting in the world, I'm not an unconstrained "free" creature "without inertia"; neither am I the passive victim of external causes and determining forces. Neither mechanical determinism nor libertarian freedom can really make sense of our being-in-the-world because our freedom is both "conditioned and conditional." Both our perception and our action are conditioned, but as conditioned, it is possible for both to be spontaneous and improvisational. I learn how to constitute my world from others, but I learn how to constitute *my* world. The "I" that perceives is always already a "we." My perception is communal, a debt I owe.

What if we thought of the goal of Christian education and formation, not in terms of the acquisition of a Christian "worldview," but instead as the acquisition of a Christian *habitus*? Might we not better capture the essence of Christianity in the "between" concept of *habitus*—as an orientation to the world that is carried in a way of life and oriented fundamentally toward action, toward tangible being-in-the-world? We would then need to attend to the nexus of belief and the body.

Belief and the Body: The Logic of Practice

You'll notice that Bourdieu regularly bumps up against the limits of a lexicon. When it comes to philosophical anthropology (and even "folk" anthropologies—the functional views of humans that we assume in everyday practice), our vocabulary tends to be dualistic and reductionistic: intellect *or* instinct, freedom *or* determinism, minds *or* bodies, rational *or* irrational, conscious *or* unconscious, and so forth.[19] Bourdieu, like Merleau-Ponty, is trying to honor the messy complexity of our being-in-the-world that is *between* all of these and thus in danger of falling between the cracks because we lack appropriate concepts and terms to even name what's operative here. So he resorts to an old, dead language and invokes *habitus* to name this "between" way of intending the world that is not quite "knowledge" but enough *like* knowledge to still be named in that ballpark. This is why he also continues to avail himself of the language of "logic," even as he's describing something that is a million miles from what we usually associate with logic. So Bourdieu adopts two heuristic terms in his analysis of *habitus*: "practical sense" and "the logic of practice." On the one hand, there's something wrong with each of these terms; on the other hand, we need *some* concepts to articulate a theory of practice as practice. Let's unpack each of these in turn so we might better understand the dynamics of *habitus*. What will emerge is something like Bourdieu's (quasi) epistemology.

"Practical sense," Bourdieu stipulates, "is a quasi-bodily involvement in the world which presupposes no representation either of the body or of the world, still less of their relationship. It is an immanence in the world through which the world imposes its imminence, things to be done or said, which directly govern speech and action. It orients 'choices' which, though not deliberate, are no less systematic, and which, without being ordered and organized in relation to an end, are none the less charged with a kind of retrospective finality" (*LP* 66). "Practical sense" is the know-how that resides in the body, that unique sort of understanding of the world that is identified with a *habitus*. In this dense definition, Bourdieu highlights important features of this comportment to the world. First, as we'd expect, it is a *bodily* orientation to and involvement in the world. Practical sense is not an intellectual or mental processing of objective inputs; it is more a kind of adept immersion in an environment. This is why it is not representational: it's not a distanced observation of objects by a body, or images generated on the internal screen of my consciousness. Practical sense is not that sort of knowledge; it is more a kind of proficiency, a mastery—what Bourdieu

19. Mark Johnson also notes this lexical constraint in his discussion of John Dewey who, like Merleau-Ponty and Bourdieu, was trying to evade the dualism of the Western philosophical tradition. Out to refuse dichotomies of cognition/emotion, thought/feeling, mind/body, Dewey coined the hyphenated phrase "body-mind," without much improvement (or traction). Johnson rightly comments: "Even our language seems to be against us in our quest for an adequate theory of meaning and the self" (*MB* 7).

calls "a feel for the game" (*LP* 66). To have acquired practical sense is a matter of being *adroit* rather than having some encyclopedic knowledge.

He also describes practical sense as an "immanence," something that "exists," for lack of a better term, *in* our relationship to the world, not in some mind that is "above" the world. Practical sense, in that respect, isn't really "in" me—it's not located in some interiority; rather, it is a kind of halo effect that is forged *between* me and my environment, enacted in my being-alongside-the-world. This is why Bourdieu describes practical sense as an immanence "through which the world imposes its imminence"—the urgency of "things to be done or said," the nitty-gritty necessities that call for a response from me and thus "directly govern speech and action." It is practical sense that clarifies the million little invitations and invocations that call to me each day, whether it's responding to the whistle of the teakettle or responding to a deranged neighbor banging on my door at three in the morning. Practical sense is operative across a wide spectrum of *praxis* and action, from the mundane to the moral.[20] It is the submerged operations of practical sense that effect a "take" on these situations and thus generate action on my part. So it is in this manner that practical sense "orients [my] 'choices.'" Bourdieu puts the scare quotes around "choices" because these are *intentional* actions, and they are actions for which I am *responsible*; but they are *not* actions that are outcomes of rational deliberation, nor are they *consciously* "chosen." They are "chosen" in the sense that they are actions prompted from me in response to a situation; they are actions I undertake because practical sense has unconsciously surveyed a situation and my *habitus* has already inclined me toward certain ends.[21] They

20. Indeed, this spectrum is not easily divided. All sorts of seemingly mundane actions are charged with moral significance. Take, for example, the daily habit of putting vegetable scraps in the compost pile: Is that just a mundane action of home management? Or, with a scheme of tending God's creation and pursuing shalom, could this be a *moral* matter, a *just* practice? If all of life is lived *coram Deo*—before the face of God—it's hard to sort out what actions don't have transcendent significance. For a concrete consideration, see Wendell Berry, *Home Economics* (San Francisco: North Point Press, 1987).

21. In this respect Bourdieu bumps up against our default libertarianism, which thinks an action is only "free" if it is deliberately chosen without any constraint—even the constraint of habit (just the model that Bourdieu finds—and criticizes—in Sartre). In contrast, Bourdieu refuses such libertarian accounts, while also refusing to lapse into a determinism. In this respect, Bourdieu's account of choice and freedom is more like Augustine's or Jonathan Edwards's or—more proximately—Hegel's, particularly his discussions of freedom in *Elements of the Philosophy of Right*, trans. H. B. Nisbet (Cambridge: Cambridge University Press, 1991). As Robert Pippin succinctly summarizes, "For Hegel freedom consists in being in a certain reflective and deliberative relation to oneself (which he describes as being able to give my inclinations and incentives a 'rational form'), which itself is possible . . . only if one is also already in a certain relation (ultimately institutional, norm-governed relations) to others, if one is a participant in certain practices" (in *Hegel's Practical Philosophy: Rational Agency as Ethical Life* [Cambridge: Cambridge University Press, 2008], 2). Pippin goes on to note, in ways resonant with Bourdieu's

are actions generated by the dispositions I've acquired that have made me the *kind of person* who is inclined to respond in certain ways in certain situations because I've absorbed a sensibility that "makes sense" of the world—and to functionally "see" the world in that way is already a practical, ethical take on the world.

So practical sense is still a kind of "sense" (*sens*)—a way of *meaning* the world, a way of "making sense of" the world. But it is a "making sense" that is not consciously, mentally processed or even thought about. It is, Bourdieu suggests, more like a feel for the game. And one can have a masterful feel for the game without ever being able to articulate what one "knows" in that respect. There are all kinds of virtuoso players who make terrible coaches, precisely because their practical sense and feel for the game does not necessarily translate into the ability to communicate and teach what they know. The didactic expression required to coach is of a different order than the feel for the game one needs in order to play.

Working in this "between" space with boundary concepts, Bourdieu is willing to describe practical sense as a kind of "belief"—the sort of belief that is "an inherent part of belonging to a field" (*LP* 67). This is not that sort of belief we define as assent to propositions but rather a functional, enacted trust and entrustment to a context and a world. In fact, for Bourdieu, this belief is something that resides in the body:

> Practical belief is not a "state of mind," still less a kind of arbitrary adherence to a set of instituted dogmas and doctrines ("beliefs"), but rather *a state of the body*. Doxa is a relationship of immediate adherence that is established in practice between a *habitus* and the field to which it is attuned, the pre-verbal taking-for-granted of the world that flows from practical sense. Enacted belief, instilled by the childhood learning that treats the body as a living memory pad, an automaton that "leads the mind unconsciously along with it," and as a repository for the most precious values, is the form *par excellence* of the "blind or symbolic thought" which Leibniz refers to, . . . and which is the product of quasi-bodily dispositions, operational schemes, analogous to a line of verse whose words have been forgotten. (*LP* 68–69, emphasis original)

So practical sense is a "belief" in the sense that it is a disposition of the body to inhabit its world in certain ways. It is an attunement to the world that is a "pre-verbal taking-for-granted." But such "enacted belief" is not just mundane, like counting on the table to hold up my soup or trusting that the buses will run on time. Such a "state of the body" is also "a repository for the most precious values." It's not just trivial or mundane beliefs

---

claim above, that "my" action is "mine" not if I am the sole, autonomous cause of the action but if I can *own* the action upon later reflection (and justification) (ibid., 36–37).

To Think About: Newman on Faith *as* Love

Bourdieu's unconventional notion of "belief" might seem to depart from Christianity. But in fact it deeply resonates with premodern (and therefore pre-epistemological) under-standings of faith. This more holistic model of belief is well articulated in Cardinal John Henry Newman's *Grammar of Assent*, in which he also relativizes the propositional and expands faith to include other modes of intentionality. This was recently encapsulated by Terry Eagleton.

> Militant atheists today regard religious faith as a question of subscribing to certain propositions about the world. Newman countered this theological ignorance, pervasive in his own time too, with the Romantic claim (and this from one of the towering intellects of the Victorian age) that "man is not a reasoning animal; he is a seeing, feeling, contemplating, acting animal. . . . It is the concrete being that reasons."[1] It is the imagination, he holds, which is primary in matters of faith. Yet this passionate subjectivity was never whimsical subjectivism. How could it be, in a Catholic thinker for whom faith and truth were communal and institutional rather than a matter of private intuition? Newman, like Kierkegaard, recognised that religious faith is a kind of love, and like love engages intellect, emotion, experience and imagination together. There is a "notional" kind of knowledge, Newman argues in *An Essay in Aid of a Grammar of Assent*, by which he means a knowledge of abstract ideas, and there is "real" assent, which involves one's whole personality.[2]

1. John Henry Newman, *An Essay in Aid of a Grammar of Assent* (London: Longmans, Green & Co., 1903), 294.
2. Terry Eagleton, "Washed in Milk," *London Review of Books*, August 5, 2010, 10–11.

---

that are "carried" in the body, as it were, it is also our ultimate beliefs, our defining beliefs, our "most precious values." It's not that beliefs about can openers and changing diapers are housed in the body while big, ethical, metaphysical beliefs about God and justice are reserved for the mind. On Bourdieu's account, practical sense is comprehensive.

Practical sense, then, is a communal *habitus* that has been absorbed to such an extent that it now orients my perception of the world without me realizing it. To have acquired a practical sense[22] is to have imbibed embodied beliefs in such a way that I "naturally" relate to my world and my environment on those terms.[23] Practical sense (*sens*), as Bourdieu summarizes, is "social necessity turned into nature, converted into motor schemes and body automatisms, is what causes practices, in and through what makes them obscure to the eyes of their producers, to be *sensible*, that is, informed by

22. The indefinite article here ("*a* practical sense") is important: Bourdieu is not saying that there is *one* practical sense, "the" practical sense, some universal practical sense. What *counts* as practical sense is relative to a community of practice and is indexed to a *habitus*.
23. "The body believes in what it plays at. . . . It does not represent what it performs" (*LP* 73).

a common sense" (*LP* 69). A "common" sense is precisely what "we" can normally take for granted, what is widely *shared*, the sense and understanding that is a communal heritage and possession. To have acquired a practical sense is to have absorbed communally shared plausibility structures that constitute the world in certain ways—not just "seeing" the world from a certain perspective but intending the world as an environment that calls for certain responses and invites us to certain kinds of projects. To have acquired practical sense is to know more than you think. Practical sense is that "sense" that is operative *in action.* It's not just knowledge *so that* I can act; it is to know *by* acting.[24] This is not "practical knowledge" in the sense of mental, propositional content that I can then "apply" in practice; it is a unique "sense" that is *enacted* belief (*LP* 68). "It is because agents never know completely what they are doing that what they do has more sense than they know" (*LP* 69).

Practice has a logic of which "logic" knows nothing (to invoke a fittingly Pascalian dictum). Or as Bourdieu puts it, "Practice has a logic which is not that of the logician" (*LP* 86)—"a logic that is performed directly in bodily gymnastics" (*LP* 89). It's not just that practical sense is a clunky, unrefined version of "real" logic.[25] His point is that practical sense has its own irreducible "logic": what "makes sense" on the order of practice conforms to standards of sensibleness that are fundamentally different from discursive rationality. Something can "make sense" on the order of *habitus* that cannot be diagrammed as a syllogism. If we fail to recognize this, then we will end up "asking of [practice] more logic than it can give, thereby condemning [ourselves] either to wring incoherences out of it or to thrust a forced coherence upon it" (*LP* 86).

For example, practical sense is a mode of understanding and orientation that operates without concepts.[26] The logic of practice "dispenses with all the operations required by the construction of a concept. Practical sense 'selects' certain objects or actions, and consequently certain of their aspects, in relation to 'the matter in hand,' an implicit and practical principle of pertinence" (*LP* 89–90). You might say practical sense operates with the "so what?" meter dialed *way* up. It is inherently pragmatic, not in the sense

24. "The logic of practice . . . understands only in order to act" (*LP* 91).

25. This is the error he calls "logicism," a cousin to the "theoreticism" and "theoretization effect" we noted earlier. Logicism is a kind of logical imperialism that mistakenly thinks that all modes of sense and understanding must ultimately bow to syllogistic standards of what counts as "rational." "The logicism inherent in the objectivist viewpoint inclines one to ignore the fact that scientific construction cannot grasp the principles of practical logic without forcibly changing their nature" (*LP* 90).

26. This is at the heart of Dreyfus's critique of McDowell in "Overcoming the Myth of the Mental: How Philosophers Can Profit from the Phenomenology of Everyday Expertise," *Proceedings and Addresses of the American Philosophical Association* 79 (2005): 47–65.

of being cynically instrumentalizing, but in the sense of being primarily concerned with action, with not just being-in-the-world but *doing*-in-the-world. This is why any attempt to theoretically understand practice is fraught, because "the concepts that the analyst is forced to use . . . to give an account of the practical identifications that ritual acts perform are quite alien to practice" (*LP* 90). So if the scientist puts conceptual questions to a practitioner, the answers almost *have* to be false. Indeed,

> there is every reason to think that as soon as he reflects on his practice, adopting a quasi-theoretical posture, the agent [i.e., practitioner] loses any chance of expressing the truth of his practice, and especially the truth of the practical relation to the practice. Academic interrogation inclines him to take up a point of view on his own practice that is no longer that of action, without being that of science, encouraging him to shape his explanations in terms of a theory of practice that meshes with the juridical, ethical or grammatical legalism to which the observer is inclined by his own situation. Simply because [the practitioner] is questioned, and questions himself, about the reasons and the *raison d'être* of his practice, he cannot communicate the essential point, which is that the very nature of practice is that it excludes this question. (*LP* 91)

Like those Native Americans who are categorized as "unemployed" only when a consumer economy defines what counts as "work," so the practitioner is only "irrational" once a rational*ism* has defined what counts as "sense." Bourdieu, in contrast, is trying to avoid this "theoretization effect" by beginning with a theory of practice *as* practice, which recognizes—and, in a way, *honors*—the irreducible logic *of* practice. But he also realizes that he's straining against the limits of his lexicon.

> The idea of practical logic, a "logic in itself," without conscious reflexion or logical control, is a contradiction in terms, which defies logical logic. This paradoxical logic is that of all practice, or rather of all practical sense. Caught up in "the matter in hand," totally present in the present and in the practical functions that it finds there in the form of objective potentialities, practice excludes attention to itself (that is, to the past). It is unaware of the principles that govern it and the possibilities they contain; it can only discover them by enacting them, unfolding them in time. (*LP* 92)

Practical logic, then, is distinguished from "logical logic"—the rational, deliberative, deductive logic of *thinking*. Practical sense *makes sense*, but it does so according to different rules. Indeed, one can have a practical "intelligence" without ever being able to propositionally articulate such knowledge. It is a know-*how* that is enacted. As such, practical logic "can only be grasped in action"—whereas "the professional dealers in *logos* want practice to express something that can be expressed in discourse, preferably logical" (*LP* 92).

Bourdieu's case in point here is of direct relevance to our present concerns. First, he considers "rites" to be the instance par excellence of practices that resist conceptualization. "Rites, even more than most practices," he emphasizes, "might almost be designed to demonstrate the fallacy of seeking to contain in concepts a logic that is made to do without concepts[,] of treating practical manipulations and bodily movements as logical operations" (*LP* 92). A ritual logic defies conceptualization in a particularly intense way, almost to the extent that rites seem "designed" to point up the limits of conceptual analysis and articulation. They are not "expressing" what can be known by other means; rites affect what they do. A rite is "a performative practice that strives to bring about what it acts or says" (*LP* 92). So rites are a particularly intense mode of practice that, "even more than most practices," resist analytic paraphrase.[27] "Rites take place because, and only because, they find their *raison d'être* in the conditions of existence and the dispositions of the agents who cannot afford the luxury of logical speculation, mystical effusions or metaphysical *Angst*" (*LP* 96).[28]

With this claim in mind, Bourdieu then invokes a specific example (one that even resonates with the cover of this book): "the religion of the knights" (*LP* 295n8). In this case, Bourdieu, following Georges Duby, is critical of the "mentalism" that dominates religious studies,[29] taking religion to be a system of ideas and propositions. But as Duby points out,

27. On this point Bourdieu himself takes a shot at "the speculations par the theologians" whom he sees as particularly guilty of theoretical replications, imposing their own prejudices onto the integrity of religious practice *as* practice: "Always tending to project their own states of mind into the analysis of the religious, they have moved on without difficulty, through a reconversion homologous with that of the analysts of literature, to a spiritualized form of semiology in which Heidegger or Congar rub shoulders with Lévi-Strauss or Lacan or even Baudrillard" (*LP* 295n9)—perhaps even Bourdieu! Herein lie my concerns about the rising influence of "analytic theology": while there might be appropriate parameters for such analytic clarification, analytic theology will always run the risk of "the heresy of paraphrase" (and I'm not convinced that Eleonore Stump's corrective in "The Problem of Evil: Analytic Philosophy and Narrative," in *Analytic Theology: New Essays in Philosophical Theology*, ed. Oliver Crisp and Michael Rea [New York: Oxford University Press, 2009], 251–64, is sufficient to curtail this).

28. It's hard not to recall here that moving scene in Cormac McCarthy's *The Road* (New York: Vintage, 2006), in which the father, teetering on the brink of survival with his son, responds ritually: "The boy sat tottering. The man watched him that he not topple into the flames. He kicked holes in the sand for the boy's hips and shoulders where he would sleep and he sat holding him while he tousled his hair before the fire to dry it. All of this like some ancient anointing. So be it. Evoke the forms. Where you've nothing else construct ceremonies out of the air and breathe upon them" (74).

29. In a way very similar to Dreyfus's critique of mentalism in "Overcoming the Myth of the Mental."

The religion of the knights "came down entirely to a matter of rites, gestures and formulae," and he emphasizes the practical, bodily character of ritual practices: "When a warrior took an oath, what counted most in his eyes was not the commitment of his soul but a *bodily posture*, the contact that his hand, laid on the cross, the Scriptures or a bag of relics, had with the sacred. When he stepped forward to become the liege man of a lord, it was again an *attitude, a position of the hands*, a ritual sequence of words which only had to be uttered in order to bind the contract." (*LP* 295n8, emphasis original)[30]

It's not that the knights were insincere or "didn't mean it"; such concerns about sincerity are still operating with a dualism that assumes we "go through" rituals because "inside" we first *believe* something—that rituals externally "express" some prior, mental interiority. But that fails to recognize (and honor) the integrity and irreducibility of the logic of practice. "By cutting practices off from their real conditions of existence, in order to credit them with alien intentions, out of a false generosity conducive to stylistic effects, the exaltation of lost wisdom dispossesses them of everything that constitutes their *raison d'être*, and locks them in the eternal essence of a 'mentality'" (*LP* 96). In contrast, Bourdieu wants to honor the distinctive logic of practice by recognizing the irreducibility of *enacted* belief. Ritual is the way we (learn to) believe with our bodies.

In*corpor*ation and Initiation: Writing on the Body

We've unpacked in more detail the dynamics of *habitus*. But we still haven't quite answered the question above: how do we *acquire* a *habitus*? *Habitus*, we've seen, is Bourdieu's shorthand concept for that nexus of dispositions that makes it possible for us to perceive the world, to experience our environment, to constitute a context, and *act* therein. It is the visceral plausibility structure by which we make sense of our world and move within it. But the question is, how is such a visceral plausibility structure learned and absorbed?

To invoke a metaphor we encountered earlier, this is the same as asking, how does one *become* a "native"?[31] We can now say that being a "native" is a matter of having acquired a *habitus* that has become second nature—which is also a matter of one's having absorbed, and been absorbed into, the plausibility structures of a people. "Because native membership," says Bourdieu, "implies a feel for the game in the sense of a capacity for practical

30. Bourdieu is drawing on Georges Duby's study, *Le temps des cathedrals: l'art et le société de 980 à 1420* (Paris: Gallimard, 1976), 18.

31. Again, there are direct implications here for thinking about Christian initiation and sanctification. That's why part 2 below is concerned with "sanctified perception."

anticipation of the 'upcoming' future contained in the present, everything that takes place in it seems *sensible*" (*LP* 66). You know you've become a native when you know what's coming next, when you can anticipate the next move in social discourse because you are now acclimated to a "world" on a level that no longer requires conscious deliberation or processing. You now make sense of your world *with* others, but in a way you no longer notice because it's become "natural" for you. You also act accordingly: since you are now primed to automatically perceive the world in habituated ways, you're also inclined to act in certain ways because your perception of the world enables you to perceive what's at stake, what's required of you, what you're called to—not because you're thinking about relevant rules but because, as a "native," you now can't imagine seeing the world otherwise. It will just seem that this is "the way things are," and you will generally act accordingly.

We shouldn't forget, however, that becoming a native is in fact a kind of cultural accomplishment. It is the cumulative effect of habituation that shapes you *as* a native. While you can be born into a community, no one is born a "native" in Bourdieu's sense because "nativity" is not genetic—it's not just a matter of blood or location. You are formed into a native. And even if you *want* to join, you cannot simply *choose* to do so: "one cannot enter this magic circle by an instantaneous decision of the will, but only by birth or by a slow process of co-option and initiation which is equivalent to a second birth" (*LP* 68).[32] In putting it this way, Bourdieu is just a little sloppy, since even if I am born into a community, I am not born *with* its *habitus*; that will also require a "slow process of co-option" and in*corpor*ation—an "initiation." It's just that if I am born into the community, this will seem like the only option, the natural path. But if I am a "convert" of sorts—if I am going to acquire a *new habitus* when I have already absorbed others—then that process of co-option and incorporation is also going to bump up against my prior (or concurrent) formation by other communities of practice. There will be other *habitus* already inscribed within me.

The acquisition of a *habitus*, then, is described by Bourdieu as a slow process of co-option, initiation, and incorporation. But how exactly does that work? *How* are we co-opted? What are the means and dynamics of initiation? How is incorporation accomplished? In answering such questions,

---

32. Recall Bourdieu's specific target: methodological issues in the social sciences. If the goal of anthropology, for instance, is to work with a theory of what it is to be "native," and if becoming a native is a "slow process of co-option," then there are going to be inherent challenges for any participant observer who is not a "native" of the community being studied. On the other hand, if the anthropologist *is* a native, then she faces a different challenge: breaking out of the accomplished naïveté of native membership (*LP* 67) in order to achieve objectivity (which Bourdieu is not willing to give up on).

Bourdieu develops a notion of embodied pedagogy that provides unique resources for us to conceive how liturgical formation works, including how secular liturgies tacitly form in us a distinctive *habitus*.

Not surprisingly, my incorporation into a social body is effected through the *social* body co-opting *my* body. The dynamics of initiation are kinaesthetic. The operation is almost Proustian: "Every social order systematically takes advantage of the disposition of the body and language to function as depositories of deferred thoughts that can be triggered off at a distance in space and time by the simple effect of re-placing the body in an overall posture which *recalls* the associating thoughts and feelings, in one of the inductive states of the body which, as actors know, gives rise to states of mind" (*LP* 69). States of the body "give rise" to states of mind: here is the refusal of intellectualism and the recognition that our most fundamental orientations to our world (*habitus*, practical sense) are embedded in our bodies. So a social order or social body recruits me by conscripting

---

To Think About: Schooling as Ritual Performance

Social and educational theorist Peter McLaren documents a striking example of how we "learn" an entire social imaginary in entirely unconscious ways. The example, interestingly enough, comes from a classroom in an urban school.

From extensive ethnographic analysis of classrooms and pedagogical practice, McLaren developed the notion that every teacher has a "power spot" in his or her own classroom, "a place where he does most of his instructing and where he most often retreats when feeling unsure or threatened."[1] From this power spot the teacher commanded respect and taught with authority. The power spot was a functional center of the classroom's pedagogical universe.

One day when McLaren was observing a class he'd visited a number of times before, the teacher was called away briefly and asked McLaren to supervise. As usual, when the proverbial cat's away, the mice begin to play—and chatter and carouse and bounce around. So as McLaren "took charge," the classroom atmosphere almost immediately began to break down. But "as soon as I approached Barbie's power spot, the noise began to dim. But when I actually entered the power spot, one of the kids shot up his hand: 'Are you the teacher now?!'"[2]

Even if the teachers might have intentionally cultivated a power spot, the students "learned" this in entirely unconscious ways. Nonetheless, this unconscious education was entirely effective: they had tangibly picked up on a social order, in their bodies and in the placement of the teacher's body.

1. Peter McLaren, *Schooling as Ritual Performance: Toward a Political Economy of Educational Symbols and Gestures* (Lanham, MD: Rowman & Littlefield, 1999), 112. I'm grateful to David Smith for pointing me to this rich analysis.
2. Ibid.

my body through the most mundane means: through bodily postures, repeated words, ritualized cadences. The body politic implants in me a *habitus* by immersing me in an array of tangible movements and routines that effectively "deposit" an orientation within. This is the mechanics of initiation and incorporation: to incorporate bodies into the social body and to inscribe a common *habitus* into our bodies in such a way that we "sense" this in ways we don't know. In this way, the very posture of our body can be a kind of cognizance—and our body can "know" even when our conscious mind might be otherwise engaged. Indeed, the posturing of our body can call up an entire world of "sense," a web of associations and understandings that reframe our being-in-the-world. When a social body has successfully incorporated me through ritual formation, then what I "know" in this way is triggered by the same movement and postures, even "at a distance" from ritualized space. (This is Proust's madeleine, of course.)[33] The embodied, ritualized formation begins to spill over, shaping and priming my perception of the world in other spheres of experience.[34] In other words, the ritual is not an end in itself or merely a script for one "compartment" of a life. Because it effectively implants a *habitus* in the body, that *habitus* begins to govern action *across* one's life. "Thus the attention paid to staging in the great collective ceremonies derives not only from the concern to give a solemn representation of the group," Bourdieu notes, "but also, as many uses of singing and dancing show, from the less visible intention of ordering thoughts and suggesting feelings through the rigorous marshaling of practices and the orderly disposition of bodies" (*LP* 69). By putting the body through these paces, the social body marshals *my* body to act as a kind of organ of that wider body—and so primes my

33. "Many years had elapsed during which nothing of Combray, save what was comprised in the theatre and the drama of my going to bed there, had any existence for me, when one day in winter, as I came home, my mother, seeing that I was cold, offered me some tea, a thing I did not ordinarily take. I declined at first, and then, for no particular reason, changed my mind. She sent out for one of those short, plump little cakes called 'petites madeleines,' which look as though they had been moulded in the fluted scallop of a pilgrim's shell. And soon, mechanically, weary after a dull day with the prospect of a depressing morrow, I raised to my lips a spoonful of the tea in which I had soaked a morsel of the cake. No sooner had the warm liquid, and the crumbs with it, touched my palate than a shudder ran through my whole body, and I stopped, intent upon the extraordinary changes that were taking place. An exquisite pleasure had invaded my senses, but individual, detached, with no suggestion of its origin. And at once the vicissitudes of life had become indifferent to me, its disasters innocuous, its brevity illusory—this new sensation having had on me the effect which love has of filling me with a precious essence; or rather this essence was not in me, it was myself." Marcel Proust, *Swann's Way*, trans. C. K. Scott Moncrieff (New York: Vintage, 1970), 34.

34. Drawing on the work of Carl Plantinga, I have elsewhere discussed how film viewing trains our emotions to construe the world in extra-cinematic contexts. See James K. A. Smith, *Thinking in Tongues: Pentecostal Contributions to Christian Philosophy* (Grand Rapids: Eerdmans, 2010), 73–80.

> ### To Think About: Slouching toward Ritual
>
> That kind of self-respect is a discipline, a habit of mind that can never be faked but can be developed, trained, coaxed forth. It was once suggested to me that, as an antidote to crying, I put my head in a paper bag. As it happens, there is a sound physiological reason, something to do with oxygen, for doing exactly that, but the psychological effect alone is incalculable: it is difficult in the extreme to continue fancying oneself Cathy in *Wuthering Heights* with one's head in a Food Fair bag. There is a similar case for all the small disciplines, unimportant in themselves; imagine maintaining any kind of swoon, commiserative or carnal, in a cold shower.
>
> But those small disciplines are valuable insofar as they represent larger ones. To say that Waterloo was won on the playing fields of Eton is not to say that Napoleon might have been saved by a crash program in cricket; to give formal dinners in the rain forest would be pointless did not the candlelight flickering on the liana call forth deeper, stronger disciplines, values instilled long before. It is a kind of ritual, helping us remember who and what we are. In order to remember it, one must have known it.[1]
>
> 1. Joan Didion, *Slouching towards Bethlehem* (New York: Farrar, Straus & Giroux, 1968), 146–47.

action in ways that resonate with the vision of the social body well beyond the specific ritualized sites.

In ways that resonate with my description of cultural practices as "pedagogies of desire," Bourdieu describes these formative cultural rituals as pedagogies with "cosmic" dimensions. "One could endlessly enumerate the values given body, *made* body, by the hidden persuasion of *an implicit pedagogy which can instill a whole cosmology*, through injunctions as insignificant as 'sit up straight' or 'don't hold your knife in your left hand,' and inscribe the most fundamental principles of the arbitrary content of a culture in seemingly innocuous details of bearing or physical and verbal manners, so putting them beyond the reach of consciousness and explicit statement" (*LP* 69, emphasis added). This implicit pedagogy is not didactic; it is kinaesthetic. The cosmology is instilled, not through the dissemination of ideas and beliefs and doctrines, but through more oblique measures that operate on the body and thus bypass consciousness. While a child is learning to sit straight or hold her knife she is unconsciously absorbing a social imaginary, a picture of social order, a vision of the good life—even if her "teachers" might not realize they are passing it on. To learn how to stand or how to walk is to learn how to comport oneself to the world, which is, in turn, to learn how to *constitute* one's world. We are being taught *how* to perceive the world when we are taught to sit up straight; we are learning how to constitute our social world when we're trained to line up in single file; and when we are enjoined to kneel for confession an entire cosmology is instilled in us. "The body," he rightly notes, "takes metaphors seriously" (*LP* 71–72).

"The cunning of pedagogic reason," Bourdieu concludes, "lies precisely in the fact that *it manages to extort what is essential while seeming to demand the insignificant,* such as the respect for forms and forms of respect which are the most visible and most 'natural' manifestation of respect for the established order, or the concessions of politeness, which always contain political concessions" (*LP* 69, emphasis added). He later invokes an example: "The Kabyle woman setting up her loom is not performing an act of cosmogony; she is simply setting up her loom to weave cloth intended to serve a technical function. It so happens that, given the symbolic equipment available to her for practically thinking her own practice—in particular her language, which constantly refers her back to the logic of ploughing—she can only think what she is doing in the enchanted, that is to say, mystified, form that spiritualism, thirsty for eternal mysteries, finds so enchanting" (*LP* 96). This is not a criticism of the Kabyle woman but a caution to those who would try to (theoretically) understand her practice: there is a distinct *meaning* to her practice because of its placement in a wider ritual network. This is not something she could necessarily articulate, nor is it something she's been instructed in by didactic means. By learning to weave she has woven the fabric of a world, a world that is also woven into her.

Such pedagogies are effective precisely *because* they work this way, not in spite of the fact. Values are "given body, *made* body." And it is because they are *incarnate* pedagogies that they are "cunning," operative even when we're not setting out to be trained or formed. These are pedagogies that "teach" us even when—and perhaps especially when—we haven't signed up to be taught.[35] Rhythms that are "seemingly innocuous" are, in fact, fundamentally formative; while seeming to demand only the insignificant, in fact they are extorting what is essential. Our bodies are students even when we don't realize it, and because we are so fundamentally oriented by this *habitus*, this incarnate education ends up being the more powerful. The effect of such implicit pedagogies is that these dispositions become "possessed" by the body—what Bourdieu, availing himself of another Aristotelian notion, calls a "bodily hexis." "Bodily hexis is political mythology realized, *em-bodied*, turned into a permanent disposition, a durable way

35. One might worry that this undercuts the liturgical ideal of "full, conscious, active participation"; but I don't think that's true. Let's remember: I'm trying to get an account of how liturgies work, *including secular liturgies*. While Christian worship practice invites us to full, conscious, active participation, there is always *more* formation going on than what we're "conscious" of. Similarly—and perhaps even more significantly—the formative power of secular liturgies does not seem to require "full, conscious, active participation" to be quite powerfully effective.

of standing, speaking, walking, and thereby of feeling and thinking" (*LP* 69–70). In this way a worldview is materialized, incarnated.

It is just to the extent that a social body—and its social vision—is incarnated that it will be pedagogically successful, able to incorporate members into the body politic and inscribe in them the *habitus* that defines a people or a polis. So my acquisition of a *habitus* is always at the same time a matter of my being acquired *by* a people or a polis. I am incorporated into the body politic just to the extent that the social vision of the community is embedded in my body. *Habitus* is acquired, is learned, by incarnate pedagogies that in oblique, allusive, cunning ways work on the body and thus orient the whole person. "What is 'learned by the body' is not something that one has, like knowledge that can be brandished, but something that one is" (*LP* 73). To have been so educated is to have become a new person.

Picturing the Pedagogy of Insignificance with Carson McCullers

Bourdieu helps us to see that learning what seems insignificant can be training us for (and about) what's essential—that what's ultimate can unwittingly be at stake in what appears to be innocuous. Pedagogies are "cunning" just when they extort what is essential from what seems banal—which means, of course, that *nothing* is banal, nothing is insignificant. Even the most mundane can instill a whole cosmology.

Which is to say that we learn to love from the little stuff. There is a habituation and training of our desire in our relation to the most mundane. This is beautifully pictured in Carson McCullers's celebrated short story, "A Tree, A Rock, A Cloud."[36] In the early morning hours at a streetcar café, a young boy stops in for a coffee as he nears the end of his paper route. A number of the regulars are there in the respectful quiet of pre-dawn, some just finished the night shift, others on their way to the mill. Hunched in the corner is an unfamiliar man, his nose in his beer, making the others nervous. As the boy pays up, the strange man calls out, "Son! Hey Son!"

The older man buttonholes the boy as if he were the Ancient Mariner with a life-or-death tale to tell. Grasping him by the shoulders, then turning the boy's face from side to side, the old man says slowly, "I love you."

Guffaws come from the counter while the boy sidles away, sheepish and awkward. Seeing the boy's distance, the old man seeks to explain. What follows is a story of love lost—of a woman who got away. But the man offers it as the culmination of his learning, offering the findings from his empiricial observation. "I am talking about love," the man said. "With me it is a science." These findings were hard won, for he had much to learn.

> "It was like this," the man continued. "I am a person who feels many things. All my life one thing after another has impressed me. Moonlight. The leg of a pretty girl.

---

36. Carson McCullers, "A Tree, A Rock, A Cloud," in *The Ballad of the Sad Café and Other Stories* (Boston: Houghton Mifflin, 1979), 143–52.

One thing after another. But the point is that when I had enjoyed anything there was a peculiar sensation as though it was laying around loose in me. Nothing seemed to finish itself up or fit in with the other things. Women? I had my portion of them. The same. Afterwards laying around loose in me. I was a man who had never loved.

But then *she* came along, the woman who, the man said, "was something like an assembly line for my soul. I run these little pieces of myself through her and I come out complete. Now do you follow me?"

The boy did not. He didn't know what to think.

And, of course, the old man is here with his nose in a mug because this woman—this assembly line for his soul—left him. At first he searched valiantly, frantically, frenetically, around the country, for two years. But in the third year of her absence, he says, "a curious thing began to happen to me." He began to forget her. He could no longer picture her. He would try to think about her and his mind would be a blank. "But a sudden piece of glass on a sidewalk. Or a nickel tune in a music box. A shadow on a wall at night. And I would remember. It might happen in a street and I would cry or bang my head against a lamppost."

The boy continued to be puzzled, "A piece of glass?" he mused, quizzically.

"Anything," the man said. "I would walk around and I had no power of how and when to remember her. You think you can put up a kind of shield. But remembering don't come to a man face forward—it corners around sideways. I was at the mercy of everything I saw and heard. Suddenly instead of me combing the countryside to find her she begun to chase me around in my very soul. *She* chasing *me*, mind you! And in my soul."

But it was not until the fifth year of her absence that he finally hit upon his science—a strange science, almost like a "logic" of practice. And while it's "hard to explain scientifically," the old man gives it his best shot for the sake of the boy. He is a veritable evangelist for his science of love that begins with recognizing "what is wrong with us."

"'Men fall in love for the first time. And what do they fall in love with? . . . A woman,' the old man said. 'Without science, with nothing to go by, they undertake the most dangerous and sacred experience in God's earth. They fall in love with a woman.'"

"They start at the wrong end of love. They begin at the climax. Can you wonder it is so miserable? Do you know how men should love?"

The old man reached over and grasped the boy by the collar of his leather jacket. He gave him a gentle little shake and his green eyes gazed down unblinking and grave.

"Son, do you know how love should be begun?"

The boy sat small and listening and still. Slowly he shook his head. The old man leaned closer and whispered:

"A tree. A rock. A cloud."

For six years since, he has schooled himself differently. He has approached love from the other end: he has learned to love a tree, a rock, a cloud, and has thus trained himself for bigger things. He has learned to love the insignificant and in so doing has prepared himself to love what's ultimate. "For six years now," he continues, "I have gone around by myself and built up my science. And now I am a master. Son. I can love anything. No longer do I have to think about it even. I see a street full of people and a beautiful light comes in me. I watch a bird in the sky. Or I meet a traveler on the road. Everything, Son. And anybody. All stranger and all loved!"

Our erotic habits and inclinations are cultivated by the mundane. We learn to love by pedagogies of (seeming) insignificance. And the God who is Love meets us in our banalities and teaches us to love from our end. Word. Wine. Bread.

PART 2

Sanctified Perception

Part 1 was oriented by a working axiom: that a liturgical anthropology is rooted in both a kinaesthetics and a poetics—an appreciation for the bodily basis of meaning (kinaesthetics) and a recognition that it is precisely this bodily comportment that primes us to be oriented by story, by the imagination (poetics). Ultimately this axiom is rooted in a theological claim about the sorts of creatures we are: created in the image of God, and called to image the Son who is the image of the invisible God, we, too, are *incarnate* in a sense. We are sacramental animals. However, this Christian theological intuition can be elucidated and unpacked by utilizing the resources of theorists such as Merleau-Ponty and Bourdieu. We might think of part 1 as an attempt to build a theoretical toolbox that gives us conceptual resources and a fresh lexicon to be able to name and articulate a Christian liturgical anthropology. Now, in part 2, we use this toolbox to understand how worship works. This toolbox should help us appreciate, and account for, the something like the incarnate conditions of liturgical formation. And that is of interest for two reasons. On the one hand, a Christian liturgical anthropology should "hit the ground" by giving us insight into the force of "secular" liturgies. One might even say that this should enable us to construct a phenomenology of *temptation*, or at least an account of how *mis*-formation happens. On the other hand, both the outline of a liturgical anthropology and an appreciation for how secular liturgies "work" should encourage a new intentionality in the practices of Christian worship, a recognition that the Spirit renews and transforms us in and through our embodied comportment to the world. In particular, we will unpack the centrality of the imagination and the importance of the arts in sanctifying our perception for the sake of Christian action—for the sake of the kingdom.

3

"We Tell Ourselves Stories in Order to Live"

How Worship Works

... all these things think through me, or I think through them (for, in the grandeur of reverie, the *I* is soon lost); they think, I say, but musically and picturesquely, without quibble, without syllogism, without deduction.[1]

Picturing Secular Liturgies in Nicholson Baker's *The Mezzanine*

Sitting on my desk, Wallace's *Infinite Jest* and Nicholson Baker's *The Mezzanine* are a stark contrast: the 1100-page *Infinite Jest* dwarfs the tiny, 135-page *Mezzanine*.[2] Whereas *Infinite Jest* ranges across years and regions, *The Mezzanine* recounts a trip up an escalator. And while *Infinite Jest* gives us a peek into exotic, strange, unseen worlds that surround us (like the secluded Enfield Tennis Academy or Ennet House drug rehab center), *The Mezzanine* looks at what we see every day, right under our noses: the banal world of office buildings, men's rooms, and CVS drug stores. However, what the books share in common is an appreciation of the ritual formation of our identity. Thus we follow Howie, a young office worker at the end of his lunch break, ascending the

---

1. Baudelaire, "The Artist's Confiteor," in *Paris Spleen: Little Poems in Prose*, trans. Keith Waldrop (Middletown, CT: Wesleyan University Press, 2009), 7.
2. David Foster Wallace, *Infinite Jest* (1996; repr., New York: Back Bay Books, 2006); and Nicholson Baker, *The Mezzanine* (New York: Vintage, 1988); hereafter cited as *Mezz.*

escalator to his office on the mezzanine level. In fact, the novel is a faux memoir, written in the most unctuous language by this budding ad man, allowing us to bore into his consciousness while he shares with us his "take" on the world he inhabits. And while it's easy to simply delight in his prose and almost wallow in his attention to the world, it seems to me that the novel is begging us to ask some questions: Who is this guy and where did he come from? What *made* him?

Unlike Wallace, Baker doesn't provide any soliloquies or expositions on these themes. Instead, this is pictured as the cumulative effect of patient, attentive observation of our workaday world. Indeed, Baker's project in *The Mezzanine* could be seen as a kind of hallowing of artifice. Whereas the Romantics penned odes to natural beauty, Baker offers paeans to plastic straws and the ingenuity of perforation.[3] Indeed, one might suggest that there is no sacred/secular distinction in *The Mezzanine* because *everything* is holy; while the novel is riddled with the trivial, the fact of its being narrated makes it no longer trivial.[4] Even the printed text on a restroom hand dryer (". . . Pollution-Free Warm Air Hand Dryers to protect you from the hazards of disease . . .") is an occasion for rhapsodic praise:

> When I was little it bespoke the awesome oracular intentionality of prophets whose courage and confidence allowed them to scrap the old ways and start fresh: urban renewal architects; engineers of traffic flow; foretellers of monorails, paper clothing, food in capsule form, programmed learning, and domes over Hong Kong and Manhattan. I used to read it to myself as if I were reciting a quatrain from the *Rubáiyát*, and I read it so many times that now it holds for me some of the Ur-resonances of Crest's "conscientiously applied program of oral hygiene and regular professional care." (*Mezz* 88–89)

We are treated to similar meditations on the physics of shoelace wear, scrupulous accounts of men's-room social interactions, and almost lubricious hymns of praise for various pieces of office equipment and the simple machines of modern life like novelty coffee mugs. The whole of *our* constructed, artificial world—the glass and steel and plastic and brand-name world of "civilization"—is here baptized and sanctified by

3. On the fascination with developments in drinking straw technology, see *Mezz* 4n1; on perforation, see *Mezz* 74n1. (Footnotes in a novel are another point of contact between Wallace and Baker.)

4. This can be attributed to what the narrator himself describes as the "background" effect discovered in childhood: the fact that "anything, no matter how rough, rusted, dirty, or otherwise discredited it was, looked good if you set it down on a stretch of white cloth, or any kind of clean background." In short, "anytime you set some detail of the world off that way, it was able to take on its true stature as an object of attention" (*Mezz* 38). Heidegger, of course, would disagree about whether this is the "true stature" of the object; for him, when the object is de-sedimented from its concernful use within an "understood" environment and made to be something "present-at-hand," there's a certain forgetting of what the "thing" is (*pragmata*). See Heidegger, *Being and Time*, trans. John Macquarrie and Edward Robinson (San Francisco: Harper & Row, 1962), 95–104.

attention and description.[5] Under the narrator's gaze, the banal becomes bedazzling. The cold, anonymous environs of the downtown business district are hallowed, and the monotonous routines of corporate commuter life are bathed with a sanctifying attention.

But then, if you step back just a little, you begin to wonder again: Who is this guy? What's he *about*? What matters to him? What's he after? What does he care about? And you start to realize that he himself is a product of artifice—that he's the quintessential "modern man" constituted by this consumer, corporate world. While he's hymning encomiums to what we've made, we start to realize that this plastic civilization has also made him. The memoiristic divulgences from his interiority reveal to us an imagination stocked largely with the fuel of advertising images and brand-name narratives.[6] The rhythms and spaces of the office and its products have come to constitute his entire identity. He is not just a neutral, passive observer of his environment; rather, his attention is selective and his gaze constitutes the world in a certain way. This isn't just a particularly attentive description of our consumerist culture; it is a particularly consumerist take on our culture. We might say that there is a *hermeneutic* that emerges from his identity: he construes the world *as* a collection of commodities and inventions because he's been trained to do so. His lauding take on late modern culture is the product of a certain "discipleship of the eye."[7]

The novel provides its own account of how this happens precisely because it appreciates the orienting power of the unconscious and is attentive to the habituation of ritual. Howie sees the world and orients himself within it because he has absorbed

---

5. "Nature" barely makes a showing, and when it does, it is squelched and squeezed by the concrete of culture. Consider the contrasts in this passage:

> Under the impetus of a big-necked man and a rushed woman behind him, the revolving door from the lobby had been circulating a little too fast; when my turn came, I took advantage of the existing momentum by milling through my slice of its pie chart without contributing any additional force, rolling up a sleeve. Outside, it was noontime, noontime! Fifteen healthy, coltish slender trees grew out of the brick plaza a short way into the blue sky in front of my building, each casting an arrangement of potato chip–shaped shadows over its circular cast-iron trunk collar. ("Neenah Foundry Co. Neenah, Wis.") Men and women, seated on benches in the sun near raised beds of familiar corporate evergreens (cotoneaster, I think) were withdrawing wrapped delicacies from dazzling white bags. (*Mezz* 105)

Nature is ringed and framed by cast-iron artifice; the metaphors for trees derive from consumer culture; and even the basic "natural" act of eating is wrapped in plastic.

6. There are exceptions to this: he carries "a black Penguin paperback" (an edition of Aurelius's *Meditations*), makes reference to the *Rubáiyát* (as we noted above), refers to a biography of Wittgenstein he read (*Mezz* 121n1), and notes someone else reading *Readings in the Philosophy of the Social Sciences* (*Mezz* 120n1). But he notes that he had "come to history first through the backs of record albums" (*Mezz* 123) and that he had "read no more than twenty pages of" any of the other Penguin classics he had purchased. Is it very far from here to the world of Shteyngart's *Super Sad True Love Story*, where no one reads books but only "scans texts"?

7. For more on this notion, see James K. A. Smith, *The Devil Reads Derrida: And Other Essays on the University, the Church, Politics, and the Arts* (Grand Rapids: Eerdmans, 2008), chap. 23.

hermeneutic horizons that condition his construal already at the level of the unconscious. The daily rhythms of our behavior and action are driven not primarily by conscious, intentional "choices" but by a million unconscious, involuntary prompts that
carry their own "vision" of what we're about. Thus on the very first page, the narrator
notes: "When I drew close to the up escalator, I involuntarily transferred my paperback
and CVS bag to my left hand, so that I could take the handrail with my right" (*Mezz* 4–5).
This is just one in "a fairly long sequence of partially forgotten, inarticulable experiences" that carry within them their own "tiny understanding" that, only later, can be
consolidated and "tagged as knowledge" (*Mezz* 8–9). His foot, like the hand, exhibits
the same unintended independence: "As I had worked, then, my foot had, without any
sanction from my conscious will, slipped from the untied shoe and sought out the text
of the carpeting" (*Mezz* 12). Later he finds himself having "unintentionally" bought a
bag of popcorn (*Mezz* 105). His body has its own desires and goals and carries them out
without consulting the "control center" of consciousness.

At the end of the book, he creates a catalog of thoughts and their "periodicity"
over a life, rated in terms of the "Number of Times Thought Occurred per Year" (*Mezz*
127–28). For instance, thoughts of girlfriend and family rate high (580 and 400, respectively), and then a precipitous drop-off to third on the list, "brushing tongue" (150),
descending slowly to "Kant, Immanuel" (0.5)—the sign, no doubt, of a solid liberal arts
education. Behind this little exercise is the hypothesis that "if we could assign a periodicity number in this way to every recurrent thought a person had," we would "know
the relative frequency of his thoughts over time, something that might prove to be
more revealing than any statement of beliefs he might offer" (*Mezz* 126–27). Perhaps.
The idea is that frequency of thought occurrence equals significance. But the rest of the
book has suggested something else entirely: that significance is not determined at the
level of "thought" or belief because significance is not cognitively determined. Significance is more fundamentally determined at the level of our unconscious, unintentional
construal of the world that happens before "thought" ever gets to work. Howie's world
is constituted by the rhythms of ritual that he constantly engages in "without thinking
about it."

Thus the novel is replete with attention to mundane ceremonies and "automatic
subroutines" (*Mezz* 51): from the intricate, never-before-thought-about ritual of tying
his shoelaces to the automatic dexterity exhibited in putting on a shirt and tie to "the
ritual aspects of bagging" (*Mezz* 119) to "all the little ceremonies of elevator behavior"
(*Mezz* 76). Consider the restrained exuberance in his account of a familiar morning
ritual:

> There are often unexpected plusses to some minor new development. What
> sugar-packet manufacturer could have known that people would take to flap-
> ping the packet back and forth to centrifuge its contents to the bottom, so that
> they could handily tear off the top? The nakedness of a simple novelty in pre-
> portioned packaging has been surrounded and softened and *made sense* of by
> gesticulative adaptation (possibly inspired by the extinguishing oscillation of a

> match after the lighting of a cigarette); convenience has given rise to ballet; and the sound of those flapping sugar packets in the early morning, fluttering over from nearby booths, is not one I would willingly forgo, even though I take my coffee unsweetened. (*Mezz* 95n1)

And it's not just that "ritual" is a literary way to describe banal regularities; rather, when coupled with the appreciation of the directive role of the unconscious, these routines are charged with formative power. Through rituals an unarticulated but directive comportment to the world seeps into us. These routines train the unconscious. What better place to see this than in Howie's relation to escalators. As he recounts, based on early, sporadic, department-store experiences, he "had gradually developed strong beliefs as to the proper way to ride them. Your role was to advance at the normal rate you climbed stairs at home, allowing the motor to supplement, *not replace*, your own physical efforts" (*Mezz* 100). "But," he goes on to note, "a year of riding the escalator to work changed me."

> Now I was a passenger on the machine four times a day—sometimes six or more. . . . My total appreciation for the escalator deepened, eventually becoming embedded along my spinal column, but each individual ride was no longer guaranteed to trigger a well-worn piece of theory or state of irritation. I began to care less whether the original intent of the invention had been to emulate the stairway or not. And when I went back to department stores after those early months of work, I regarded the big motionless back of shoppers ahead of me on the crowded slope with new interest, and I relaxed with them: it was natural, it was understandable, it was defensible to want to stand like an Easter Island monument in this trance of motorized ascension through architectures of retailing. (*Mezz* 101–2)

Indeed, that is the triumph of ritual: what is learned and acquired becomes so habituated and absorbed—"embedded along [the] spinal column"—that it is taken to be "natural."

But one wonders whether Howie fully appreciates the force of this intuition. In particular, while he's able to, in a way, externalize these ritualizations in order to comment on them, recognizing that they're acquired over time and have become part of the fabric of his identity, he doesn't seem to be able to manage the same observational distance about his own observation. In other words, he doesn't seem to appreciate that his attentive, hallowed praise of the commercial world is shaped by a commodified, name-brand consciousness precisely because the world according to Crest and Jiffy Pop has been embedded along his spinal column. The practices of a corporate, consumer world have had a trumping effect: they have evacuated his identity of pretty much anything else. As a result, a particular social imaginary has seeped into his pre-observational consciousness, shaping how he sees the world and how he construes what matters. His perception has been primed by practices. Rituals make the man who makes the world.

Imaginative, Narrative Animals

Nicholson Baker offers us a story that narrates the story-making power of unconscious, formative rituals—a compressed little narrative that shows rather than tells us the embodied rituals that shape our very identities. In short, Baker tells a story about how mundane routines conscript us into a larger story that begins to shape who we are, what we love, and hence what we do. Our hearts traffic in stories. Not only are we lovers; we are storytellers—and story-listeners. As the novelist David Foster Wallace once put it, "We need narrative like we need space-time; it's a built-in thing."[8] We are narrative animals whose very orientation to the world is fundamentally shaped by stories. As both Merleau-Ponty and Bourdieu suggest, we live at the nexus of body and story—a "between" space where the aesthetic force of a narrative or poem captures our imagination because it resonates with the bodily attunement that so fundamentally governs our being-in-the-world. The imaginative logic of *poiesis* plucks our deepest heartstrings, and such aesthetic resonances reverberate in deep corners of our unconscious, attuning us in ways we are not even aware of. We're less convinced by arguments than moved by stories; our being-in-the-world is more aesthetic than deductive, better captured by narrative than analysis.[9] Indeed, the philosopher Alasdair MacIntyre says that stories are so fundamental to our identity that we don't know what to do without one. As he puts it, I can't answer the question, "What ought I to do?" unless I have already answered a *prior* question, "Of which story am I a part?"[10] It is a story that provides the moral map of our universe. It is narrative that trains our emotional perceptual apparatus to perceive the world as meaningful.

The essayist and incisive cultural critic Joan Didion captured our narrative nature in her 1970s journal, *The White Album*, though with a more cynical take: "We tell ourselves stories in order to live. . . . We look for the sermon in the suicide, for the social or moral lesson in the murder of five. We interpret what we see, select the most workable of the multiple choices. We live entirely, especially if we are writers, by the imposition of a narrative line upon disparate images, by the 'ideas' with which we have learned to freeze the shifting phantasmagoria which is our actual experience."[11] Stories are like the air we breathe. Narrative is the scaffolding of our experience.

8. David Foster Wallace, "Fictional Futures and the Conspicuously Young," *Review of Contemporary Fiction* 8.3 (1988): 8.

9. So Brooks, following the psychologist Jerome Bruner, distinguishes "paradigmatic thinking" that traffics in logic and analysis from the "narrative mode" that weaves together our world on the level of the imagination (*The Social Animal: The Hidden Sources of Love, Character, and Achievement* [New York: Random House, 2011], 54–55).

10. MacIntyre, *After Virtue*, 2nd ed. (Notre Dame: University of Notre Dame Press, 1984), 216.

11. Joan Didion, *The White Album* (New York: Farrar, Straus & Giroux, 1979), 11.

And as we saw with both Merleau-Ponty and Bourdieu, stories "mean" on a register that is visceral and bodily, more aesthetic than analytic, "made sense of" more by the imagination than the intellect. Stories are something we learn "by heart" in the sense that they *mean* on a register that eludes articulation and analysis. A whole world(view) can be compressed in even the most minimal narrative because the story is "working" aesthetically—it *means* in its cadence and rhythm, in what is said and what is left unsaid, in its tensions and resolutions. I "understand" a story in ways I don't know.

This philosophical anthropology, which sees the (affective, preconscious) imagination as the "center of gravity" of human action, thus accords a central role to *story* or narrative.[12] This is why a liturgical anthropology—recognizing that we are "liturgical animals" whose fundamental longings and desires are shaped by liturgical practices (whether "secular" or Christian)—must take seriously this body/story nexus. This is why any adequate liturgics needs to appreciate the interplay of kinaesthetics and poetics. Our identity and love are shaped "liturgically" precisely because liturgies are those rituals and practices that constitute the embodied stories of a body politic. If liturgies are "rituals of ultimate concern" that form identity, that inculcate particular visions of the good life, and that do so in a way that means to trump other ritual formations,[13] they do so because they are those story-laden practices that are absorbed into our imaginative epicenter of action and behavior. Liturgies are compressed, repeated, performed narratives that, over time, conscript us into the story they "tell" by showing, by performing. Such orienting narratives are not explicitly "told" in a "once-upon-a-time" discursive mode—as if the body politic invites us to passively sit at the proverbial librarian's feet for "story time" while she walks us through a picture-book narration. No, these stories are more like dramas that are enacted and performed. The stories of a body

12. James K. A. Smith, *Desiring the Kingdom: Worship, Worldview, and Cultural Formation* (Grand Rapids: Baker Academic, 2009), 52–54. In this respect, my project resonates with others working in the philosophy of social sciences, particular Alasdair MacIntyre, Charles Taylor, and Christian Smith, all of whom emphasize the centrality of narrative or story in the formation of both individual and communal identity—and in shaping our action and ethical behavior. If our actions and behavior are driven by an affective, preconscious, imaginative construal of our world, then the aesthetic register of stories has a better "fit" with our adaptive unconscious. In short, stories shape and influence our action. Hence, MacIntyre, Taylor, and Christian Smith also emphasize the need for social-scientific research of human action to recognize that humans are "narrative animals." As Christian Smith comments, "For all our science, rationality, and technology, we moderns are no less the makers, tellers, and believers of narrative construals of existence, history, and purpose than were our forebears at any other time in human history." Even more than that, he adds, "We not only continue to be animals who make stories but also animals who are *made by* our stories." Christian Smith, *Moral, Believing Animals* (Oxford: Oxford University Press, 2003), 64.

13. As defined in *Desiring the Kingdom*, 86.

politic become inscribed in our body through that "pedagogy of insignificance" noted by Bourdieu—all the mundane little micropractices that
nonetheless "carry" a big Story. And insofar as we are immersed bodily
in these microperformances, we are, over time, incorporated into a Story
that then becomes the script that we implicitly act out. The Story becomes
the background narrative and aesthetic orientation that habitually shapes
how we constitute our world. We don't memorize the Story as told to us;
we imbibe the Story as we perform it in a million little gestures.

So the liturgical anthropology first sketched in *Desiring the Kingdom*
is here supplemented with a new appreciation for the aesthetic or poetic
force of liturgies and the narratives that are "carried" in worship—both
"secular liturgies" and intentional Christian worship. My hope is that
Merleau-Ponty's phenomenology of incarnate significance and Bourdieu's
account of the "logic of practice" have given us a new appreciation for just
how such liturgies activate—and act upon—our bodily comportment to
the world. More specifically, it is my hope that the theoretical analyses of
part 1 have provided us with a lens and toolbox we can now use to reflect
upon the liturgies in which we finds ourselves immersed—to appreciate
"how worship works."

The Primacy of Metaphor and the Aesthetics
of Human Understanding

Merleau-Ponty and Bourdieu both prompt us to appreciate what Mark
Johnson calls "the bodily basis of meaning"—or more specifically, the
aesthetics of human understanding.[14] Johnson, translating Merleau-Ponty's
claim about "incarnate significance," says that "what and how anything is
meaningful to us is shaped by our specific form of incarnation" (*MB* ix).
This requires that we attend to "the bodily depths of human meaning-
making through our visceral connection to the world"—"the vast, submerged continents of nonconscious thought and feeling that lie at the
heart of our ability to make sense of our lives" (*MB* x). "Meaning," on
this account, is not restricted to the propositional or the conceptual; rather,
our bodies make meaning on an "aesthetic" register, without the discursive
mediation of words, concepts, or propositions. This "bodily basis of meaning" is rooted in "image schemas" (what he'll later call "conceptual metaphors," discussed further below). These image schemas (such as UP-DOWN

---

14. Johnson emphasizes that this entails a "generalization" of aesthetics beyond art or "the
beautiful": "Instead, aesthetics becomes the study of everything that goes into the human capacity to make and experience meaning." In this sense, "an aesthetics of human understanding
should become the basis for all philosophy." *The Meaning of the Body: Aesthetics of Human
Understanding* (Chicago: University of Chicago Press, 2007), x; hereafter cited as *MB*.

or Into-Out of[15]) correspond to bodily movements and constitute the most basic ways that we "make sense" of our experiences at an implicit level. But they are not concepts: they are fundamental structures of interaction with our environment that both govern and generate meaning-making (*MB* 10, 21). So, for example, the way we *move* fundamentally shapes how we can and do experience our world. This is generated from "processes of organism-environment interaction that operate beneath our felt awareness and that make that felt awareness possible": "these meanings cannot just pop into existence (arise in our consciousness) out of nothing and from nowhere. Instead, they must be grounded in our bodily connections with things, and they must be continuously 'in the making' via our sensorimotor engagements" (*MB* 25). To appreciate the bodily basis of meaning is to appreciate the bodily conditions of meaning-*making*. There is a creational, almost incarnational impulse here: a desire to honor the finite (and good!) conditions of our being-in-the-world—just those conditions to which God condescends in meeting us and revealing himself to us, and the same conditions by which the Spirit molds and (re)makes us. As Johnson summarizes, "We must see how our bodies, our brains, and our environments *together* generate a vastly meaningful milieu out of which all significance emerges for creatures with bodies like ours" (*MB* 31). Or as he later puts it, more explicitly: "In order to have human meaning, you need a human brain, operating in a living human body, continually interacting with a human environment that is at once physical, social, and cultural. Take away any one of these three dimensions, and you lose the possibility of meaning: no brain, no meaning; no body, no meaning; no environment, no meaning" (*MB* 155).[16] Our bodies, brains, and environments function together as the three-legged stool of our experience; any meaning is generated at the nexus of all three.[17] This is simply to recognize the conditions of creaturehood to which God condescends to meet us and mold us.

15. The capitalization of certain words and phrases in this chapter reflects Johnson's usage in *Meaning and the Body*.

16. Theologically, we should note that if this is an accurate account of our embodiment, and hence the conditions of our experience, then these would also be the conditions under which God's revelation would have to be manifest. For further discussion of this incarnational dynamic, see James K. A. Smith, *Speech and Theology: Language and the Logic of Incarnation*, Radical Orthodoxy (London: Routledge, 2002), 153–79.

17. Johnson later connects this threefold axiom to our specific concern with ritual formation: Meaning requires a functioning brain, in a living body that engages its environments—environments that are social and cultural, as well as physical and biological. Cultural artifacts and practices—for example, language, architecture, music, art, ritual acts, and public institutions—preserve aspects of meaning as objective features of the world. Without these cultural artifacts, our accumulated meaning, understanding, and knowledge would not be preserved over time, and each new generation would have to literally start over from scratch. Fortunately, because of social and cultural cognition, we do not have

So even though humans are those unique creatures who can "mean" the world unlike any other creatures, at the root and basis of those meaning-making and meaning-receiving capabilities is the bodily dynamics of organism-environment interaction.[18] Or as Johnson provocatively puts it, "Adults are big babies" because "the many bodily ways by which infants and children find and make meaning are not transcended and left behind when children eventually grow into adulthood. On the contrary, these very same sources of meaning are carried forward into, and thus underlie and make possible, our mature acts of understanding, conceptualization, and reasoning" (*MB* 33).[19] In this context, he specifically emphasizes the role that "feeling" plays in meaning, referring not to emotions but rather to a tactile "sense" of things. "There is a way it feels," for example, "to stick out your tongue, and there is a distinctive quality to the experience of sucking a pacifier with protruding nubs that is different from the quality experienced with a smooth pacifier. Feeling is one of the most notoriously difficult aspects of our experience to describe, and consequently we tend to overlook it in our accounts of meaning and thought. Nevertheless, it lies at the heart of all meaning" (*MB* 43). For lack of a better term, the tongue "knows" something that can't be expressed, and all experience has this "feel" and "quality" to it that is meaningful and differentiated, even if it can't be articulated or propositionalized. Following Daniel Stern, Johnson describes this as a "vitality-affect contour" (*MB* 43) akin to what Suzanne Langer, also struggling to find the right term, called "vital import": the *meaning* of feeling.[20] Here is a way of constituting the world that is learned

---

to relearn the meaning of our world. Each child, and each social group, can appropriate those objects and activities in which a culture's meanings and values are sedimented. However, we must keep in mind that those sociocultural objects, practices, and events are not meaningful in themselves. Rather, they become meaningful only insofar as they are enacted in the lives of human beings who *use* the language, *live by* the symbols, *sing* and *appreciate* the music, *participate* in the rituals, and *reenact* the practices and values of institutions. (*MB* 152, emphasis original)

Anyone who's worried that there's no room for God to show up here should consider more carefully: God's revelation and presence can constitute part of the *environment* of our experience, and our intersubjective relationship to God is the most fundamental aspect of "social" cognition. So to accept Johnson's threefold conditions of experience is far from accepting a naturalism: it can be a way of recognizing the conditions of the goodness of creation—conditions God deigns to inhabit in an "incarnational" move, both in the Incarnation and in his self-revelation.

18. Johnson also emphasizes that this is always already a "*body-based intersubjectivity*—our being with others via bodily expression, gesture, imitation, and interaction" that is "constitutive of our identity from our earliest days, and it is the birthplace of meaning" (*MB* 51).

19. Or, as Alasdair MacIntyre puts it, even philosophers are still animals. *Dependent Rational Animals: Why Human Beings Need the Virtues* (Chicago: Open Court, 1999), 36.

20. See Suzanne Langer, *Mind: An Essay on Human Feeling* (Baltimore: Johns Hopkins University Press, 1967). Johnson comments: "Because Langer was writing at a time when logical empiricism permitted only conceptual and propositional structures to be part of cognitive

at our mother's breast, but also never leaves us because it is both primary and primal. It continues to orient our being-in-the-world and is the basis for all of the other "higher" orders of meaning-making we engage in. So, for that reason, we are "big babies": "what Stern identifies as being at the heart of an infant's sense of itself and the meaning of its experience also lies at the heart of meaning in an adult's experience. The vitality-affect contours that make up a large part of an infant's meaningful experience continue to operate pervasively in adults. We never abandon or transcend our early meaning-making ways; we only extend and build upon them" (*MB* 44). But the import of this reaches to the highest levels of significance because vitality-affect contours play a role in determining what we feel called to *do*: "Vitality affects are meaningful to us at the most primordial levels of our bodily understanding of our world and our experience. They are meaningful because they give our experience motivation, direction, and intensity. They constitute the erotic, desire-full character of a particular situation that makes it matter to us" (*MB* 45). What *matters*—what's *at stake*—is determined by this *feel* for the world.

At the basis of our meaning-making is an action-oriented comportment to our environment. We are in the world primarily as *doers*, not thinkers—and even our thinking serves, and grows out of, our doing. We are certainly *more* than our bodies, but we are never *less* than that: while we can make and receive meaning on complex registers, we are only able to do so because of a fundamental "organism-environment coupling" by which we navigate being-in-the-world. And what Johnson helpfully emphasizes is the way that these baseline bodily interactions constitute the environment in which we would pursue "meaningful" action. If our most basic perception of a "situation" already "loads" an environment as a certain kind of situation calling for a certain sort of action, then the constitution of a *moral* situation is also rooted in these bodily dynamics of organism-environment interaction.

Indeed, we might even speak of the bodily basis of *holiness*. Sanctification will require the rehabilitation of such embodied perception. For example, the Holy Spirit will need to reconfigure what Johnson describes as our "neural maps." Neural maps are constellations of neural cells that "fire sequentially when a stimulus moves across adjacent positions within a sensory field" (*MB* 127). On the one hand, there are biological realities that constrain such neural maps. For example, the placement of a frog's eyes in relation to its head (and its prey) governs how its neural map can be formed, just as there are constraints on the formation of my neural

meaning, she had to coin a new term, 'vital import,' to identify the kind of significance she was pointing to. She knew, but wasn't then permitted to say, that vital import was just as much a part of human meaning as an abstract 'cognitive content' of propositions or sentences" (*MB* 44).

maps given that my eyes are on the front of my head, about five feet off the ground, and so on. On the other hand, there is a significant degree of *plasticity* or malleability in the formation of neural maps. So if we have forged a neural map but then experience injury to the eye or brain, a neural map can be reconfigured and can adjust for the change, enabling us to once again be able to navigate our environment. These neural maps significantly determine the shape of our experience: "Like the frog," Johnson summarizes, "we live in the world significantly (but not totally) defined by our maps. Topologically speaking, our bodies are our minds" (*MB* 130).

In fact, Johnson suggests, "mind" is not a given, a priori reality and should not be thought of as a substance. "*Mind emerges*," he emphasizes: "Mind is an achievement, not a pre-given faculty" (*MB* 151, 152). While we are created and born with capacities to navigate our world—to create and receive meaning, and thus function as cultural animals—"we are not born with minds fully formed and ready for thinking. Instead, we acquire 'minds' through coordinated sharing of meaning and our concomitant ability to engage in symbolic interaction" (*MB* 151). Thus our capacities *become* "mind," as something acquired. This picture might also change what we think it is to have "the mind of Christ" (1 Cor. 2:16): perhaps the mind of Christ is also something that is *acquired* through practice and formation, something that emerges as a result of sanctification rather than an informational deposit.

We can further reflect on this dynamic by considering Johnson's account of the concurrent formation of our neural maps: "alternative learned and normal circuits can coexist in this network" (*MB* 128). In other words, our minds can contain *worlds*—we can simultaneously be forging multiple neural maps that each constitute the world differently. Consider a strange but fascinating study that Johnson cites involving owls:

> Like frogs, owls have developed an extremely accurate method of catching prey. The owl hears a mouse rustling on the ground and locates the mouse primarily in the owl's retinotectal map, and the diving owl then looks to find the exact location of its prey as it strikes. Eric Knudsen put prismatic glasses on adult and juvenile owls that distorted the owls' vision by twenty-three degrees. After wearing the glasses for eight weeks, the adult owls never learned to compensate, although juveniles were able to learn to hunt accurately. However, when the glasses were reintroduced to adult owls who had worn them as juveniles, they were able to readjust to the glasses in short order. (*MB* 128)

There was a plasticity to the juvenile owl neural maps that permitted them to adjust for the prismatic glasses; they learned to constitute their world anew by reconfiguring their neural map. However, what's most intriguing is the parliament of owls that had worn the glasses as juveniles, then lived without them, and finally had the glasses reintroduced to their "habit-body" as adults. This group was able to reactivate the neural maps that had been formed in their earlier experience, though they had gone dormant. Nonetheless, they remained there to be reactivated under the right conditions.

Following Gerald Edelman, Johnson introduces the notion of "repertoires" to describe this phenomenon. *Primary* repertoires are formed by "normal" environmental conditions[21]—those conditions that prevail most of the time and thus stimulate the relevant neural pathways more often. They will "fire together and wire together in a process of axonal sprouting and synaptogenesis" (*MB* 130). This becomes the dominant neural map and hence the primary repertoire by which we constitute and interact with our environment. Other neuronal groups "will fail to find useful topological connections, and they eventually die and are crowded out by the successful neuronal groups" (*MB* 130). But then there is a third category that Edelman describes as *secondary* repertoires: "In the adult organism, these *latent* axonal arbors remaining from only partly successful attempts to wire together lie dormant, ready to reorganize the map as needed by means of further synaptogenesis" (*MB* 130, emphasis added). These latent maps remain possibilities for the adult organism. They have been lightly inscribed on the brain, but they lack the density of primary repertoires simply from lack of use and stimulation. The brain is subject to competing formations, and the competition is won by those environmental conditions that most regularly stimulate relevant neural pathways.

If our being-in-the-world is significantly bound up with the bodily basis of meaning, and our embodied intentionality is governed by such repertoires, then it seems that this could be part of an account of how various cultural liturgies "trump" others. The rhythms and routines of an environment shape my habitual orientation toward and perception of the world in no small part because they form the neural maps that govern that perception of the world. Those rhythms and routines and rituals that constitute "regularities" in my environment—that are experienced as normal and dominant—will determine what counts as a "primary" repertoire. Concurrent, competing formations can inscribe "secondary" repertoires, but those will be pressed by the dominance of primary repertoires. However, not all is lost: secondary repertoires that become dormant can also be reactivated, and if the environment and constancy of stimuli change—if the balance of competing rituals shifts—there also seems to be the possibility that the ordering of primary and secondary repertoires could be reversed, though this will have to fight against the overwhelming inertia and density of those primary configurations. What Johnson gives us is an

21. What constitutes "normal" conditions, of course, will not be universal.

embodied way to think about the dynamics of conversation, initiation, and sanctification.[22]

As we noted earlier, Johnson is arguing that there is a fundamental *aesthetics* of human understanding. This is because our fundamental "feel for the world" makes sense of our experience in a way that is more like poetry than propositional analysis. This doesn't mean that our experience is "merely" aesthetic or boils down to just "beauty." "Aesthetics is not just art theory," Johnson emphasizes, "but rather should be regarded broadly as the study of how humans make and experience meaning" (*MB* 209).[23] And the reason to describe this as fundamentally *aesthetic* is because the modes of inference and meaning-making that characterize our embodied being-in-the-world operate according to a "logic" that is more akin to understanding a story than solving an algebra problem. For example, in analyzing an erotic poem by Pablo Neruda ("Gentleman without Company"), Johnson remarks: "One hesitates to comment on this image, for fear of diminishing its incarnate realization of sexual longing. The meaning that is 'working' here, as Gendlin would say, is the meaning of the body, developed through various senses (sight, hearing, smell, taste), and dependent on the precise rhythm of the images, sounds, pauses, and intensifications that define what is inadequately known as the 'form' of the poem" (*MB* 220–21). One "gets" this poem not by analysis but by immersion: to understand it is to be pulled into the *feel* that it evokes, to resonate with the corporeal significance conveyed, even if that meaning can never quite be put into words. "These aspects of bodily meaning," he concludes, "are not, for the most part, propositional, and it therefore follows that meaning cannot be primarily linguaform and propositional" (*MB* 213). Understanding how our experience "means" is not like diagramming a sentence or parsing a syllogism; it's more like making sense of how Thomas Wilfred's mesmerizing light in *Opus 161* affects us, and what this haunting light *means* in the narrative arc of Terrence Malick's *Tree of Life*. When Johnson presses the "aesthetic" of human understanding, he is pointing to the irreducible affectivity that governs (and undergirds) our experience of the world—our entire "environment" (which, of course, includes God and others). So "instead of isolating the 'aesthetic' as merely one autonomous dimension of experience, or merely one form of judgment, we must realize that aesthetics is about the conditions of experience as such, and art is a culmination of the possibility of meaning in experience" (*MB* 212).

22. And given the recognition of pliability of juvenile neural maps, we have a bodily basis for appreciating the importance of early childhood *faith* formation.

23. We should remember that our term *aesthetic* owes its origin to the Greek αἰσθάνεσθαι, which simply referred to perception by the senses. The narrowing of the term to the realms of art and beauty is a modern phenomenon.

As an "aesthetics" of human understanding, Johnson's account culminates in his argument regarding the primacy of *metaphor* in the way we make sense of our world.[24] Metaphor is a kind of association or analogy by which we understand one thing in terms of another. The force of metaphor is always just slightly more than what we can analyze—there's a certain "genius" to a metaphor that generates a power of meaning with a sort of *je ne sais quoi*, an excess of meaning that I "get" without being able to say.[25] The metaphorical sum is greater than the analytic parts. There is a unique, "aesthetic" mode of inference by which we understand the metaphor. Metaphors generate meaning by confrontation, as a sort of chemical reaction that results from bringing together things not usually associated. Jeremy Begbie helpfully considers a Shakespearean metaphor: "Juliet is the sun." "The different terms of the metaphor," he observes, "each draw on a whole range of connotations and associations of the words" to generate a "surplus of meaning" that could not be *meant* in any other way.

A metaphor generates a whole set of new[26] meanings for us, and just because they are generated this way, these meanings can be apprehended only

24. One can see Johnson's *Meaning of the Body* as an advance from his earlier work, with George Lakoff, *Metaphors We Live By* (Chicago: University of Chicago Press, 1980), which begins with the claim that "metaphor is pervasive in everyday life, not just in language but in thought and action" (3). (The aesthetic trajectory of his later work is hinted at on pp. 235–36. It seems to me that in *Metaphors We Live By*, Johnson had not yet made the "pragmatist" turn that would release him sufficiently from "representationalist" paradigms.) The earlier work argued for the centrality, even primacy, of metaphor but didn't yet tease out the implication of this: that if this is true, then our account of human understanding and experience must be fundamentally an *aesthetics*—more of a "poetics" than an epistemology.

25. Or as Paul Ricoeur puts it, "The metaphorical meaning of a word is nothing which can be found in the dictionary." *Hermeneutics and the Human Sciences*, trans. John B. Thompson (Cambridge: Cambridge University Press, 1981), 169. Ricoeur also delineates the reasons for this. First, metaphor is *contextual*: "metaphorical use must be solely contextual, that is, a meaning which emerges as the unique and fleeting result of a certain contextual action" (169). Second, and because of this, metaphorical meaning is *interactive*: it is produced "between" different senses, and between the author and reader (170). Ricoeur's understanding of metaphor is nicely summarized by Henry Venema: "Metaphorical statements are not decorative devices in which one simply substitutes one lexical meaning for another; they are genuine creations of meaning that have not yet been added to the virtual system of semiotic signifiers. The production of metaphorical meaning through semantic interaction is irreducible to the dictionary meaning of its semiotic elements." Venema, *Identifying Selfhood: Imagination, Narrative, and Hermeneutics in the Thought of Paul Ricoeur* (Albany: SUNY Press, 2000), 81.

26. Though I don't think novelty is an essential aspect of metaphoricity. Granted, some metaphors will be powerful precisely because they are innovative, but other metaphors do not seem to lose their meaning or force just because of repetition. Indeed, metaphors can have an enduring meaning that can take you by surprise, even after much repetition. It is precisely the play and range and allusivity of metaphor that enables a metaphor to *keep* generating meaning. Or, similarly, a metaphor can be a powerful force of memory—it can bring back worlds to us. I was happy to discover that Iain McGilchrist makes the same point. "Metaphor does not have

through this metaphor, by being drawn into its life. Thus a metaphor is irreducible: it cannot be translated into another form of language without loss of meaning. As we all know, you cannot convert a metaphor into a literal statement without robbing it of its content and power. ("He is a tiger" must communicate more than "he is ferocious"; otherwise we would likely not bother to use the metaphor.)[27]

Given the play and can't-be-pinned-down-ness of metaphor, it's not surprising that the dynamics of metaphor are at the very heart of "the aesthetic." What is true of art in particular is, we begin to see, characteristic of our very incarnate existence. Calvin Seerveld suggests that "peculiar to art is a parable character, a metaphoric intensity, an elusive play in its artifactual presentation of meanings apprehended."[28] But that parable character and metaphoric intensity are not confined to "art" narrowly; they are also characteristic of the aesthetic aspect of human being-in-the-world. Thus metaphor is powered by that "allusivity" that characterizes not only art but our aesthetic being-in-the-world.[29] Metaphor is a kind of shorthand for the aesthetic.

Insofar as our being-in-the-world is navigated metaphorically, we can appreciate why Johnson posits a fundamental *aesthetics* of human understanding.[30] Even more strongly, Johnson will argue that our higher order "conceptual" thinking is nonetheless indebted to—and dependent upon—primary metaphors that are linked to the bodily basis of meaning. So abstract concepts "are defined by conceptual metaphors that recruit the semantics and inference patterns of sensorimotor experience" (*MB* 176). He pictures a nested relationship, beginning with the image schemas that arise from our bodily engagement, which in turn give rise to "primary" metaphors, which then generate "conceptual" metaphors, eventually yielding concepts proper. So our concepts are *emergent*, growing out of what is ultimately a body-based interaction with our environment.

to be new: in fact the best ones never can be. They are like the language of love, as old as the hills yet fresh with every new lover. The trick of the poet is to make what seemed feeble, old, dead come back to life. True metaphor is a union like love." Ange Mlinko and Iain McGilchrist, "This Is Your Brain on Poetry," *Poetry* 197 (October 2010): 44.

27. Jeremy Begbie, *Resounding Truth: Christian Wisdom in the World of Music* (Grand Rapids: Baker Academic, 2007), 50. Begbie goes on to note that music's meaning is just this sort of irreducible metaphoricity (52).

28. Calvin Seerveld, *Rainbows for the Fallen World: Aesthetic Life and Artistic Task* (Toronto: Tuppence, 1980), 27.

29. Ibid., 125–35.

30. McGilchrist makes the same point: "the importance of metaphor is that it *underlies all forms of understanding whatsoever*, science and philosophy no less than poetry and art" (*The Master and His Emissary: The Divided Brain and the Making of the Western World* [New Haven: Yale University Press, 2010], 71, emphasis original). What I, following Johnson, am describing as "aesthetic," McGilchrist would call "right-brained."

Johnson's account of the primacy of metaphor is a suggestive (and, I think, accurate) picture that enables us to articulate anew the relationship between "worship" and "worldview," the nested relation between liturgy and theology. It also prompts us to think about Christian faith not simply as a set of fundamental beliefs but also as a fund of primary *metaphors* that attune us to the world on an "aesthetic" register. Following Johnson's account will enable us later to consider how liturgies, broadly speaking—and Christian worship, more specifically—function not just on a conceptual (didactic) level but also at the level of conceptual metaphor; indeed, we might think of worship as a constellation of conceptual metaphors.[31] Let me unpack Johnson's account before further exploring this notion of Christian faith as a constellation of conceptual metaphors.

1. We *acquire* "primary metaphors" from our sensorimotor experience of enacted meaning. So we need to first appreciate that these primary metaphors are acquired, not hardwired and not possessed a priori. These are not Kantian "categories" that come pre-installed. These primary metaphors are acquired through immersion in an environment or environments. While there might be wide commonality in these metaphors, we must also recognize the contingency of different contexts and environments. So primary metaphors are not necessarily universal, though they can be widely shared (and *could* be functionally universal).

2. Immersion in an environment creates a context of repeated exposure and experience that becomes the basis of absorbing primary metaphors. For example, "the repeated co-activation of neural patterns associated with the subjective experience of intimacy and the sensorimotor experience of being physically close establishes the cross-domain neural connections that define the primary metaphor PSYCHOLOGICAL INTIMACY IS PHYSICAL CLOSENESS" (*MB* 178). The acquisition of this basic association (that is, intimacy equals physical closeness) becomes the basis for a conceptual map. The primary metaphorical relation then shapes how we conceive relationships: "We used to be so close," or "He seems distant," or "They're drifting apart." The conceptual metaphors for interpersonal relationship are rooted in, and grow out of, our bodily experience of physical closeness. There is no "literal" language for relationality or psychological intimacy because even alternatives would also be rooted in other primary metaphors. In a sense, it's metaphor all the way down.

31. In suggesting this, I think that Johnson's account of primary metaphors—as I'm extending it here—could supplement Nathan Mitchell's important discussion of the "logic of metaphor" in Christian worship in *Meeting Mystery*, 189–227.

To Think About: Metaphor as Godfire

As I noted early on, this book—and the Cultural Liturgies project in general—walks a delicate, almost hypocritical tightrope: I am making an allusive argument (I hope) for the irreducibility of the aesthetic. I am providing an intellectual analysis of why and how incarnate significance eludes our intellectual grasp. I'm trying to convince you of the fact that we are more fundamentally *moved* than convinced. I'm offering you the laborious detail of a "philosophical anthropology" and a "liturgical theology of culture" to prompt you to consider that God gets hold of us in stories and poems and the performed narrative of liturgies. Which is why you'll find me regularly pointing you to aesthetic works—novels, poems, films—to help picture what we're talking about. What better way to picture the elusive power of metaphorical meaning-making than Jeanne Murray Walker's marvelous poem "Staying Power," which ventures quite a unique metaphor for God. (I encourage you to read the poem aloud to yourself or, even better, to a friend.)

Staying Power

In appreciation of Maxim Gorky at the International Convention of Atheists, 1929

Like Gorky, I sometimes follow my doubts
outside and question the metal sky,
longing to have the fight settled, thinking,
I can't go on like this, and finally I say

*All right, it is improbable—all right, there
is no God*. And then as if I'm focusing
a magnifying glass on dry leaves, *God* blazes up.
It's the attention, maybe, to what isn't

there that makes the notion flare like
a forest fire until I have to spend the afternoon

---

3. "People will acquire hundreds, or even thousands, of primary conceptual metaphors just by going about the daily affairs of their lives. These metaphors are formed primarily because of the nature of our bodies (with their brains, sense organs, motor systems, and emotions) as they interact with our environments."[32] They "arise naturally" and, in some sense, cannot *not* be acquired.[33] "Most of the time they are activated automatically and unconsciously to structure our

---

32. Other examples he discusses include Affection Is Warmth, Important Is Big, Purposes are Destinations, Time Is Motion, and many others (*MB* 179).

33. This is not to say that all people acquire the same primary metaphors: again, we would have to recognize the differences in environmental contexts. One can easily appreciate how different environments would yield different primary metaphors. What Johnson doesn't

spraying it with the hose to put it out. Even
on an ordinary day when a friend calls,

tells me they've found melanoma,
complains that the hospital is cold, I whisper *God*.
God, I say as my heart turns inside out.
Pick up any language by the scruff of its neck,

wipe its face, set it down on the lawn,
and I bet it will toddle right into the godfire
again, which—though they say it doesn't
exist—can send you straight to the burn unit.

Oh, we have only so many words to think with.
Say God's not fire, say anything, say God's
a phone, maybe. You know you didn't order a phone,
but there it is. It rings. You don't know who it could be.

You don't want to talk, so you pull out
the plug. It rings. You smash it with a hammer
till it bleeds springs and coils and clobbered-up
metal bits. It rings again. You pick it up

and a voice you love whispers hello.[1]

No analysis will substitute for the affective power of the poem, which is bound up not only with its metaphors and diction, but also its cadence and timbre. What this poem *means* is not merely "between the lines"; its meaning is generated like that fire *in* the reading.

1. Jeanne Murray Walker, "Staying Power," in *New Tracks, Night Falling* (Grand Rapids: Eerdmans, 2009), 54–55. Reprinted by permission of the publisher; all rights reserved.

understanding of situations and events" (*MB* 178). Such metaphors, then, would condition our perceptual evaluation and appraisal of situations.

4. These primary metaphors are the building blocks of more complex, high-level, systematic metaphors. These more complex metaphors "build on, blend and extend our primary metaphors" (*MB* 178–79).[34] So if we think of concepts as "containers," this is rooted in primary

---

entertain is the possibility that one could simultaneously acquire "competing" primary metaphors.

34. This is akin to Bourdieu's claim regarding "logical logic" versus the "logic of practice." To translate Johnson's argument into Bourdieu's language: logical logic is a derivation from the logic of practice.

metaphors of INSIDE-OUTSIDE, and given our experience of something's being either "in" the container or outside of it, we bring to the concept-as-container metaphor certain predispositions and a "bodily" understanding of how concepts work. So "abstract" concepts don't drop from the sky; they bubble up from our embodied experience. Concepts are more like distillations of our experience than pristine, Form-like categories that descend upon our experience.[35]

5. At the heart of Johnson's analogical argument is the claim that there is a "logic" to metaphor; metaphors "make sense" of our experience and carry within them a kind of coherence and logic that entails certain kinds of inferences. For example, I have a bodily experience with CONTAINMENT, and "there is a definite spatial or bodily logic of containment that arises in our experience with containers"—that is, "an entity is either inside the container or outside of it, but not both at once." So "our bodily encounters with containers and objects that we observe and manipulate teach us the spatial logic of containers" (MB 179). Image schemas or primary metaphors, "which arise recurrently in our perception and bodily movement, have their own logic" (MB 181). The logic of metaphor is a kind of felt inference.

6. This "bodily logic" of metaphor is then "recruited" and articulated in a conceptual logic, like the law of the excluded middle or the law of noncontradiction—conceptual logical "rules" that trace back to sensorimotor experience. "We have not developed two separate logical and inferential systems, one for our bodily experiences and one for our abstract concepts and reasoning (as pure logic). Instead, the logic of our bodily experience provides all the logic we need in order to perform every rational inference, even with the most abstract concepts" (MB 179).[36]

Johnson gives us some resources to see anew what's at work—and at stake—in "liturgical" formations (which include both the sorts of "secular" liturgies I've analyzed in Desiring the Kingdom and Christian liturgical formation).[37] On one level, meaningful liturgies will recruit and employ primary metaphors precisely because we are embodied actors. Any practices that are going to be "inhabitable" by us will have to honor the embodied

35. This will have implications for how we think about dogmas and doctrines. If doctrines are on the order of complex metaphors and concepts, then in some sense they bubble up from primary metaphors forged in practice. I hope to explore this dynamic in more detail in James K. A. Smith, Who's Afraid of Relativism? Taking Wittgenstein, Rorty, and Brandom to Church, Church and Postmodern Culture Series (Grand Rapids: Baker Academic, forthcoming).

36. See, for example, George Lakoff and Rafael Núñez, Where Mathematics Comes From: How the Embodied Mind Brings Mathematics into Being (New York: Basic Books, 2000).

37. See Desiring the Kingdom, chaps. 3 and 5, respectively.

ways that we interact with our environment. Insofar as such liturgies create "worlds" for us, they will have to be worlds cut to the measure of our meaty existence. Because we first and foremost *mean* the world as incarnate actors, any meaningful liturgy is going to "activate," as it were, some of our primary metaphorical orientations: touch will resonate with INTIMACY IS CLOSENESS; rhythms of movement will activate our sense that PURPOSES ARE DESTINATIONS; the presentation of narratives will find tangible ways to build on our primary metaphorical sense that TIME IS MOTION; and so forth. Rather than trafficking in abstract concepts that descend from on high, meaning-full liturgies that "make sense" for us on this deep, aesthetic, metaphorical level successfully meet us in our embodiment and build upon the *praktognosia* we carry in our bones.

On another level, such liturgies—insofar as they offer opportunity for "repeated co-activation of neural patterns"—will constitute part of our "environment" and thus will build on primary metaphors in order to habituate us to *conceptual* metaphors that will then seep into our background and shape how we (nonconsciously) intend and constitute the world. In other words, such liturgies are not simply meaningful *in themselves*; they also become funds of meaning as "horizons of expectation" that then govern and condition the way we constitute the "extra-liturgical" world, as it were. Just as we "cannot avoid acquiring these [primary] metaphors" because they are the oxygen of our mundane experience—"activated automatically and unconsciously to structure our understanding of situations and events" (*MB* 178)—so too the conceptual metaphors that are "carried" in liturgical practices will, over time, sediment into our background in ways that are more aesthetic than logical, more poetic than didactic. Carried in such practices will be conceptual metaphors that prime us to immediately see God, the world, and others in certain ways. These will not be conscious judgments we make but rather our primary perception of the world that is already evaluative. Different operative metaphors give us a very different world—and different callings within it. There will be secular liturgies, for example, that find their metaphorical power and center in a picture of egocentricity: they will functionally tell the story that *I* am the center of the universe; that the world—and perhaps even God—exists for my pleasure; that "nature" is a fund of resources available for my use and disposal; that there is a kind of centripetal force tending toward *me* at the center. There are primary metaphors that can reinforce this take on the world. Indeed, the very fact that I can only ever experience *my* experience is a powerful embodiment that has a centripetal feel to it. Various narratives and metaphors and practices can build conceptual metaphors upon this reality that, over time ("repeated co-activation of neural patterns"), inscribes in me a habitual orientation to the world in which I am the center of the universe.

In contrast, it is easy enough to imagine liturgies that activate and build upon very different primary metaphors, and thus generate a different constellation of conceptual metaphors. Such liturgies would perhaps build on our primary metaphors of interaction, sociality, and dependence. INTIMACY IS CLOSENESS and AFFECTION IS WARMTH, for example, are primary metaphors that are deeply relational and thus can displace our tendency to egoism. Building on such primary metaphors, one could generate conceptual metaphors that "picture" the world as a home shared with others—a place that makes a claim upon me, shared with others who are both gifts and responsibilities, who bear the image of their Creator.[38] In other words, we would have two very different liturgies that generate contrasting metaphorical universes: the world as "nature" versus the world as "creation." And our orientation—and hence our "understanding" of our calling—would be fundamentally shaped at the level of conceptual metaphor. We don't "decide" to "see" the world as creation or nature; we imbibe a metaphorical inclination, almost unavoidably, by being immersed in liturgical environments.

A General Poetics: Imagination, Metaphor, Narrative

A liturgical anthropology recognizes the primacy of "incarnate significance." For finite, embodied creatures like us, meaning is fundamentally rooted in metaphor because that is the inferential "logic" of the body.[39] As I suggested in this book's introduction, an adequate *liturgics* needs to be rooted in a phenomenological appreciation of a kind of *kinaesthetics* that is, in turn, the basis for appreciating the *aesthetics* of human understanding. In other words, at the heart of a liturgical anthropology is a recognition of not just the centrality of desire but also the centrality of the imagination. It is because I imagine the world (and my place in it) in certain

38. I think this is exactly what Emmanuel Levinas accounts for in his phenomenology of "living from . . ." in *Totality and Infinity*, trans. Alphonso Lingis (Pittsburgh: Duquesne University Press, 1969), 110–21, 147–51. For relevant discussion, see Jeffrey Bloechl, *Liturgy of the Neighbor: Emmanuel Levinas and the Religion of Responsibility* (Pittsburgh: Duquesne University Press, 2000). Consider also Steven Bouma-Prediger and Brian Walsh's analysis of the significance of construing creation as "home" in *Beyond Homelessness: Christian Faith in a Culture of Displacement* (Grand Rapids: Eerdmans, 2008).

39. McGilchrist helps us appreciate the "mechanics" of this, as it were, by a kind of triangulation. As he suggests, the right hemisphere of the brain is the "between" of body and (left-brained, analytic) mind: "The right hemisphere is in general more intimately connected with the limbic system, an ancient subcortical system that is involved in the experience of emotions of all kinds, and with other subcortical structures, than is the left hemisphere" (*The Master and His Emissary*, 58). The right hemisphere is that part of the brain that negotiates metaphorical inference (71) as well as the understanding of narrative (76).

ways that I am oriented by fundamental loves and longings. It is because I "picture" the world as *this* kind of place, this kind of "environment," that I then picture "the good life" in a certain way that draws me toward it and thus construe my obligations and responsibilities accordingly.[40] While my actions and behavior are, in a sense, "pulled" out of me because of my passional orientation to some *telos*—some vision of the good life and what it means to be human—my love and longing for that "good life" is itself a signal that I conceive that "kingdom" as something that attracts me. So, in some sense, imagination precedes desire. My longings are not simply "chosen" by me; they are not self-generated "decisions." I don't wake up on a Monday morning and say, "From now on, I am going to long for X." We don't choose desires; they are *birthed* in us. They are formed in us as habits, as *habitus*. And as Merleau-Ponty helped us to see, the acquisition of such habits is ultimately a rearrangement of our corporeal schema—a reconfiguration of how we imagine ourselves and our places in the world. Or as Bourdieu would put it, to acquire a *habitus* is to have been incorporated into a social body and its vision of a way of life. And that in*corpor*ation marshals our embodied nature. In short, the way to the imagination is through the body.

We become a people who *desire* the kingdom (or some other, rival version of "the kingdom") insofar as we are a people who have been trained to *imagine* the kingdom in a certain way. Once we appreciate this interplay of desire and imagination, we can finally address a criticism that has sometimes been leveled against my argument in *Desiring the Kingdom*. The critique would be formulated as a question: Before I *love* something, don't I need to *know* what I'm loving? So doesn't that mean that knowledge precedes love, and hence that intellect is prior to affect? Therefore shouldn't education still be fundamentally about equipping students with knowledge—with propositional content about what they *ought* to love? And shouldn't the heart of worship be the sermon, which didactically instructs us so that we *know* what we ought to love, whom we ought to follow, and hence what we ought to *do*? Doesn't the "right order of love" (per Augustine) require *knowing* what I ought to love?

Not quite. What I'm suggesting is that we first *imagine* what we ought to love, because significance, for creatures like us, is first and foremost "incarnate." Such imagination is clearly "cognitive" insofar as it is an intentional mode of consciousness—it is "about" something, it is aimed at something, and there is a "content" to what I imagine. However, imagination is not intellection. And being able to "imagine" a kingdom is different

40. There is a basically Aristotelian intuition here: an agent always acts for his own good. But now there's a kind of aesthetic qualifier: it's not primarily that we *know* this good but that we *imagine* the good.

from "knowing" it—for just the sorts of reasons that Merleau-Ponty emphasizes the priority of *praktognosia* to analysis or that Johnson points to the priority of metaphor to propositions. So it's not as simple as saying that I first have to *know* what I love, and hence knowledge precedes desire. The relevant sort of "knowing" here is not propositional knowledge but rather an *aesthetic* know-how. It is what Merleau-Ponty called an "erotic comprehension" of a situation. It's more like "knowing" that someone is flirting with you than knowing someone's shoe size. I imagine a *telos* or vision of the good life on an aesthetic, metaphorical, poetic register. And that is why a "vision" of the kingdom is birthed in me or inscribed in me through aesthetic means. I come to imagine the kingdom in certain ways—and come to desire that kingdom in unconscious, automated ways—because I have drunk up the stories of a people or a culture. I am incorporated into the *habitus* of a people, and that *habitus* in inscribed in me, because I have been immersed in the stories of the body politic. Liturgical animals are imaginative animals who live off the stuff of the imagination: stories, pictures, images, and metaphors are the poetry of our embodied existence.[41]

So we might say that a liturgical anthropology yields a "general poetics,"[42] in the sense and spirit of Aristotle's *Poetics*—but now expanded beyond "aesthetics" or the narrow realm of art to account for the aesthetics of human understanding in general.[43] A general poetics is a way of recognizing the fundamentally aesthetic way that we intend the world, that meaning is primarily metaphorical for us.[44] To say we are liturgical animals is

41. Thus Charles Taylor emphasizes that a "social imaginary" is "carried in images, stories, and legends." *Modern Social Imaginaries* (Durham, NC: Duke University Press, 2004), 23.

42. I'm playing here on the notion of a "general hermeneutics" (following Hans-Georg Gadamer) that expands the scope of interpretation to experience "in general." For discussion, see James K. A. Smith, *The Fall of Interpretation: Philosophical Foundations for a Creational Hermeneutic*, 2nd ed. (Grand Rapids: Baker Academic, 2012), 159–63.

43. While I cannot do justice to it here, in the ballpark are conversations internal to the Reformational tradition of aesthetics in the philosophical heritage stemming from Herman Dooyeweerd. With Dooyeweerd, I'm emphasizing that there is an aesthetic "aspect" of all human existence; but I agree with Calvin Seerveld's suggestion that "Dooyeweerd's placement of aesthetic structure in the order of modal complexity needs reworking since aesthetic affairs are much more fundamental an underground in human experience than Dooyeweerd seems to admit." Seerveld, "Dooyeweerd's Legacy for Aesthetics: Modal Law Theory," in *The Legacy of Herman Dooyeweerd: Reflections on Critical Philosophy in the Christian Tradition*, ed. C. T. McIntire (Lanham, MD: University Press of America, 1985), 41–79 (quote at 68).

44. This resonates with, but also differs from, William Dyrness's project in *Poetic Theology: God and the Poetics of Everyday Life* (Grand Rapids: Eerdmans, 2011). It seems to me that Dyrness's project is fundamentally an apologetic—a cultural theology that takes the arts ("the poetic") seriously in order to discern in our artistic endeavors what is really a longing for God (see esp. 201, 246). Dyrness also expands the "poetic" to include "everyday" endeavors, but then does so by linking such cultural projects to beauty. In sum, I find the meaning of "poetic" in his

simultaneously to emphasize that we are metaphorical animals, imaginative animals, poetic animals, "storied" animals. We act in the world more as characters in a drama than as soldiers dutifully following a command.[45] We are acting out a script, improvising in an unfolding drama, taking on a character in a story that has captivated us at a level we might not even be aware of. We come to "see" ourselves in a certain way, not by introspection or reflection, but because we have absorbed a narrative that now functions as the background drama of our existence. So it's not so much that I "see" myself in this way as that I *act* in accord with the character I've assumed. This is not an identity that I have chosen; it is more like an orientation I have assumed—a mode of comportment to the world that grows out of my implicit, tacit sense of who I am within an overarching story of the world. And such stories captivate and orient me not primarily didactically or instructively, but affectively and unconsciously: such stories are "understood" by the imagination at a "gut level" that turns out to be the incarnate core of my existence.

A "general poetics," then, is a phenomenology of our being-in-the-world that recognizes that meaning-making is, for us, a primarily aesthetic matter. At this level, poetry and story, metaphor and narrative, are bound together because they *do* the same thing: they give meaning—and give us the ability to make meaning—on a register that reverberates with our bodies. Both metaphor and narrative resonate with the imagination, which is why a general poetics sees imagination as central to our being-in-the-world.[46] The dynamics of metaphor and the dynamics of story are

---

project to be equivocal. For my critique of Dyrness, see James K. A. Smith, "Erotic Theology," *Image* 69 (2011): 118–20. My "general poetics" is focused on the fundamentally aesthetic mode in which we constitute our worlds. Dyrness is also more focused on affirming what's *good* in "secular liturgies" (emphasizing "common grace"), whereas I have tended to emphasize the antithesis between the vision of the good life carried in secular liturgies and the vision of *shalom* that is performed in Christian worship. However, my antithetical account is not a "total" critique. Following Augustine, I would advocate nuanced, ad hoc evaluation of particular cultural practices. For a relevant discussion, see James K. A. Smith, "Reforming Public Theology: Two Kingdoms, or Two Cities?," *Calvin Theological Journal* 47 (2012): 122–37. These themes will be addressed in much more detail in volume 3 of Cultural Liturgies.

45. For a discussion of how stories can be normative, see N. T. Wright, *Scripture and the Authority of God* (San Francisco: HarperOne, 2011), 24–25.

46. Johnson notes the ambiguity of Kant's legacy in this regard. On the one hand, "nowhere is the derogation of the aesthetic more pronounced than in the impressive aesthetic theory of Immanuel Kant. . . . His adherence to a faculty psychology that rigidly demarcates cognitive from noncognitive mental acts made it impossible for him to ever fully embrace imagination (and feeling) as the key to meaning and understanding." In fact, "his reduction of the aesthetic to feeling alone and his exclusion of feeling from cognition and knowledge were carried forward most fatefully into twentieth-century aesthetic theory" (*MB* 211). On the other hand, "In his *Critique of Judgment* (1790), Kant toyed with the pervasiveness of blended imaginative-feeling-thinking processes in how we experience meaning, but he was never able to give up

both "logics" whose modes of inference are aesthetic, and because they are aesthetic they resonate with our bodies. "Poetry engraves itself in the brain: it doesn't just slip smoothly over the cortex as language normally does. It has all the graininess of life, as it rips into being from deep within the limbic system, the ancient seat of awareness and affective meaning."[47] We "know" and "make sense" of a story or a poem in that "between" space of our incarnation.[48] And I'm suggesting that liturgies "work" on us—shape us and form us and grab hold of us—because they also operate on that "between"-ness of incarnate significance. Liturgies marshal the aesthetic dynamics of metaphor and narrative, the "literary" force of poems and stories. This is why a liturgical philosophical anthropology needs to incorporate a general poetics in order to account for (at least some of) the formative power of liturgies, whether secular or Christian.

In this respect, I resonate with Paul Ricoeur's career-long project of unpacking the significance of the imagination for human being-in-the-world.[49] "The mediating role of imagination," he once told Richard Kearney, "is forever at work in lived reality."[50] Thus Ricoeur "generalizes" phenomena that are usually narrowly associated with art, fiction, and poetry to develop an account of "the imaginative core of human existence."[51] For Ricoeur, "to participate in the mystery of incarnate existence means to adopt the internal rhythm of *drama*."[52] One can then plot the trajectory of Ricoeur's work from *metaphor* to *narrative* as a continuous attempt to get at this imaginative core of human existence. These are two different portals into the imagination, two angles of approach to the "dramatic" nature of our being-in-the-world. On one approach, an appreciation for metaphor

---

his architectonic of cognitive functions, and so he always pulls back from acknowledging the embodiment of mind, thought, and language." And so we have a missed opportunity. But "Kant's profound treatment of imagination" could be "substantially revised to place imagination at the core of all experience, understanding, and reasoning" (*MB* 211). Gilles Deleuze seems to suggest something similar in his meta-reading of Kant's project, suggesting that the insights of the *Critique of Judgment*, which makes the imagination central, should have a kind of retroactive impact on the earlier *Critiques*. See Gilles Deleuze, *Kant's Critical Philosophy: The Doctrine of the Faculties*, trans. Hugh Tomlinson and Barbara Habberjam (Minneapolis: University of Minnesota Press, 1964).

47. McGilchrist, "Four Walls," in *Poetry*, vol. 196, no. 4 (July/August 2010), 335.

48. Recall that Schneider was unable to understand a story because he lacked this "between," this "antepredicative" knowledge. Maurice Merleau-Ponty, *Phenomenology of Perception*, trans. Colin Smith (London: Routledge, 1962), 153.

49. For discussion, see Venema, *Identifying Selfhood*, 39–40.

50. Richard Kearney, *Dialogues with Contemporary Continental Thinkers: The Phenomenological Heritage* (Manchester: Manchester University Press, 1986), 24.

51. Venema, *Identifying Selfhood*, 41.

52. Paul Ricoeur, *Freedom and Nature: The Voluntary and the Involuntary*, trans. Erazim Kohak (Evanston, IL: Northwestern University Press, 1965), 17, quoted in Venema, *Identifying Selfhood*, 46.

opens up "the poetic power of the imagination,"[53] since metaphor is at the heart of poetry. Indeed, "metaphor is taken as a *poem in miniature*." But Ricoeur's interest is to extend and expand the operation of metaphor: "The proposed working hypothesis is that if a satisfactory account can be given of what is implied in this kernel of poetic meaning, it must be possible equally to extend the same explication to larger entities, such as the entire poem."[54] Indeed, Ricoeur will expand even further to consider the metaphorical and poetic meaning of human existence *as such*. It is this same interest in appreciating the imaginative core of human existence that later propels Ricoeur's interest in the dynamics of narrative, which isn't just a concern with textuality or with a sequential organization of events or identity. At work in narrative is also a fundamentally imaginative way of meaning the world and our place in it.[55] Like poetry, narrative is also a way of making meaning (and receiving meaning) that is fundamentally aesthetic because it is fundamentally metaphorical.[56] The entire realm of human experience is "one vast poetic sphere that includes metaphorical utterance and narrative discourse."[57]

What I'm calling a "general poetics" is just a way of honoring the fundamental aesthetics of human understanding, which is both poetic and narrative. And this aesthetics is rooted in our embodied comportment to the world, at the nexus of body and story. This is why, as Didion puts it, "we tell ourselves stories in order to live." We need stories like we need food and water: we're *built* for narrative, nourished by stories, not just as distractions or diversions or entertainments but because we constitute our world narratively. It is from stories that we receive our "character," and those stories in turn become part of our background, the horizons within which we constitute our world and engage in action. I cannot answer the

---

53. Venema, *Identifying Selfhood*, 82.

54. Paul Ricoeur, *The Rule of Metaphor: Multi-disciplinary Studies in the Creation of Meaning in Language*, trans. Robert Czerny (Toronto: University of Toronto Press, 1977), 94 (emphasis original).

55. Elsewhere Ricoeur describes this as the "configurational" operation of narrative. While sequence or chronology is part of narrative, it is not the sole defining feature—which is why nonlinear narrative is still narrative. The "configurational dimension, present both in the art of narrating and the art of following a story," is a kind of aesthetic mode of constitution bound up with narrative. "This complex structure implies that the most humble narrative is always more than a chronological series of events and, in turn, that the configurational dimension cannot eclipse the episodic dimension without abolishing the narrative structure itself." Ricoeur, "The Narrative Function," in *Hermeneutics and the Human Sciences*, 278–79.

56. "[T]he narrative function repeats the conceptual pattern Ricoeur developed in *The Rule of Metaphor*: the production of linguistic innovation that unifies identity and difference." Venema, *Identifying Selfhood*, 92. Thus Venema sees Ricoeur's *Time and Narrative* as "forming a pair with *The Rule of Metaphor*" (91).

57. Paul Ricoeur, *Time and Narrative*, vol. 1, trans. Kathleen McLaughlin and David Pellauer (Chicago: University of Chicago Press, 1984), xi, quoted in Venema, *Identifying Selfhood*, 92.

To Think About: I Can't Say; Let Me Tell You a Story

We have already seen that the novelist David Foster Wallace, in his own unique—even "secular"—way, appreciates the dynamics of liturgical formation and the inextricable link between worship and love. We've also seen that he appreciates our nature as narrative animals, suggesting that we need stories like we need air. He also appreciates the irreducibility of aesthetic meaning that is carried in a story. As he says at one point in his conversation with David Lipsky: "Like if I could articulate it, then there wouldn't be any need to make up stories about it, you know?"[1]

1. David Foster Wallace, quoted in David Lipsky, *Although Of Course You End Up Becoming Yourself: A Road Trip with David Foster Wallace* (New York: Broadway Books, 2010), 40.

---

question, what do I love? without (at least implicitly) answering the question, what story do I believe?[58] We tell ourselves stories in order to live.

Indeed, there is an increasing literature in cognitive science that suggests we are *wired* for stories.[59] And these discussions can help us appreciate just how worship works insofar as liturgies are "performed stories" of a sort.

Before drawing on the wells of cognitive science of literature, however, we should first note two different schools of thought in this emerging field. Let's call one school of thought "literary Darwinism"[60] and refer to the other as "cognitive narratology"[61] (for lack of a better term). (Readers uninterested in the implications need not linger on these next couple of pages.)

- **Literary Darwinism** is the (over)confident extension of evolutionary psychology to the realm of literature. Assuming the paradigm of evolutionary psychology, literary Darwinism accepts the baseline model of evopsych: that "our modern skulls house a stone age mind."[62] So what's actually assumed here is a distinctly evolutionary theory of

58. Though we need to keep in mind that the sort of "belief" we're talking about here is what Bourdieu described as "practical belief"—the sort of belief that is "a state of the body" (*LP* 68).

59. See, for example, Brian Boyd, *On the Origin of Stories: Evolution, Cognition, Fiction* (Cambridge, MA: Harvard University Press, 2009); Jonathan Gottschall and David Sloan Wilson, eds., *The Literary Animal: Evolution and the Nature of Narrative* (Evanston, IL: Northwestern University Press, 2005); and Joseph Carroll, *Literary Darwinism: Evolution, Human Nature, and Literature* (New York: Routledge, 2004).

60. Brian Boyd also calls this "evocriticism" in "For Evocriticism: Minds Shaped to Be Reshaped," *Critical Inquiry* 38 (2012): 394–404.

61. See James Phelan, "Narrative Theory, 1966–2006: A Narrative," a new chapter in the fortieth anniversary edition of Robert Scholes and Robert Kellogg, *The Nature of Narrative* (Oxford: Oxford University Press, 2006), 283–336.

62. As famously phrased by Leda Cosmides and John Tooby, "Evolutionary Psychology: A Primer," University of California Santa Barbara, Center for Evolutionary Psychology, http://www.psych.ucsb.edu/research/cep/primer.html, principle 5.

mind: namely, that the fundamental shape (or components) of the "minds" that we operate with today—which help us understand and navigate our late modern world—was actually forged and solidified in an "environment of evolutionary adaptation." So, according to this paradigm, we still carry around hunter-gatherer habits of mind in our twenty-first-century environment. Evolutionary psychology is bent on explaining the current operation of human cognition as a reflection of our *adaptation* in the Pleistocene Era. In other words, while our "stone age minds" might seem a tad outdated, they have endured precisely because they were successful: they reflect successful adaptations that enable our survival. So any "explanation," in terms of evolutionary psychology, is a reduction to adaptive success.[63] Human minds evolved to recognize faces, for example, because that ability contributed to in-group recognition, which contributed to survival. The interests of literary Darwinism are similar. The overarching question it asks is, how did a capacity for storytelling contribute to the survival of the human species? What sort of adaptive advantage was provided by story or fiction or literature?

As you might imagine, the returns on such a question are not what usually interests those who care about literature. Consider just a few problems with this school of thought. First, what we get in the name of "explanation" is a number of "just-so" stories that tell a sweeping narrative about how we came to tell stories in order to survive. Second, the very particularities of story and narrative are shunted aside for vague, sweeping talk about metarepresentation, the ability to imagine nonexistent states of affairs, and the adaptive ability to empathize. The result is a bland formalist criticism that, as Kramnick puts it, is "relentlessly *thematic*." Every story and artifact of literature is treated as something that can be paraphrased without loss. "At the extreme, the theme is a kind of microversion of the story of natural selection itself. The Darwinian saga somehow becomes the very story of most fictions."[64] Third, and as a result of the above, literary Darwinism tends to ignore just what is unique and irreducible about narrative, metaphor, and story, instead reducing stories to conduits of information to help us "succeed" (i.e., reproduce). Boyd, for example, is fixated on distinguishing "fiction"—"stories that neither side believes"—from "true narration."[65] This distinction itself indicates that Boyd's interest

63. In an incisive critique, Jonathan Kramnick argues that literary Darwinism appropriates a problematic model of "adaptation," which creates problems at the ground floor of this school of thought. See Kramnick, "Against Literary Darwinism," *Critical Inquiry* 37 (2011): 315–47, esp. 324–33.
64. Kramnick, "Against Literary Darwinism," 344.
65. Boyd, *On the Origin of Stories*, 129.

is not properly "literary." In other words, he's not interested in the dynamics of *narration* as a distinctive way to constitute meaning; rather, he is interested in stories that are "not true"—fictions that do not correspond to reality. He reduces story to pretense. Smuggled into his analysis, then, is already a narrow definition of truth as correspondence (hence fiction is "not true," is make-believe) as well as a narrow understanding of storytelling as a means of representation. In short, what Boyd gives us is an entirely "intellectualist" account of stories, as if they were merely containers or conduits for information—just the sort of model subjected to critique by Merleau-Ponty, Dreyfus, and Taylor. Boyd's stories are the sorts of stories Schneider would understand—which is to say that they are not characterized by the irreducible metaphoricity that we "know" with our bodies. This is because Boyd, like other literary Darwinists, fails to appreciate the *truth* of story and is only interested in the representational truths ("strategic information")[66] that stories might convey.

- **Cognitive narratology** is a very different engagement between literature and cognitive science. Like literary Darwinism, cognitive narratology takes seriously the biological affordances of human beings that make us able to both create and understand stories.[67] But the goal is not the sort of "just-so" stories that we tend to get from literary Darwinism. As Kramnick rightly points out, "You don't have to be a fan of the adaptive story about literature . . . to be excited about recent, interdisciplinary ventures between the humanities and the sciences."[68] Instead, cognitive literary criticism is interested in how fiction works—how stories and narratives, as well as the specific forms and elements of specific stories and novels, *work* on human cognition given our embodied minds and our inherited habits of perception. As Phelan summarizes it, cognitive narratology takes classical narratology's fundamental question—what are the underlying rules of narrative's textual system?—and revises it to ask, What are the mental tools, processes, and activities that make possible our ability to construct and understand narrative? This includes a focus on "narrative itself as a tool of understanding, that is, on how narrative contributes to human beings' efforts to structure and make sense of their experiences"— how the "frames" and "scripts" we learn through story contextualize our experience differently.[69] So rather than explaining away story as

66. Ibid., 130.
67. Overlooked in recent conversations are Simon Lesser's prescient insights about the intersection of science and literature in "A Note on the Use of Scientific Psychological Knowledge in Literary Study," an appendix to *Fiction and the Unconscious* (Boston: Beacon Hill, 1957), 294–308.
68. Kramnick, "Against Literary Darwinism," 346–47.
69. Phelan, "Narrative Theory, 1966–2006," 290.

a merely adaptive strategy, cognitive narratology is interested in the particulars of how stories, novels, and novelists generate meaning for readers whose bodies and brains afford certain ways of being-in-the-world.[70] Cognitive narratology, in other words, is interested in the biological affordances that make literary and poetry unique modes of meaning—unique modes *of truth*.

Insofar as a liturgical anthropology requires the articulation of a general poetics, I think we would find constructive resources for advancing this project by staging further dialogue between theology, liturgics, and cognitive literary criticism. If liturgies "work" by means of story—including metaphor, allusivity, and the fuel of the imagination—then understanding how story works would also give us insight into the conditions and dynamics of liturgical formation.[71]

These explorations at the intersection of biology and narratology—at the intersection of bodies and stories—get at that "between"-ness disclosed by Merleau-Ponty and Bourdieu and McGilchrist. Like them, cognitive narratology is interested in the unique "logic" of story and the imagination, the sort of visceral induction that characterizes our narrative sense. Stories have reasons of which Reason knows nothing, but about which our bodies know almost everything. When we emphasize that metaphor and narrative are irreducible modes of meaning, we are not contenting ourselves with fabrications—as if we tell ourselves stories in order to live because the truth is too hard to face.[72] It's not a matter of choosing either stories or truth. To the contrary, stories are true in a unique and irreducible way. What interests us about narrative and metaphor is precisely that they are unique modes of truth. Stories and poems (and liturgies) are not "true"

70. See, for example, Alan Richardson, "Of Heartache and Head Injury: Reading Minds in *Persuasion*," *Poetics Today* 23 (2002): 141–60; and Mark J. Bruhn, "Shelley's Theory of Mind: From Radical Empiricism to Cognitive Romanticism," *Poetics Today* 30 (2009): 373–422.

71. I am obviously only hinting at what could be a lifelong research agenda. Consider just two concrete examples. Lisa Zunshine explores the "cognitive underpinnings" of A. L. Barbauld's eighteenth-century *Hymns in Prose for Children* to discern the way Barbauld's "catechist" approach "mobilizes the contingencies of our evolved cognitive architecture." Understanding how a "catechist" approach marshals cognitive underpinnings could give us insight into how Christian catechetical instruction might do the same. See Zunshine, "Rhetoric, Cognition, and Ideology in A. L. Barbauld's *Hymns in Prose for Children* (1781)," *Poetics Today* 23 (2002): 123–39. More recently, Marco Caracciolo has suggested that the phenomenological model of "enacted" cognition can help us appreciate "how the production and interpretation of stories can shape the value landscape of those who engage with them." This seems an obvious avenue to consider how stories help Christians "imagine" their world as one laden with God's presence and call. See Caracciolo, "Narrative, Meaning, Interpretation: An Enactivist Approach," *Phenomenology and Cognitive Science*, August 4, 2011, http://www.springerlink.com/content/764065387174464v/fulltext.html.

72. Though Didion perhaps means to suggest this in her famous opening phrase from *The White Album*, which I've recontextualized as the title for this chapter!

in the way that a newspaper article or surveillance video may be "true." Nor are they "true" because they are vehicles to convey a "message" that is true. The "truth" of journalism and surveillance cameras and articulated propositions might not be the most interesting or most important sort of truth. What I know to be true through a novel or poem might be more significant than the litany of true "facts" that can be endlessly Googled. The truth of art—the truth of the aesthetic aspect of our existence[73]—does not reduce to mere representation or correspondence. A story or poem does not merely communicate "a truth" that I can also "get" in some other way. Rather, the truth of a story or poem is carried in its form, in the unique affect generated by its cadences and rhythm, in the interplay and resonances of the imaginative world it invokes, in the metaphorical inferences that I "get" on a gut level.[74] If we are going to appreciate the distinctive force of metaphor and narrative—if we are going to understand how fiction works and, analogically, how worship works—then we will need to expand our notions of truth beyond representation and correspondence. We will need to stop restricting ourselves to "propositionally inflected correspondence theories of truth" and expand our epistemic models to include and honor what Lambert Zuidervaart describes as "artistic truth."[75] We will need to throw off the narrow constraint that sees all truth as subject to what Bourdieu calls "logical logic" and instead recognize modes of truth that are subject to a different logic—a "story logic."[76] To understand the logic of a story is to have intuited a flow and an arc, to have absorbed a world and lived with characters, to have dwelt in a world of words whose

73. This is an important point to keep in mind: what we refer to as "art" is an intensification of the aesthetic aspect that characterizes being-in-the-world more broadly, and more fundamentally. Again, see Seerveld, "Dooyeweerd's Legacy for Aesthetics."

74. McGilchrist's critique of modernism in art is that it requires too much *dis*engagement from our immersion in experience: it is art that is too self-conscious, thus resonating with (and requiring) intellectual reflection that shunts aside our aesthetic sense. For example, in a modernist poem by John Ashberry, "There is a tension between what has to engage our conscious debating minds and what must carry us into a realm beyond any ratiocination. An excessive fear of being direct, and the worship of the difficult, endemic in Modernism, threaten at times to undermine the direction that poetry inevitably takes, away from what we have to 'work out' for ourselves toward what we thought we knew already, but in fact never understood" ("This Is Your Brain on Poetry," 45).

75. Lambert Zuidervaart, *Artistic Truth: Aesthetics, Discourse, and Imaginative Disclosure* (Cambridge: Cambridge University Press, 2004), 203. Zuidervaart very helpfully distinguishes theories of truth that are "nonpropositionalist" (which do not see propositions as the only or primary bearers of truth) and "antipropositionalist" theories, which seem to leave no room to affirm that propositions can be true. With Zuidervaart, I am a nonpropositionalist. We relativize propositional truth without rejecting it.

76. See David Herman, *Story Logic: Problems and Possibilities of Narrative* (Lincoln: University of Nebraska Press, 2002); and Catherine Brady, *Story Logic and the Craft of Fiction* (New York: Palgrave Macmillan, 2010).

connotations and resonances play on the strings of our imagination to generate meaning. "To follow a story," Ricoeur says,

> is to understand the successive actions, thoughts and feelings as displaying a particular *directedness*. By this I mean that we are pushed along by the development and that we respond to this thrust with expectations concerning the outcome and culmination of the process. In this sense, the "conclusion" of the story is the pole of attraction of the whole process. But a narrative conclusion can be neither deduced nor predicted. There is no story unless our attention is held in suspense by a thousand contingencies. Hence we must follow the story to its conclusion. So rather than being *predictable*, a conclusion must be *acceptable*.[77]

The conclusion to a story is not something that is "valid," but it will "make sense" according to the implicit logic of story. And at the end of a story that has "worked," we find the world and its characters continuing to reverberate with(in) us, and we come back to our own worlds with a different angle, a different horizon, a transformed "background" that now changes our perception of the world in ways we can't quite name.

What we've hit upon is the dynamic of aesthetic truth that characterizes both art and bodily meaning more generally—a mode of "imaginative disclosure" that opens up the world for us in powerful ways precisely because it breaks into our own bodily composure. Aesthetic truth is invasive because it is not content to merely present itself as an idea to be impartially considered by the mind. Such imaginative disclosure is visceral and kinaesthetic and won't leave our bodies alone, which is why it gets under our skin and lodges itself in our memories, becoming sedimented in the background of our consciousness. Consider an example of such imaginative disclosure highlighted by Lambert Zuidervaart:

> A brilliantly illuminated sculpture stands on nine blocks of wood in the center of an artist-run gallery in Toronto. It is opening night for a three-woman show on loss and retrieval titled *Speak on Memory*. People crowd around the sculpture but keep their distance, struck by its stark complexity. A young corkscrew willow has been cut off before it could flourish, its dead leaves removed, its bare branches disassembled. Now it stands forcibly reconstructed, twisting within and through a skeletal cage of whittled maple translucently twined. The willow's branches, their ends carved into spears, have been rejoined with sharp wooden rivets into the simulacrum of a tree. Snakelike, they writhe through each other as their trunk stands rootless in a nest made from tiny interlaced twigs. The nest lies on a bed of pointed lateral branches arranged in two crosswise layers. Cemented sand fills the

---

77. Ricoeur, "The Narrative Function," in *Hermeneutics and the Human Sciences*, 277 (emphasis original).

nest, blasted soil where something once grew. Graying rocks, circling the
tree trunk like petrified eggs, are all that remains. The gnarled but youthful branches of this caged and nested and refabricated tree spiral upward
toward an elevation they will never reach. The piece, by Joyce Recker, is
titled *Earth's Lament*.[78]

Zuidervaart at this point does *not* ask, what does this piece mean? Instead,
he rightly asks something more like, *how* does this work of art mean?

> Why does the sculpture so visibly move its public on this occasion, calling
> its attention and prompting conversation? It makes no direct statement and
> asserts no propositions. Yet it offers more than an innovative treatment of
> nontraditional materials that, under proper lighting and in the right space,
> creates wonderful juxtapositions of angles and curves, of light and shadow,
> of the found and the fabricated. It is simultaneously an open-ended meta-
> phor for hope amid loss, for renewal amid destruction. And the import it
> offers comes through the sculpture's own imaginative and self-referential
> structure, even as it testifies to the artist's vision of art and life and interacts
> with a public's need for echoes of earth's lament. The piece is a work of
> imaginative disclosure, one that can meet the multidimensional expectation
> of artistic truth.[79]

The work is a kind of revelation, not because it deposits new information
into our minds like tablets inscribed with propositions, but because the work
of art stages an encounter with the world that "speaks" to us in metaphors
we can never speak. The encounter and engagement with *Earth's Lament*
embodies a truth about the brokenness of a good creation; it "teaches"
us of the Spirit's groaning (Rom. 8) in ways we could never have "known"
before. These are chemical reactions of meaning absorbed at subterranean
levels of our consciousness. But precisely because aesthetic truth "works"
on us at that depth, it shakes our foundations, reconnoiters our being-in-
the-world, seeps into that subcortical core of our being. And because of
that, we leave such an experience with a "rearrangement of our corporeal
schema," Merleau-Ponty might say, in the sense that we now carry the truth
of this embodied metaphor as part of our background. The experience of
imaginative disclosure now reconfigures the very horizons of our ongoing
experience. The truth of the aesthetic encounter is not merely an "event,"
a sort of artistic high; it is a truth that we absorb in a way that governs
and conditions our erotic comprehension of the world.

Our incarnate significance, our imaginative being-in-the-world, is governed by the dynamics of metaphor and narrative, poetry and story, which

---

78. Zuidervaart, *Artistic Truth*, 217–18. A photograph of a similar work by Recker appears
on the cover of Zuidervaart's book.
    79. Ibid., 218.

is precisely why formative liturgies are practiced poems, embodied stories, performed dramas. Liturgies—those formative rituals of ultimacy—marshal exactly these dynamics. Liturgies are formative because—and just to the extent that—they tap into our imaginative core. As compressed narratives and tactile poems, the formative power of liturgies (whether secular or sacred) is bound up with their aesthetic force. Such liturgies are pedagogies of desire that shape our love because they *picture* the good life for us in ways that resonate with our imaginative nature. Over time, we are formed as a people who desire a certain *telos* because we have been immersed in liturgies that have captured our imagination by aesthetic means. This isn't a matter of simply learning new ideas and content; it is a matter of *tuning*. We are *attuned* to the world by practices that carry an embodied significance.[80] We are conscripted into a Story through those practices that enact and perform and embody a Story about the good life. To recall Bourdieu's account, we could now say that we are incorporated into a social body when the stories of a people become the dominant landscape of our imaginative background—when those stories have worked their way into our "practical sense" in such a way that they now (automatically) govern how we perceive the world. In other words, this is how we "become native": because "nativity" is absorbed at the level of affect, on an aesthetic register. This is how worship works.

The iPhone-ization of Our World(view): Compressed Stories and Micropractices

Liturgies are formative because they are both kinaesthetic and poetic, both embodied and storied. Liturgies are covert incubators of the imagination because they play the strings of our aesthetic hearts. Liturgies traffic in the dynamics of metaphor and narrative and drama as performed pictures of the good life, staged performances of some vision of the kingdom that capture our imagination and thus orient our love and longing. By an aesthetic alchemy, these liturgies implant in us a vision for a world and way of life that attracts us so that, on some unconscious level, Liz Lemon–like, we say to ourselves: "I want to go to there." And we *act* accordingly.

Indeed, that is the real upshot of our concern: as I have been emphasizing, what's ultimately at stake in a liturgical anthropology is a philosophy of action. Liturgical formation is a way of describing the intense formative dynamic that shapes our imagination and forms our background horizons,

---

80. I further develop this theme of "attunement," in dialogue with Heidegger, in James K. A. Smith, "Secular Liturgies and the Prospects for a 'Post-Secular' Sociology of Religion," in *The Post-Secular in Question*, ed. Philip Gorski, David Kyuman Kim, John Torpey, and Jonathan VanAntwerpen (New York: New York University Press, 2012), 159–84.

To Think About: War Games

The dynamics of a sentimental education can be marshaled to all sorts of different ends. Not all sentimental educations are salutary. Indeed, de-formation utilizes the same dynamics and marshals the same mechanics.[1] "The powers" also employ those cunning pedagogies that extort the ultimate while seeming to demand only the insignificant (*LP* 69). Indeed, our entertainments and distractions can be implanting in us a worldview, a social imaginary, conscripting us into a story through routines and practices that seem banal and harmless. If Waterloo was won on the playing fields of Eton, could wars be won on the pixilated fields of *Madden NFL 12* and *Modern Warfare*? Might the games we play, like the loom of the Kabyle woman (*LP* 69), perform a "cosmogony," enact a worldview, implant in our imaginations a vision of the world that, over time, molds and makes us into a certain kind of person? Could it be that Cavanaugh's "provincial farm boy" we encountered in the introduction is converted into a soldier by the games he plays? Could there be an Xbox-ization of our imagination that conscripts us into imperial projects, making us subjects of kingdoms for which we become willing to kill?

This is not reactionary musing or overblown pacifist alarmism. In fact, it turns out that the U.S. military has quite intentionally co-opted the (seemingly insignificant) gaming habits of young American men in order to ask of them something much more significant: killing from a distance through "drone" warfare. When these soldiers are seated at a console somewhere in the Nevada desert, manipulating a controller that feels all too familiar to them, the screen before them enables them to peer into a building in remote Afghanistan. The familiar "drone" of unmanned aerial vehicles (UAVs) hums steadily as its cameras enable the "pilot" to see a target light a cigarette or shuffle a tin can down the street. The "point-of-view" look from the drone is exactly the angle of vision the young controller has peered through for years as he played *Halo* or *Call of Duty*. The eerie com-

which in turn affect how we constitute our world and thus what we feel ourselves *called to* in the world. To perceive the world is to always already perceive it *as* a certain kind of space: as mere "nature" or God's creation; as the flattened, disenchanted space for human self-assertion or the enchanted, sacramental realm of God's good gifts; as a competitive arena for my plunder and self-fulfillment or a shared space of neighbors who beckon to me for care and compassion; as a random assemblage for which we now claim "progress" or the stage on which is played the drama of God's gracious redemption. These loaded, valuative perceptions are enacted by my body, absorbed through (competing) stories that now govern how I constitute my experience. And these habits of perception become tied to dispositions toward action. We are inclined to action by the shape of our habit-body; we are disposed to act in certain ways, toward certain ends, by the inertia of the *habitus* we've absorbed. I become *the kind of person*

bination of focus and decontextualization is exactly the world in which he feels "at home" from years of video gaming. And as he pulls the trigger that launches Hellfire missiles to destroy his target, he might sometimes find himself frustrated that the grainy pixilation of the kill doesn't quite measure up to the HD graphics on his home console. But while this is "real," Christian Caryl notes,

> The US military does little to discourage the notion that this peculiar brand of long-distance warfare has a great deal in common with the video-gaming culture in which many young UAV operators have grown up. As one military robotics researcher tells Peter Singer, the author of *Wired for War*, "We modeled the controller after the PlayStation because that's what these eighteen-, nineteen-year-old Marines have been playing with pretty much all of their lives." And by now, of course, we also have video games that incorporate drones: technology imitating life that imitates technology.[2]

But of course, there's no restart button here. And while the pilot plays this game of ultimacy from the comfort of his air-conditioned base thousands of miles away, there's no rebooting, no second life, for those unfortunates chalked up as collateral damage in this war game.

Cavanaugh's provincial farm boy no longer has to travel to the other side of the world to kill for the state. As for imagining himself a soldier, being conscripted into the Story of the nation-state? This is a game he's played his whole life.

1. Furthermore, one could only assess a practice as *deformative* relative to norms that specify a substantive *telos* that establishes the "standards of excellence" for what counts as "good" formation (see MacIntyre, *After Virtue*, 187–92). I will explore these complicated issues in more detail in *Who's Afraid of Relativism? Taking Wittgenstein, Rorty, and Brandom to Church*, The Church and Postmodern Culture (Grand Rapids: Baker Academic, forthcoming).

2. Christian Caryl, "Predators and Robots at War," *New York Review of Books* 58, no. 14 (September 29, 2011): 55.

who sees others as threats and competitors or the kind of person who sees others as gifts and callings; I become the kind of person who is inclined to "get mine" or the kind of person who is inclined to seek the common good—all "without thinking about it." *Liturgy* is the shorthand term for those rituals that are loaded with a Story about who and whose we are, inscribing in us a *habitus* by marshaling our aesthetic nature. Liturgies are "cunning" pedagogies that extort what is essential while seeming to demand the insignificant, precisely because they are stories that are told by—and told upon—our bodies, thereby embedding themselves in our imagination, becoming part of the background that determines how we perceive the world. Liturgies are those social practices that capture our imaginations by becoming the stories we tell ourselves in order to live.

Now what I've claimed about the formative power of liturgies is true of liturgies "in general." In other words, both secular and Christian liturgies marshal and "work on" the same imaginative, aesthetic aspects of human being-in-the-world. The fact that we are "liturgical animals"—and hence imaginative, narrative animals—is a structural feature of creaturehood that cannot be effaced or erased, even by sin. Indeed, sinful systems exploit the same reality of our "incarnate existence." In chapter 4 I will specifically explore how the Triune God meets us *as* liturgical animals, "sanctifying perception" through liturgical practices that transform and reform our horizons and habits. But we also need to recognize that the same dynamics are at work underneath our *dis*ordered loves. So a liturgical anthropology not only provides a framework for appreciating the sanctification of perception; it also provides the resources for articulating a phenomenology of temptation. More specifically, it provides resources for us to discern the how and why of our assimilation to visions of the good life that are, in fact, rivals to the vision of flourishing and justice characteristic of God's coming kingdom. If discipleship is a matter of Christian formation, and specifically the formation of the imagination, then we need to realize that these same dynamics of formation also characterize *de*formation. Disordered secular liturgies, ordered to a rival *telos*, also work on the imagination.

Once again, this would require that we resist merely "intellectualist" accounts of sin, temptation, and malformation, which are problematic on two levels. First, intellectualist accounts of sin mistakenly see *all* action as the outcome of conscious, deliberative *choices*, unaware of the dynamics of formation and habituation that we've described above.[81] For the intellectualist, every sin is a deliberate choice based on either false beliefs or a lack of knowledge. To be "tempted," on this account, is always to *believe* a lie. So the corrective for sinful action would be *knowledge*: true beliefs and adequate knowledge to equip the person to make better choices. Second, and as a result, intellectualist accounts tend to be blithely unaware of the social forces and systemic factors that prime and shape our imaginations, creating dispositions and tendencies within us toward unjust action and sinful behavior. This is why intellectualist accounts also tend to be highly individualist accounts. We might say that an intellectualist model is able to register only discrete sinful *actions* but is unable to account for a sinful *way of life*—the rhythms and habits and routines that disorder a people or a culture in ways that run counter to what God envisions for creation.[82]

81. It's the "all" that's the problem here. Of course we do sometimes explicitly and even deliberately choose to sin. But intellectualist accounts think *all* sinful action can be accounted for in this way.

82. Thus it's no accident that John Piper, the author of *Think: The Life of the Mind and the Love of God* (Wheaton: Crossway, 2011), sees racism as a problem of individual responsibility rather than systemic injustice (in *Bloodlines: Race, Cross, and the Christian* [Wheaton: Crossway, 2011])—and thus advocates different *choices* and the (individualist) "miracle" of grace as the solution. For a helpful discussion of the problems with Piper's approach, see Mark Mulder,

But as I've been arguing throughout this book, much of our action is not the fruit of conscious deliberation but is rather the outcome of an acquired, habitual disposition. So the same must be true of our *sinful, disordered* action. That doesn't mean we're not responsible (which would be to lapse back into dichotomies between "freedom" and "determinism"); rather, the point is that we become habituated to ways of life that run counter to what God envisions for the flourishing of creation. By the quiet, unconscious operation of liturgical formation, we are unwittingly conscripted into stories that are rival tellings of what's in store for the world. These narratives and their metaphorical power seep into our bones in such a way that they come to dominate our "background" and thus begin to shape our very perception of the world—which, in turn, orients and governs our (habitual) action. We absorb rival gospels as *habitus*, and thus act "toward" them, as it were—pulled toward a different *telos* that rivals the coming kingdom of God. But since liturgical formation operates on our embodied unconscious and marshals the dynamics of incarnate significance, working on our aesthetic sense to implant in us stories of what "the good life" looks like, such deformation often happens under the radar of awareness—and certainly off the radar of intellectualist fixations.

Through a vast repertoire of secular liturgies we are quietly assimilated to the earthly city of disordered loves, governed by self-love and the pursuit of domination.[83] So we toddle off to church or Bible study week after week, comforting ourselves that we're devoted to "the temple of the Lord, the temple of the Lord, the temple of the Lord" (Jer. 7:4), without realizing that we spend the rest of the week making bread for idols (Jer. 7:18) because we fail to appreciate the *religious* nature of these "secular" practices. So we become the *kind of people who* are inclined to a sort of low-grade, socially acceptable greed that makes us remarkably tolerant of inequality and the exploitation of the (global) poor; or we take for granted a mobile, commuting way of life that exploits creation's resources rather than stewards them. We might be passionately devoted to ending religious persecution without for a moment considering how our "normal" way of life exploits children halfway around the globe; or we think it's just "natural" to turn a blind eye to the suffering of Christians in countries that we bomb in the name of "freedom." A way of life becomes habitual for us such that we pursue that way of life—we *act* in that way of life—*without thinking about it* because we've absorbed the *habitus* that is oriented to

---

"Right Diagnosis—Wrong Cure," *Comment*, January 18, 2012, http://www.cardus.ca/comment/article/3038/right-diagnosis-wrong-cure.

83. It's important to remember that for Augustine, the "earthly city" is *not* merely "temporal" life or "creation." The origin of the "earthly city" is the Fall, which is why the earthly city is antithetical to the city of God. For further discussion of this point, see Smith, "Reforming Public Theology."

a corresponding vision of "the good life." Indeed, because this becomes sedimented into my background, I can't even see the world otherwise; this way of seeing it just seems "obvious," and I don't even *feel* the call to be otherwise. I fail to resist temptation, not because I've simply made a bad decision, but because I've failed to recognize that I'm being *mal*formed by a constellation of cultural "disciplines" that are disciplining me otherwise. And such rival discipleship is effected through the most banal practices. As Bourdieu put it, such liturgies are pedagogies of insignificance: they co-opt us to an ultimate vision by simply demanding what seems to be insignificant.

Consider, for example, the pervasive role that certain technologies now play in the everyday life of a middle-class North American. Every technology is attended by a mode of bodily practice. So even if the computer is primarily an information processor, it can never completely reduce us to just "thinking things" because it requires some mode of bodily interface: whether we're hunched over a desk, glued to a screen; looking downward at a smartphone, our attention directed away from others at the table; or curled up on a couch touching a tablet screen, in every case there are bodily comportments that each sort of device invites and demands. Apple has long understood the bodily nature of this interface. In this respect, we already take for granted how revolutionary the touch screen is: a new, differently tactile mode of bodily interface, a heretofore-unimagined level of intimacy with machines.[84] Indeed, working on a laptop feels distant and disconnected compared to the fingertip intimacy of the iPhone or the iPad or other tablets. (Do you ever thoughtlessly try to touch your laptop screen? Then you know what I'm talking about.) The technology affords and invites rituals of interaction.

How you handle your phone might seem to be a rather banal concern. Are the practices of how we interface with a small metal device really worthy of analysis? What's next: a philosophical analysis of how I put on my socks or a ritual analysis of how I hold my fork?

Let's not forget what we learned from Bourdieu: "the hidden persuasion of an implicit pedagogy . . . can instill a whole cosmology, through injunctions as insignificant as 'sit up straight' or 'don't hold your knife in your left hand'" (*LP* 69).[85] The seemingly innocuous "manners" of a society extort what is essential by commanding what seems insignificant. If we

---

84. Walter Isaacson recounts the emergence of Apple's touchscreen technology for the iPhone in *Steve Jobs* (New York: Simon and Schuster, 2011), 465–75. The final description is telling: "The new look was austere, yet also friendly. You could fondle it" (473). Not surprisingly, it's in this same chapter that Alan Keyes is quoted as saying, "Steve understands desire" (474). Indeed, has any company better understood the erotics of design?

85. We might also recall Bertie being forced to write with his right hand in *The King's Speech* (see chap. 1).

follow Bourdieu's insight here, then what appear to be "micropractices" have macro effects: what might appear to be inconsequential microhabits are, in fact, disciplinary formations that begin to reconfigure our relation to the wider world—indeed, they begin to *make* that world. One could suggest that our interface with the iPhone (or any other smartphone) is just this sort of microtraining that subtly and unconsciously trains us to be more like Milton's Satan, rather than conforming us to the image of the Son—and not because of the *content* communicated via the iPhone but because of how I interact with the device and the subtle pedagogy of the imagination effected by that intimate interface with a tiny machine. The iPhone brings with it an invitation to inhabit the world differently—not just because it gives me access to global internet resources in a pocket-sized device, but precisely in how it invites me to interact with the device itself. The material rituals of simply handling and mastering an iPhone are loaded with an implicit social imaginary. To become habituated to an iPhone is to implicitly treat the world as "available" to *me* and at my disposal—to constitute the world as "at-hand" for me, to be selected, scaled, scanned, tapped, and enjoyed.[86]

As is so often the case, this zeitgeist is succinctly pictured in a rather inane Michelob Ultra commercial in which the world obeys the touch commands of an iPhone screen. Don't like that car? *Swipe* for a different one. Wish the scenery was different? *Swipe* for an alternative. Wish you could be somewhere else? Just *touch* the place you want to be. Wish you could see *her* just a little better? *Zoooooom* with the slide of a couple of fingers. A way of relating to a phone has now become a way of relating to the world. The practices for manipulating a small device are now expanded to show how we'd really like to manipulate our environment to serve our needs and be subject to our whims. And while we don't go around swiping our hands in front of us to change the scenery, we perhaps nonetheless unconsciously begin to expect the world to conform to our wishes as our iPhone does. Or I implicitly begin to expect that I am the center of my own environments, and that what surrounds me exists *for* me. In short, my relation to my iPhone—which seems insignificant—is writ large as an iPhone-ized relation to *the world*, an iPhone-ization of my world(view).

In similar ways, we might underappreciate the rituals—yea, liturgies—that are part and parcel of social media. Unlike an iPhone or an iPad, Facebook and Twitter are *software*. They don't necessarily require specific patterns of bodily interface. Because they aren't identified with specific

---

86. In fact, one might wonder whether the basic orientation to the world that is "carried" and learned in this micropractice isn't analogous to the "training" one would receive from viewing pornography, whereby (predominantly) men unconsciously learn to construe women as objects available to be selected, viewed, touched, and enjoyed at the whim of the user.

material devices (there is no particular device that comes with the same quasi-sacramental sheen of the iPhone or iPad),[87] it might be a little more difficult to imagine them as fostering defined rituals that we could describe as "liturgies." And yet.

I should confess to my own short-lived Facebook experiment. A couple of years ago, several years behind the curve, I finally caved and created a Facebook account. After about three months, I deleted the account as a result of the sort of "practices audit" I suggested in *Desiring the Kingdom*.[88]

Now at this point I'm supposed to make the obligatory observation that no cultural artifact is necessarily evil—that cultural systems and products are latent with possibilities that can be used, proverbially, "for good or ill." Such provisos and qualifications want to resist simplistically demonizing any particular cultural phenomenon. So they put the onus for disorder on *users*: if Facebook became a problem for me—if it began to function as a disordering liturgy—then the problem lies with me as a user. But shouldn't we concede that cultural artifacts also come loaded with the intentions of their creators, and that they also take on a life of their own that can outstrip the intentions of even their creators *and* users?[89] Cultural phenomena and systems can be laden with an implicit vision of the good life that is inscribed in the very structure, in the warp and woof, of the cultural artifact itself. In that case, not even the best of intentions on the part of users will be able to undo the teleological (dis)order that is built into the system. Or at the very least, users can severely underestimate the (de)formative power of cultural artifacts, approaching them with just a little bit too much confidence, assured that they are masters of the technology when it might be the technology that is slowly mastering them. Social media—despite the good uses to which it can be put—might be just this sort of disordering liturgy. Signing up for Twitter or Facebook is not a neutral decision to simply employ a "medium": it is to insert oneself in an environment of practice that inculcates in us certain habits that then shape our orientation to the world—indeed, they *make* our worlds.

87. I recently encountered a probing evaluation of our relationship to technology from the playwright Tony Kushner that is directly relevant here: "Capitalism has done exactly what Marx said it does—it gives the inorganic machine the qualities of the living beings who created it and makes it seem like a living thing itself, not a dead thing created by human labor. We're trained through market research and the dark genius of advertising to develop increasingly erotically charged relationships with the inorganic. You develop the feeling that you can't live without your iPhone or your iPad because they're sold to you as having souls, as magical manna from heaven, instead of what they actually are, which is just stuff that people put together." "The Art of Theater No. 16: Tony Kushner," *The Paris Review* 201 (Summer 2012): 118.

88. *Desiring the Kingdom*, 84.

89. For illuminating analysis and wisdom, see Brad J. Kallenberg, *God and Gadgets: Following Jesus in a Technological World* (Eugene, OR: Cascade Books, 2011), esp. 82–105.

For example, both Facebook and Twitter can seem to foster habits of self-display that closely resemble the vice of vainglory.[90] Or at the very least, they amplify the self-consciousness and ironic distance that characterizes late modern capitalism—to a debilitating degree. Indeed, I do not envy our four teenagers in the least: far from carefree, their adolescence is a tangled web of angst that is, I think, qualitatively different from that of past generations. The difference, I suggest, stems from a unique constellation of cultural habits that has exacerbated their self-consciousness to an almost paralyzing degree.

Granted, self-consciousness is part of the rite of passage that is adolescence. The hormonal effects on teenaged bodies make them realize they *are* bodies in ways that surprise them. They inhabit their bodies as foreign guests, constantly imagining that all eyes are upon them as they go to sharpen their pencil or climb the stairs at a football game. Such self-consciousness has always bred its own warped ontology in which the teenager is the center of the universe, praying both that no one will notice and that everyone would.

The advent of social media has amplified this exponentially. In the past, there would have been spaces where adolescents could escape from these games, most notably in the home. Whatever teenagers might have thought of their parents, they certainly didn't have to put on a show for them. The home was a space to let down your guard, freed from the perpetual gaze of your peers. You could almost forget yourself. You could at least forget how gawky and pimpled and weird you were, freed from the competition that characterizes teenagedom.

No longer. The space of the home has been punctured by the intrusion of social media such that the competitive world of self-display and self-consciousness is always with us. The universe of social media is a ubiquitous panopticon. The teenager at home does not escape the game of self-consciouness; instead, she is constantly aware of being on display—and she is regularly aware of the exhibitions of others. Her Twitter feed incessantly updates her about all of the exciting, hip things she is *not* doing with the "popular" girls; her Facebook pings nonstop with photos that highlight how boring her homebound existence is. And so she is compelled to constantly be "on," to be "updating" and "checking in." The competition for coolness never stops. She is constantly aware of herself—and thus unable to lose herself in the pleasures of solitude: burrowing into a novel, pouring herself out in a journal, playing with fanciful forms in a sketch pad.

90. For a helpful discussion of vainglory in the context of pedagogy and formation, see Rebecca Konyndyk DeYoung, "Pedagogical Rhythms: Practices and Reflections on Practice," in *Teaching and Christian Practices: Reshaping Faith and Learning*, ed. David I. Smith and James K. A. Smith (Grand Rapids: Eerdmans, 2011), 24–42.

More pointedly, she loses any orientation to a *project*. Self-consciousness is the end of teleology.

Catholic philosopher Charles Taylor provides a framework for cultural analysis in this regard. In *A Secular Age*, Taylor suggests that ours is the "age of authenticity," an age governed by an expressive individualism. To get at this, he homes in on fashion as a kind of case study. While fashion is a medium of *expression* for my individuality, it is also something that is inescapably relational, almost parasitic: "The space of fashion is one in which we sustain a language together of signs and meanings, which is constantly changing, but which at any moment is the background needed to give our gestures the sense they have."[91] This is no longer a space of common action but rather a space of *mutual display*—another way of "being-with" in which "a host of urban monads hover on the boundary between solipsism and communication." This breeds a new kind of self-consciousness: "My loud remarks and gestures are overtly addressed only to my immediate companions, my family group is sedately walking, engaged in our own Sunday outing, but all the time we are aware of this common space that we are building, in which the messages that cross take their meaning."[92] In other words, we all behave now like thirteen-year-old girls.

With the expansion of social media, *every* space is a space of "mutual self-display." As a result, every space is a kind of visual echo chamber. We are no longer seen doing something; we're doing something to be seen. Something similar was pointed out twenty years ago by the novelist David Foster Wallace. In a somewhat neglected essay, "Fictional Futures and the Conspicuously Young," Wallace pointed out how he and his generation of writers (the "conspicuously young") emerged in the echo chamber of self-consciousness described by Taylor. And this inevitably influenced American fiction.

In particular, Wallace points out that the conspicuously young (Wallace, Jay McInerney, Brett Ellis, and others) were the first generation of writers to grow up with the ubiquity of television. "The American generation born after, say, 1955 is the first for whom television is something to be *lived with*, not just looked at." Here lies an important difference between Philip Roth, John Updike, and Saul Bellow, on the one hand, and David Foster Wallace, Jonathan Franzen, and Zadie Smith, on the other: "We quite literally cannot 'imagine' life without [television]. As it does for so much of today's developed world, it presents and so defines our common experience; but we, unlike any elders, have no memory of a world without such electronic definition. It's built in."[93]

---

91. Charles Taylor, *A Secular Age* (Cambridge, MA: Harvard University Press, 2007), 481.
92. Ibid., 482.
93. Wallace, "Fictional Futures," 3.

It may seem quaint to carp on television today ("So *analog*!"), but Wallace's analysis is prescient. For it is already with television that we see a reconfiguration of social space as a space of mutual display: "A mysterious beast like television begins, the more sophisticated it gets, to produce and live by an antinomy, a phenomenon whose strength lies in its contradiction: aimed ever and always at groups, masses, markets, collectivities, it's nevertheless true that the most powerful and lasting changes are wrought by TV on *individual persons*, each one of whom is forced every day to understand himself in relation to the Groups by virtue of which he seems to exist at all."[94] The gaze of the camera on some becomes the ubiquitous gaze under which we all constantly live. "Prolonged exposure to broadcast drama," Wallace notes, "makes each one of us at once more self-conscious and less reflective." When all of us are constituted as an audience, then all the world becomes a TV. "We, the audience, receive unconscious reinforcement of the thesis that the most significant feature of persons is *watchableness*, and that contemporary human worth is not just isomorphic with but rooted in the phenomenon of watching." Here is that unique and distorted mode of "being-with" observed by Taylor: to be is to be seen. It is Wallace who situates this in a philosophical heritage: "Imagine a Berkleyan *esse-est-percipi* universe in which God is named Nielsen."[95]

What neither Taylor nor Wallace appreciates is how paralyzing this self-consciousness can be. In a world in which we are always and everywhere *seen*—where camera phones are ready to capture every gaffe and failure, and Jon Stewart is at the ready to cynically mock us in front of a broadcast audience—who would ever venture to *do* anything? When you have grown up watching twenty-four-hour highlight reels on ESPN, your halting attempts to hit a golf ball become excruciating embarrassments better avoided by inaction. You no longer feel permission to be an amateur because in our age of mutual display, everyone is on television. And so you are never free to learn a craft or master a new skill because the horror of someone seeing you fail paralyzes you. When your whole world is one giant YouTube clip, every action is an act of self-display—and hence fodder for criticism, mockery, and rejection. Constantly conscious of being watched, you freeze like a deer in the headlights: "Maybe if I don't move they won't notice me."

David Brooks's snapshot of human nature in *The Social Animal* can help us diagnose the problem here: in self-consciousness, we are both the "deer" *and* the "headlights." Such self-consciousness is debilitating precisely because it forces us to constantly inhabit that "conscious" part of the mind that is more primed for analysis than action, more comfortable observing

94. Ibid., 6.
95. Ibid., 7.

than doing. More specifically, self-consciousness draws us out of the orienting impulses of our automated *preconsciousness*—that unconscious "feel" for the world that governs most of our action. Self-consciousness compromises the ability to inhabit our habits, to live toward a *telos*, to pursue a project and act toward an end. In sum, such self-consciousness is the end of *action*.

So the very nature of social media encourages a certain social ontology; it comes primed with a social imaginary, and to inhabit the Facebook world is to play by its rules. Over time, this becomes a formative exercise. In tangible but implicit ways, it inculcates in us dispositions and inclinations that lean toward a configuration of the social world that revolves around *me*—even if we tell ourselves we're interested in others. It is a classic example of a "pedagogy of insignificance" that extorts the essential from the seemingly insignificant. While it purports to be simply a "medium," it comes loaded with a Story about what matters, and *who* matters. And as we inhabit these virtual worlds—clicking our way around the environment, constantly updating our "status" and checking on others, fixated on our feed, documenting our "likes" for others to see—we are slowly and covertly incorporated into a body politic with its own vision of human flourishing: shallow connections for instant self-gratification and self-congratulation. And all of this happens precisely because we don't think about it.

Gary Shteyngart's disturbing and satirical novel *Super Sad True Love Story* can be read as a prophetic mirror showing us where such a culture of self-display and voyeurism might be headed: what would the world look like, and what would *we* look like, if such practices continued—if the "real" world looked like the Facebook world? A quirky, dystopian story set in the not-too-distant future, comprising the diary of Lenny Abramov interspersed with the "GlobalTeens" (i.e., Facebook?) communications of his girlfriend, Eunice Park, the book extrapolates from our current cultural trends to imagine what will be left of the United States, or more specifically, New York City. It is a world where people are publicly identified by their credit ranking, where nation-states have been replaced by corporations, and where the debt-riddled United States has become entirely enfolded into China (with sections parceled out to Norway). Shteyngart's social commentary is oblique and allusive, again projecting from our current cultural habits into an imagined future. One might describe it as the ubiquitization of a Facebook sensibility, where everything is made public—our credit rankings are displayed on "credit poles" that line the street; our emotions and thoughts are made public on äppäräts dangling from our necks; shopping is the great globalized pastime; and nothing is left to the imagination as all the young women are wearing transparent "onionskin" jeans. The stark effect of all of this is the loss of any sense of a common good: moneyed tribes retreat into walled enclaves while entertained individuals retreat from civic life for private fulfillment and entertainment. The social imaginary of this body politic is the end of the *body* politic: the sinews of social interaction have dwindled to fiber-optic tethers, and any notion of a *social* good has gone the way of the American dollar, a distantly remembered dream.

Shteyngart's novel is a cautionary tale. Its futuristic despair can wake us up to a present-day concern: that these aren't just things we do; they do something *to* us. Zadie Smith makes a similar point in her review of the movie *The Social Network* alongside Jaron Lanier's manifesto, *You Are Not a Gadget*. As Smith notes, in language strikingly akin to my argument here, "We know the consequences of this instinctively; we feel them. We know that having two thousand Facebook friends is not what it looks like. We know that we are using the software to behave in a certain, superficial way toward others. We know what we are doing 'in' the software. But do we know, are we alert to, what the software is doing *to* us?"[96] Twitter and Facebook are not just "media" that are neutral, benign conduits of information and communication; they are world-making and identity-constituting. They invite and demand modes of interaction that function as liturgies. Like so many formative liturgies, they extort the essential by the seemingly insignificant, precisely by telling us a Story, capturing our imaginations to perceive the world in ways we don't even realize. We imagine more than we know.

Christian worship invites us into a very different social ontology, through a different set of rituals—a counter-liturgy. Whereas the technological rituals we just considered reinforce a social imaginary in which I am the center of the universe, only related to others as an audience for my display, Christian worship is an intentionally decentering practice, calling us out of ourselves into the very life of God. That worship begins with a *call* is already a first displacement that is at the same time an invitation: to find ourselves *in* Christ. If the rituals of social media and smartphones are involutional, the practices of Christian worship are fundamentally ecstatic—calling us out of ourselves and into the life of the Triune God, not to "lose" ourselves, but to be found in him. Granted, there is still a call to vulnerability, even a kind of "display" in the call to confession. But this is not a competitive display. It is rather a vulnerability that is met with mercy and grace: you confess your sins and are reminded once again that "you have died, and your life is hidden with Christ in God" (Col. 3:3). In a society of mutual self-display and debilitating self-consciousness, it is a special grace to be invited into a Story where we are *hidden* with Christ in God. And being found in him, we are called out of ourselves to love

96. Zadie Smith, "Generation Why?," *New York Review of Books* 57, no. 18 (November 25, 2010): 57–60 (emphasis added). See also Jaron Lanier, *You Are Not a Gadget: A Manifesto* (New York: Knopf, 2010).

neighbors and enemies, widows and orphans. In the performed story that is Christian worship, we are related to others as neighbors[97] rather than as an "audience."

And herein lies a central aspect of Christian worship: it is an alternative imaginary, a way that the Spirit of God invites us into the Story of God in Christ reconciling the world to himself. But as we've seen, if such a Story is really going to capture our imaginations, it needs to get into our gut—it needs to be written on our hearts. And the way to the heart is through the body. In the final chapter I'll utilize our theoretical toolbox developed from Merleau-Ponty and Bourdieu to "see anew" what's at stake in the formative practices of intentional Christian worship.

97. As J. Todd Billings notes, "The Lord's Supper, as an icon of the gospel, not only offers communion with Christ and with Christ's body but also directs the lives of the communicants to the 'in God' dimension of the neighbor" (*Union with Christ: Reframing Theology and Ministry for the Church* [Grand Rapids: Baker Academic, 2011], 113–14).

4

Restor(y)ing the World

CHRISTIAN FORMATION FOR MISSION

Through worship God trains his people to take the right things for granted.[1]

Sanctifying Perception: Re-Narration Takes Practice

Let's return to where we began: Christian worship and Christian education both have the same *end*. Both the church and the Christian university are institutions caught up in the *missio Dei*, recruiting the hearts and minds of the people of God into the very life of God so that we can once again take up our creational and re-creational calling—to bear God's image *for* and *to* all of creation.[2] The church and the Christian college (and Christian schools) are sites of formation that culminate in *sending*: to "go in peace to love and serve the Lord" *by* taking up our cross along with our commission to cultivate the earth.[3] Christian worship and formation, as

---

1. Stanley Hauerwas and Samuel Wells, "The Gift of the Church and the Gifts God Gives It," in *The Blackwell Companion to Christian Ethics*, ed. Stanley Hauerwas and Samuel Wells (Oxford: Blackwell, 2006), 25.
2. On the continuity between the "cultural mandate" (Gen. 1:26–31) and the "Great Commission" (Matt. 28:18–20), see James K. A. Smith, *Desiring the Kingdom: Worship, Worldview, and Cultural Formation* (Grand Rapids: Baker Academic, 2009), 205–7.
3. For clear articulation of the expansive scope of the mission of God, and hence the mission of God's people, see Christopher J. H. Wright, *The Mission of God: Unlocking the Bible's Grand*

practices of *divine* action, culminate in Christian action—being sent as ambassadors of another "city," as witnesses to kingdom come, to live and act communally as a people who embody a foretaste of God's shalom.[4] This is not to "instrumentalize" worship as merely a means to an end, nor is it to reduce worship to a strategy for moral formation; neither should it be confused with an activism that sees Christian action as some Pelagian expression of *our* abilities. Worship and the practices of Christian formation are first and foremost the way the Spirit invites us into union with the Triune God. Worship is the arena in which we encounter God and are formed by God in and through the practices in which the Spirit is present—centering rituals to which God makes a promise (the sacraments). As Boulton observes, while John Calvin persistently emphasized a "preferred suite of formative practices"[5] as "disciplines of regeneration," he also constantly emphasized that these were not routines of spiritual self-assertion or human accomplishment:

> Disciples may and do perform these sanctifying practices, but their performances are themselves divine gifts, and they take place properly and fruitfully—that is, in ways that produce genuine humility and insight for them and others—only by way of divine accompaniment and power. . . . Thus following Calvin, we may reframe "spiritual practices" as in the first place works of the Holy Spirit and Jesus Christ, the sanctifying, regenerating, restorative labor of God with us and in us. . . . Each of the church's key practices is still something human beings do, but they do it neither alone nor as the act's primary agent. Rather, in and through the practice, they participate in divine work.[6]

So in the practices of Christian worship, and in related spiritual disciplines, we encounter the Lover of our souls. We are drawn into the life of the One our hearts were made for, the Lord of heaven and earth.[7]

And it is that creating and re-creating God who tells us to *go* even as he goes with us, "even to the end of the age." Christian worship culminates

---

Narrative (Downers Grove, IL: InterVarsity, 2006); and Wright, *The Mission of God's People: A Biblical Theology of the Church's Mission* (Grand Rapids: Zondervan, 2010).

4. Consider Graham Ward's careful parsing of just what counts as "Christian action," analyzed in terms of six key elements: the agent who acts, the nature of the action, evaluation of the action, the object of the action, the effect of the action, and the intentions and affections ("pro-attitudes," after Donald Davidson) that lead to action. See Graham Ward, *The Politics of Discipleship: Becoming Postmaterial Citizens*, The Church and Postmodern Culture (Grand Rapids: Baker Academic, 2009), 181–201. In many ways, I see the present book as expanding and deepening our analysis of the sixth aspect.

5. Matthew Myer Boulton, *Life in God: John Calvin, Practical Formation, and the Future of Protestant Theology* (Grand Rapids: Eerdmans, 2011), 24.

6. Ibid., 223.

7. Augustine, *Confessions* 1.1.1: "You have made us for yourself, and our hearts are restless until they rest in you."

with a sending ("Go!") accompanied by a promise ("And as you go, you go with his blessing")—the benediction that is both a blessing and a charge, a co-*mission*-ing accompanied by the promise of the Spirit's presence. So while we are sent to act, to labor in love for God and neighbor, the Spirit of Christ goes with us so that even "our" Christian action, undertaken as we are recruited into the *missio Dei*, is never merely "ours"; we "act in communion with God."[8] Worship is not merely time with a deistic god who winds us up and then sends us out on our own; we don't enter worship for "top up" refueling to then leave as self-sufficient, autonomous actors. "In the conception of Christian praxis," Ward notes, "there is no room for such a modern notion of self-sufficiency."[9] Instead, the biblical vision is one of co-abiding presence and participation ("I in you and you in me"). In other words, our Christian action is bound up with the dynamics of incorporation. "By the act of receiving the Eucharist," for example, "I place myself *in* Christ—rather than simply placing Christ within me. I consume but I do not absorb Christ without being absorbed into Christ. Only in this complex co-abiding are there life, nourishment, and nurture because of, through, or by means of this feeding; there is both participation of human life in God's life and participation of God's life in human life."[10] So our action is not merely motivated by worship of the Triune God; rather, it is in worship that we are caught up into the life of God, drawn into union with Christ, and thus recruited into this participation that generates Christian action as we "go." "The Christian act," Ward continues, "has to be understood in terms not just of the church but also of the church's participation in Christ, the church as the body of Christ. That is, the Christian act is integral to the church's participation in the operations of the Triune God within realms created in and through Christ as God's Word. Discipleship is thus not simply following the example of Christ; it is formation within Christ, so that we become Christlike. And the context of this formation is the church in all its concrete locatedness and eschatological significance."[11]

To emphasize the s/ending of Christian worship is not to reduce worship to moral formation or to treat the presence of God as a tool for our self-improvement. Rather, the centrifugal *end* of Christian worship is integral to the Story we rehearse in Christian worship; sending is internal to the logic of the practice. To emphasize that Christian action is the end or *telos* of Christian worship is not to instrumentalize worship but is rather to "get" the Story that is enacted in the drama of worship—the

8. J. Todd Billings, *Union with Christ: Reframing Theology and Ministry for the Church* (Grand Rapids: Baker Academic, 2011), 110.

9. Ward, *Politics of Discipleship*, 184.

10. Ibid., 187.

11. Ibid., 184. As he puts it a little later, "We might characterize Christian acting as a *praxis* that participates in a divine *poiesis* that has soteriological and eschatological import" (201).

"true story of the whole world"[12] in which we are called to play our part as God's image-bearers *by* cultivating creation. Integral to that Story, and to the practice of Christian worship, is the sense that we are now enabled and empowered to take up this mission precisely because of the gift of the Spirit (Rom. 8:1–17). At the same time, the Spirit meets us where we are as liturgical animals, as embodied agents, inviting us into that "suite" of disciplines and practices that are conduits of transformative, empowering grace. So even if there is a centrifugal *telos* to Christian worship and formation, there is also a regular centripetal invitation to recenter ourselves in the Story, to continually pursue and deepen our in*corp*oration.[13] It's not a matter of choosing between worship *or* mission; nor are we faced with the false dichotomy of church *or* world, cathedral *or* city. To the contrary, we worship *for* mission; we gather *for* sending; we center ourselves in the practices of the body of Christ *for the sake of* the world; we are reformed in the cathedral to undertake our image-bearing commission to reform the city.[14] So it is precisely an expansive sense of mission that requires formation. It is the missional *telos* of Christian *action* that requires us to be intentional about the formative power of Christian practices.

This dynamic interplay between formation and action, worship and mission, is wonderfully illustrated in Matthew Boulton's lucid, provocative account of Calvin's vision for Geneva. At the heart of Calvin's vision for reform was the sanctification of ordinary life that energized the project of reforming not only the church but also the city.[15] Not only should worship be re-ordered and renewed, but all of cultural life should reflect God's designs and intentions. God is Lord not only of the soul but also of the body, the Ruler of not just heaven but also earth. The gospel is good news not just as a rescue plan for embattled souls but as a word from the

12. See Michael Goheen and Craig Bartholomew, *The True Story of the Whole World: Finding Your Place in the Biblical Drama* (Grand Rapids: Faith Alive, 2009), echoing N. T. Wright: "the whole point of Christianity is that it offers a story which is the story of the whole world" (*The New Testament and the People of God* [Minneapolis: Fortress, 1992], 41–42).

13. In a rich footnote, Boulton suggests that proposals by Willimon and Hauerwas differ from Calvin insofar as their "Anabaptist" conception of the church is more centripetal than centrifugal (*Life in God*, 219n8). I think he's right to feel a difference here; I would only caution that even the centrifugal *telos* requires persistent centripetal gathering *for* formation. In other words, centrifugal mission is only possible to the extent that we are centripetally recentered in Christ through Word, sacrament, and that repertoire of formative Christian practices. For the sake of Geneva, one might say, the saints needed to regularly gather in St. Pierre Cathedral.

14. There are a host of knotty questions and issues here regarding Christian engagement with the "politics" of the earthly city that I will address in detail in volume 3, *Embodying the Kingdom*.

15. For a discussion of the social implications of this, see Charles Taylor, *Sources of the Self: The Making of Modern Identity* (Cambridge: Cambridge University Press, 1989), 211–33, with further consideration in Taylor, *A Secular Age* (Cambridge, MA: Harvard University Press, 2007), 77–84. I will discuss this in more detail in *Haunting Immanence: Reading Charles Taylor in a Secular Age* (Grand Rapids: Eerdmans, forthcoming).

Creator who is redeeming *all* things (Col. 1:15–20). The grace of God has ripple effects not just in the church but also in the world, which is precisely why our *sending* is integral to the story. And so we get something of the "activism" that is often associated with the Calvinist tradition, seeking to claim every square inch for Christ.[16]

Not surprisingly then, Calvin articulates a critique of monasticism, that medieval institution that epitomizes the opposite sensibility: elitist withdrawal from the messiness and domesticity of ordinary life. However, as Boulton so carefully points out, what Calvin rejects in monasticism is *not* the commitment to formative practices and regular observance of spiritual disciplines.[17] What he rejects is not the "rituals" associated with monasticism but the elitism and separatism of it. Calvin "storms the monastery" as it were, not to demolish the disciplines of the community, but to *liberate* these formative practices from their separatist captivity. "For Calvin," Boulton observes, "monastics are mistaken only insofar as they make elite, difficult, and rare what should be ordinary, accessible, and common in Christian communities: namely, whole human lives formed in and through the church's distinctive repertoire of disciplines, from singing psalms to daily prayer to communing with Christ at the sacred supper."[18] The upshot of Calvin's critique of monasticism is not a de-ritualized, sermon-centric, intellectualist piety but rather a generalization of monastic practices—a celebration of the "monkhood of all believers."[19]

What's celebrated here is precisely the pedagogical wisdom implicit in the monastic disciplines, which were rooted in an even more ancient heritage of the church's wisdom about spiritual formation. The "suite" of disciplines practiced by the monastery was indebted to an ancient Christian *paideia*, "the church's ancient disciplinary treasury."[20] Immersion in the disciplines of this Christian *paideia* did not require withdrawal from the labor of the city to the isolation of the desert; but it would require remaking the city as a kind of desert: "Geneva as a whole would become a *magnum monasterium*"[21] insofar as the consistory in Geneva—at least if Calvin had his way!—would see to it that butchers, bakers, and candlestick makers would have ample opportunity to immerse themselves in these formative spiritual disciplines that were gifts of God for the people

16. For a classic summary of this vision of the Reformation as unleashing "world-formative" Christianity, see Nicholas Wolterstorff, *Until Justice and Peace Embrace* (Grand Rapids: Eerdmans, 1983).

17. I already noted Calvin's affirmation of a "holy and lawful monasticism" in *Desiring the Kingdom*, 209n118.

18. Boulton, *Life in God*, 13.

19. Ibid., 22.

20. Ibid., 23–24.

21. Ibid., 27.

of God, conduits of grace given for their sanctification. As Boulton comments, "Calvin ultimately sought to expand the sanctuary not only out to the walls of the church's worship space, but also beyond them, all the way out to the Genevan city walls—or better, out to the limits of a Christian disciple's life and work wherever she may go, and in that sense out to the limits of creation."[22] Calvin's concern was that these practices be accessible and practicable for Christians in *all* vocations[23] because they could only carry out their missional vocations in every sphere of culture insofar as they were adequately formed and shaped by the Spirit of God. And for Calvin—as for ancient Christian faith—the way to "clothe" oneself with the virtues of Christ (Col. 3:12–15) was to be immersed in the practices of prayer and worship (Col. 3:16–17). The worship practices and spiritual disciplines of the church were the "paideutic repertoire" needed to form agents who could carry out their mission and vocation in and for the world.

Again, note the interplay of the centripetal and centrifugal dynamics here: Calvin's vision of reforming is clearly creational in its scope. We are called to participate in the cosmic redemption by which Christ is redeeming all things, which is why every nook and cranny of the city *matters*—and hence all sorts of cultural labor can be taken up as expressions of the *missio Dei.* However, undertaking that cultural labor "in the name of the Lord Jesus" (Col. 3:17); that is, in a way that is rightly ordered—requires that we regularly discipline our habits and desires to God's desires for his creation. This requires that we regularly immerse ourselves in the repertoire of practices and disciplines that recenter us in Christ. And while Calvin rejects monastic withdrawal and Anabaptist "alternative societies," he still emphasizes a fundamental *antithesis* here. It is precisely because "the conventional everyday life of his time" was "deeply at odds with the needs of Christian piety"[24] that Calvin saw the need for countermeasures: regular, persistent opportunities to be immersed in counterformative Christian disciplines that would counter the formative power of other disciplines, other liturgies. So while Calvin does not advocate a retreat from "the world" to the desert, he still emphasizes the set-apart-ness of the Christian life. As Boulton so well summarizes it, "For Calvin, Christian life does involve being set apart, not via a geographical, social retreat to a monastic campus, but rather via a moral, existential brand of practical withdrawal from 'the world' and 'the depravity of disposition.' That is, Calvin envisions a reformed way of life robustly engaged in ordinary affairs that is nevertheless unconformed to

22. Ibid., 43. The latter qualification is important if we are to avoid concerns about a "theonomist" project. Again, I will take up these questions in volume 3.

23. For example, Calvin proposed a daily prayer cycle, "in effect a version of the divine office designed to be practicable to all Christians" (ibid., 39); he also advocated more frequent celebration of the Lord's Supper for the sake of Christian formation (40–42).

24. Ibid., 25.

their prevailing patterns and protocols, in effect a *dispositional deflection* from the world while remaining ensconced within it."[25]

And so we arrive at the crux of my argument. We gather to be sent, and we are sent to do—to undertake Christian action that participates in the *missio Dei.* "Mission" then is just shorthand to describe what it is for Christians to pursue their vocations to the glory of God and in ways that are oriented to the shalom of the kingdom. But as we've been emphasizing, our action flows from our *dispositions*, our *habitus*, our nonconscious passional orientation to the world. Which is precisely why any Christian emphasis on mission and vocation and culture-making has to be rooted in a more fundamental concern with "dispositional deflection." If the church is a centrifuge, sending out image-bearers to take up their commission in God's good-but-broken world, it must also be a community of practice that centripetally gathers for dispositional reformation. And other missional institutions—such as Christian schools, colleges, and universities—will also need to engage in such dispositional deflection. In sum, any missional, formative Christian institution that is bent on sending out *actors*—agents of reformation and renewal—will need to attend to the reformation of our *habitus*.

To put this in terms of Merleau-Ponty's lexicon, if we aim to form Christian actors and agents of renewal, then dispositional deflection requires sanctifying perception—for it is our bodily comportment (*praktognosia*) that *constitutes* the world in which we are called and moved to act. To shape perception is to transform action because we transform the "world" in which we find ourselves. If we are going to recalibrate our attunement to the world, and hence feel pulled by a different *call*, it is not enough to have a Christian "perspective" on the world; we need nothing less than a Christian imagination. Because our evaluation of a situation is bound up with our perception of it, and because our perception is shaped by the bodily background within which we constitute our experience, Christian action requires the sanctification of perception on the bodily register of incarnate significance. In sum, if we are going to be agents of the coming kingdom, *acting* in ways that embody God's desires for creation, then our imaginations need to be conscripted by God. It is not enough to convince our intellects; our imaginations need to be caught by—and caught up into—the Story of God's restorative, reconciling grace for all of creation. It won't be enough for us to be convinced; we need to be *moved*. Otherwise we'll just be reading Wendell Berry in Costco; we'll be convinced but not transformed.

Below I want to consider what this means for the church, and specifically for the worship practices of the church. But let's also consider the implications of this for another missional institution: the Christian

25. Ibid., 26 (emphasis added).

To Think About: Imagining the Reformation of Manners

In his historical snapshot of Calvin's vision for Geneva, Matthew Boulton emphasizes that Calvin's vision was to extend those formative practices that had been reserved for clergy and monastics to the laity as a whole, pressing not only for the priesthood of all believers but also for the "monkhood" of all believers. The hope was that the entire city of Geneva would be "enrolled, as Calvin envisions it, in a citywide program of practical formation. Now every Christian, rooted in her own particular calling and context, is to live out a life formed through disciplines only speciously reserved to cloistered specialists: Scripture reading, daily prayer regimens, psalm singing, and so on."[1] Intriguingly, this is pictured as a "reformation of manners."[2]

The phrase might strike us as a bit odd, as if the hope was that Geneva would be a place of politeness, where everyone dutifully says "please" and "thank you." But of course, manners are about more than the niceties that govern our social interaction. *Manners* and *customs* are something like the vernacular terms for what Bourdieu calls *habitus*—which is precisely why Bourdieu would emphasize that there might be more going on in those niceties than we realize (the cosmological significance, for example, of "sit up straight" and "hold your fork in your left hand"). Seeing dispositional deflection as a reformation of manners might also prime us to read Lionel Trilling's essay "Manners, Morals, and the Novel" with new interest and new eyes.[3] Trilling's attention to "manners" links them with the function of literature and the imagination in ways that resonate with our project here. In fact, Trilling suggests that we understand such a notion of "manners" in ways that we can't quite articulate. "Somewhere below all the explicit statements that a people makes through its art, religion, architecture, legislation, there is a dim mental region of intention of which it is very difficult to become aware."[4] Manners are a name we give to that "region of intention," and it is that same region that enables us to understand what we mean by "manners." Manners, as he summarizes it, "is a culture's hum and buzz of implication"—

---

university.[26] If Christian education is a holistic formation of prime citizens of the kingdom, then it needs to reshape students' perception in its fullest (Merleau-Pontian) sense: the tactile, visceral mode in which we *mean* the world in ways we can't quite say. Such an education needs to impact the *aesthetics* of human understanding. It needs to get hold of our gut and capture our imagination—that preconscious, emotional register on which we perceive the world and that, in turn, drives or "pulls" our action. Christian formation, in worship or education, must be characterized by a fundamentally aesthetic aspect—not merely in the sense that such formative practices should be "beautiful" or attractive or "pleasing," but in the

---

26. Everything I'll say here also applies to Christian schools at lower levels, and could also apply to other missional institutions of the church such as campus ministries, mental health facilities, summer camps, and more.

"the whole evanescent context in which its explicit statements are made. It is that part of a culture which is made up of half-uttered or unuttered or unutterable expressions of value. They are hinted at by small actions, sometimes by the arts of dress or decoration, sometimes by tone, gesture, emphasis, or rhythm, sometimes by the words that are used with a special frequency or a special meaning."[5] It is just to the extent that we are able to honor and recognize this "hum and buzz" that we will be attuned to what really directs a people and a culture. In other words, we will only appreciate the importance of a "reformation of manners" if we see the powerful drives that are absorbed from such an unuttered and unutterable "evanescent context."

Which is why we need novelists. For Trilling, literature is the science of manners. "The great novelists," he observes, "know that manners indicate the largest intentions of men's souls as well as the smallest and they are perpetually concerned to catch the meaning of every dim implicit hint." The novel is our imaginative form that recognizes this humming, buzzing reality *beneath* our stated ideals. "The novel, then, is a perpetual quest for reality, the field of its research being always the social world, the material of its analysis being always manners as the indication of the direction of man's soul."[6] "In the novel," Trilling concludes, "manners make men."[7] Which is precisely why the reformation of manners is nothing short of a remaking of our very comportment to the world.

1. Matthew Myer Boulton, *Life in God: John Calvin, Practical Formation, and the Future of Protestant Theology* (Grand Rapids: Eerdmans, 2011), 27.

2. Ibid., 33.

3. In Lionel Trilling, *The Liberal Imagination: Essays on Literature and Society* (1950; repr., New York: NYRB, 2008), 205–22. The gendered language is Trilling's, reflecting 1950s practice.

4. Ibid., 205.

5. Ibid., 206–7.

6. Ibid., 212.

7. Ibid., 216.

sense that such practices should tap into our incarnate significance, should pluck the strings of our embodied attunement to the world. If the practices of Christian formation are truly going to reform our manners and deflect our dispositions to be aimed at the kingdom of God, then such practices need to engender rightly ordered erotic comprehension by renewing and reorienting our imaginations.[27]

27. While I hope I have provided new warrant and impetus for the importance of the aesthetic in Christian formation, the proposal itself is not new. Indeed, I commend Calvin Seerveld's manifesto from a generation ago: "The Fundamental Importance of Imaginativity within Schooling," in *Rainbows for the Fallen World: Aesthetic Life and Artistic Task* (Toronto: Tuppence, 1980), 138–55. Seerveld frames the importance of imaginativity in Christian education in terms of "the sanctification of a person's functional complexity" (141). His "working hypothesis" is that "aesthetic life is integral to sound Christian pedagogy, deserves a curricular attention, and is the philosophical place to order the so many 'intangibles' that make a school's life thrive or

Sanctifying perception requires restor(y)ing the imagination. Note two aspects of this: first, this transformation of the imagination is a re-*story*-ing of our understanding. Sanctifying perception requires aesthetic measures that resonate with the imagination and affect us on an affective level, in the "between" of our incarnate significance. Stories are not just nice little entertainments to jazz up the material; stories are not just some supplementary way of making content "interesting." No, we learn through stories because we know *by* stories. Indeed, we know things in stories that we couldn't know any other way: there is an irreducibility of narrative knowledge that eludes translation and paraphrase.[28] And such stories are not only "told" in a "once-upon-a-time" fashion; stories are compressed into films and commercials, enacted in games and dramas, played out on playgrounds and in malls. Story is the lingua franca of incarnate significance.

In his discussion of education amongst the people of Israel, Old Testament scholar Walter Brueggemann captures the point: in the Torah, when a child asks a question, the teacher's response is "Let me tell you a story." For the people of God, he continues, story "is our primal and most characteristic mode of knowledge. It is the foundation from which come all other knowledge claims we have."[29] So it is crucial that the task of Christian education and formation is nested in a story—in the narrative arc of the biblical drama of God's faithfulness to creation and to his people.[30] It is crucial that the *story* of God in Christ redeeming the world be the very air we breathe, the scaffolding around us, whether we're at our Bunsen burners or on the baseball field, whether we're learning geometry or just learning to count. All of the work of the Christian school or college needs to be nested in this bigger story—and we need to constantly look for ways to tell that story, to teach *in* stories, because story is the first language of love. If hearts are going to be aimed toward God's kingdom, they'll be won

---

flag" (152). And in a wonderful admission that resonates with my own sense of lack, Seerveld confesses: "I have no master plan for consolidating functional features of imaginativity at this point, but I know it is important" (152).

28. Daniel Kahneman notes in *Thinking, Fast and Slow* (New York: Farrar, Straus & Giroux, 2011) that story is understood by "System 1" of our consciousness—the automated, "intuitive" register that governs so much of our action in the world (75).

29. Walter Brueggemann, *The Creative Word: Canon as a Model for Biblical Education* (Philadelphia: Fortress, 1982), 22–23.

30. This narrative intuition is what informs Sally Lloyd-Jones's evocative exercise in *The Jesus Storybook Bible*, illustrated by Jago (Grand Rapids: Zonderkidz, 2007). While one might have some reservations about this kind of improvisation on the Scriptures, those need not detain us from recognizing and affirming Lloyd-Jones's intuition: "The Bible isn't a book of rules, or a book of heroes. The Bible is most of all a Story. It's an adventure story about a young Hero who comes from a far country to win back his lost treasure. It's a love story about a brave Prince who leaves his palace, his throne—everything—to rescue the one he loves. It's like the most wonderful of fairy tales that has come true in real life!" (17).

> **To Think About: Story and the Economy of Abundance**
>
> Stories can haunt and unsettle us, and the most skilled storytellers can do this with remarkable lexical economy (think Cormac McCarthy). The imaginative expanse of a story does not depend on the quantity of words. Rather, there can be a feel *among* the words, resonances, and assonances that carry an aesthetic power disproportionate to their length. Short stories and poetry are often examples of such compressed narrative power. Perhaps nothing matches the evocative power of the six-word story said to have been composed by the master of verbal economy, Ernest Hemingway:
>
> > For sale: baby shoes, never worn.[1]
>
> In just six words the story creates—and invites us into—a whole world. One might recall another brief story with similar impact:
>
> > He is not here; he has risen, just as he said.
>
> 1. My thanks to my son Coleson for pointing me to this little gem.

over by good storytellers. Seerveld considers a case in point: What would it look like for history education to be shaped by an aesthetic appreciation for our nature as narrative animals? "Would not a 'story-telling' and 'cultural history' focus redeem much of the fact-plus-anecdote renditions of world history prevalent in so many classrooms?" he asks.[31] A narrative approach is not just a matter of the teacher being a good storyteller, however. It is a more fundamental matter of framing: "pitching historiography toward instruction of student imaginativity rather than as information of chronicled events" and approaching historical knowledge as something with a "pre-analytic quality." This raises questions about the *telos* of Christian education itself. "Such an aesthetically geared 'soft-focus' does not entail sloppy vagueness," Seerveld cautions. But "it does mean that history teaching would not be aimed at training professionally analytic historians but would attempt to give the young a sense of our time, style and location as God's people amid the nations and the ages of the world."[32]

So sanctifying perception involves re-*story*-ing our being-in-the-world. But second, the sanctification of perception for Christian action requires *restoring* rightly ordered perception—training us to take the right things for granted. So it's not just that formation and "dispositional deflection" must be fundamentally aesthetic. There is also a normative point here: our perception will be sanctified just to the extent that our "background" and imagination are recruited by a normative story—the "true story of the

31. Seerveld, *Rainbows*, 151.
32. Ibid.

whole world." Not only is our desire subject to competing formations; so too is our imagination (and it is the imagination, in some sense, that primes and aims our desire). Our imaginations are contested ground, pulled and wooed and shaped by competing stories about "the good life," tempted and attracted by affective pictures of what counts as "flourishing." The way to our hearts is through our imaginations, and the way to our imaginations is story, image, symbol, song. As Michael Budde comments, "Stories, symbols, songs, and exemplars—in our day, of course, it is not the Church that carries these to most people, even to most Christians. For people in advanced capitalist countries (and in ever-larger parts of the euphemistically labeled 'developing world'), most of their stories, narratives, images, and sounds come from centralized, for-profit transnational corporations—the so-called global culture industries."[33] Unfortunately, because the church remains fixated on content and "messages," it fails to see what's really at stake in these global culture industries: our imaginations. What can seem benign and "safe" on the Disney Channel can be a powerful co-option of imaginations for a consumerist, egocentric comportment to the world. But because we miss the affective, nonconscious way that we "get" stories—and the ways such stories can incorporate us into disordered social bodies—we will tend to simply fail to see where the battle lies. The irony, Budde concludes, is that "the commercial 'orchestrators of attention' . . . are winning a contest that church leaders scarcely recognize as underway."[34]

But if we appreciate the central, orienting nature of the imagination, then we will be poised to see what's at stake in our encounter with the stories, images, and moving icons of consumer culture; conversely, we should also appreciate anew the centrality of imagination formation to Christian discipleship and education. We will be in a place to consider how

"learning our place in the Christian story" might be a serviceable definition of Christian discipleship. It reminds us of a few important things: that we don't invent what it means to be Christian, that being Christian is a learned (not innate or "natural") condition, and that we require others to help us understand and embody the role of disciple. Mostly it draws attention to the inescapable reality that serious followers of Jesus are made, not born. They are formed by the stories, symbols, songs, and exemplars of the Christian experiment. In particular it involves the internalization of the priorities,

33. Michael L. Budde, "Collecting Praise: Global Culture Industries," in Hauerwas and Wells, *Blackwell Companion to Christian Ethics*, 124. For a trenchant analysis of the "practical aesthetic imagination" that explains "contemporary capitalism's magical powers," see Nigel Thrift, "Understanding the Material Practices of Glamour," in *The Affect Theory Reader*, ed. Melissa Gregg and Gregory J. Seigworth (Durham, NC: Duke University Press, 2010), 289–308.
34. Budde, "Collecting Praise," 125.

affections, and dispositions of Jesus of Nazareth, he through whom God reveals most fully who God is and what God desires for us.[35]

The formative power of cultural narratives cannot be adequately met or countered with mere didactics. Counterformation requires countermeasures that capture our imagination and don't just convince our intellect. (Why should the devil get all the best stories?)

On the one hand, this should be the basis for an arts manifesto rooted in that first lesson of literature: show, don't tell. We don't just need teachers and preachers and scholars and "doctors" of the church to *tell* us what to do; if the gospel is going to capture imaginations and sanctify perception we need painters and novelists and dancers and songwriters and sculptors and poets and designers whose creative work *shows* the world otherwise, enabling us to imagine differently—and hence perceive differently and so act differently.[36]

On the other hand, we need to be regularly immersed in the "true story of the whole world"; that is, our imaginations need to be restored, recalibrated, and realigned by an affective immersion in the story of God in Christ reconciling the world to himself.[37] As I suggested above, it is the particular lineaments of this Story that distinguish formative Christian practices from others. Christian practices are not just practices that Christians do; they are those practices that "carry" the true Story of the whole world as articulated in the Scriptures, centered on Christ. While secular liturgies and Christian liturgical practices (and spiritual disciplines) each touch on the same aspects of our embodied, creaturely nature as liturgical animals (that is, both secular and Christian liturgies "work" in a similar way), what fundamentally distinguishes them is the specific shape of the story carried in those practices.[38] We need to learn the true Story "by heart," at a gut level, and let it seep into our background in order to then shape our perception of the world. And that happens primarily and normatively in the practices of Christian worship—*provided that* the practices of Christian worship intentionally carry, embody, enact, and rehearse the normative shape of the Christian Story. This opportunity—and qualification—should be occasion for a new intentionality and reflection about the shape of Christian worship, not just as an arena for our expression but as the formative space that sanctifies perception. My argument should be read as an invitation to

35. Ibid., 124.
36. And by this, I don't mean art that is reduced to propaganda. For a relevant critique, see Calvin Seerveld, *Bearing Fresh Olive Leaves* (Toronto: Tuppence, 2000), 126–28.
37. For a relevant discussion of the relationship between Scripture, story, and authority, see N. T. Wright, *The New Testament and the People of God* (Minneapolis: Fortress, 1992), 139–43.
38. In other words, what distinguishes different rituals of ultimacy is the specific vision of the good life that is "carried" in them—the *telos* to which they are aimed.

reflect anew on how worship works, precisely in order to encourage both new intentionality in our planning and leadership of worship and a new intentional orientation as we enter into worship. Furthermore, insofar as sanctifying perception is crucial for Christian education, we once again have an argument for the necessary role of Christian worship and liturgical formation as the "background" of the Christian education project.

Picturing the Sanctification of Perception in Jewish Morning Prayer

Scott-Martin Kosofsky's *Book of Customs* opens with a common distinction:

> Customs are the point of departure for a Jewish life. There is a well-known expression, "Judaism is a religion of deed; Christianity is a religion of creed."[39] It's a gross oversimplification, for sure, but not without some truth. Judaism stresses that if you begin with the right actions, you'll come upon the right beliefs; Christianity works the other way around. In the Talmud, there is a passage that's considered fundamental in Jewish education, "Let a man busy himself with observing the commandments and customs even if his heart is not in them, for eventually the hand will teach the heart."[40]

As you can imagine, I take some issue with the gross oversimplification; indeed, if it were true, then I suppose my argument would be a kind of Jewish critique of Christian intellectualism. However, while I think the caricature holds for some modern forms of Christianity—and perhaps to a great degree for North American evangelicalism—in fact I think such "intellectualized" renditions of Christian faith constitute a forgetting of more ancient Christian wisdom.

No doubt that ancient Christian wisdom was deeply indebted to Jewish heritage. So perhaps it is also fitting to seek to recover a Christian affirmation of the priority of practice through engaging contemporary Jewish philosopher Peter Ochs who, in his work on "scriptural reasoning,"[41] has articulated a vision of scriptural formation that deeply resonates with what I've just described as the sanctification of perception by the Story of the gospel. In what ways and in what contexts are the Scriptures inscribed in us such that they transform our perception of the world and our very habits of thought? Ochs's landmark essay "Morning Prayers as Redemptive Thinking" articulates an answer: the condition of possibility for *scriptural* reasoning is *liturgical* formation.[42] The Scriptures

---

39. I suspect this is a post-Enlightenment distinction, after the "intellectualization" of Christianity in the German Enlightenment and its heirs.

40. Scott-Martin Kosofsky, *The Book of Customs: A Complete Handbook for the Jewish Year* (San Francisco: HarperOne, 2004), 1. My thanks to Lee Hardy for pointing me to this resource.

41. See Peter Ochs, "Philosophic Warrants for Scriptural Reasoning," *Modern Theology* 22 (2006): 465–82.

42. Peter Ochs, "Morning Prayers as Redemptive Thinking," in *Liturgy, Time, and the Politics of Redemption*, ed. Randi Rashkover and C. C. Pecknold, Radical Traditions (Grand Rapids: Eerdmans, 2006), 50–87.

are most powerfully and formatively absorbed through practices of prayer, meditation, psalm singing, and praise. In short, the condition of possibility for scriptural *reasoning* is worship. If scriptural reasoning represents a recovery of "thick" articulations of the Abrahamic traditions, it also points to "a recovery of a liturgically funded thick description."[43]

In an essay that is part ethnography, part autobiography, part philosophical meditation, Ochs carefully explicates the way in which immersion in the ritual of Jewish Morning Prayer is a mode of "training in how to make judgments."[44] More specifically, he shows how participation in Jewish Morning Prayer is a practice of redemptive thinking that "redeems the way we ordinarily misjudge the world"—a way of undoing our socialization into propositional ways of judging the world that tend to be absolutized, and thus fail to do justice to the richness and complexity of this fraught world. Jewish Morning Prayer, then, is a way to "nurture actual, everyday habits of thinking that are not dominated by this logic"—which translates into a new *philosophical* orientation when they are undertaken by a philosopher. If the philosopher's work is going to be reparative, it needs to be nurtured by prephilosophical practices that counter other formative practices of secular culture. As Ochs comments, "The colonialism that is 'writ large' into the dominant political and economic institutions of the West displays the binary logic that is 'writ small' into the way modern folks learn to make judgments about the world and one another. Morning Prayer shows how other logics can be 'writ small' into the ways we learn to make judgments and how prayer can serve as a daily exercise in these ways."[45]

43. Randi Rashkover, "The Future of the Word and the Liturgical Turn," in Rashkover and Pecknold, *Liturgy, Time, and the Politics of Redemption*, 1.

44. Ochs, "Morning Prayers," 50. The only reservation I have with Ochs's otherwise remarkable exposition of the "nurturing" effect of the practice of Morning Prayer is a lingering anthropology or model of the human person that still tends to privilege "judging" as our everyday mode of being-in-the-world. That is, my concern is that it still envisions the primary or crucial *telos* of such "alternative nurturance" to be a matter of (albeit redemptive) *thinking*, or (albeit scriptural) *reasoning*. To retain this emphasis on judgment, thinking, and cognition suggests that, even though the entire project is contesting the logical habits of "the modern West" (86), the project remains haunted by the ghosts of Descartes and Kant. In a similar way, I find the pray-er in Ochs's account is still a primarily perceiving animal in a narrow sense. We awake each day in order to *perceive* the world: "Daylight means a realm of experience in which creatures are perceivable. Losing the safety of their nighttime vagueness, they become what can be seen and what can, therefore, be received in some particular way as opposed to another way. . . . To be awake is to judge" (54). As soon as we wake up, even before we roll out of bed, Ochs pictures us as perceiving animals making judgments: "Oh, that is my breath! I am alive. Oh, that is my sock—it is on the floor." And we venture into our day to go about "perceiving, conceiving, and interpreting" (55). But is that really how we start our day? Do I immediately wake up perceiving, judging? In fact, do I even spend *most* of the day in such a spectator-like relationship to the world? Or am I rather absorbed in the world, involved with the world, making my way in the world without *thinking* about it? Before we perceive, don't we *care*? For further discussion, see James K. A. Smith, "How Religious Practices Matter: Peter Ochs' 'Alternative Nurturance' of Philosophy of Religion," *Modern Theology* 24 (2008): 469–78.

45. Ochs, "Morning Prayers," 86.

Thus Ochs points to liturgical practices such as Morning Prayer as an "alternative source of nurturance," where nurturance is "a reiterable practice that engenders integrated habits of thinking, feeling, imagining; and it means a practice that is suitable for reforming the ways of older folks, as well as bringing up the young."[46] I receive this exposition and argument as a gift for Christian teachers and learners to imagine how liturgical practices informed by our own scriptural tradition could transform and repair our habits of judgment, our patterns of discernment, and our openness to divine wisdom. In short, Ochs's exegesis of the reparative practice of Morning Prayer points to important ways to nurture alternative philosophical practice.

Redeeming Ritual: Form Matters

Let's briefly rehearse the argument to this point. If the end of worship is mission—if we gather to be sent—then Christian missional institutions (churches, schools, colleges, and universities) need to form *actors*. And given that much of our action is generated by dispositions and habits operative at a nonconscious level, the formation of Christian actors needs to form—or better, *reform*—our habits and dispositions. Christian formation will be not merely a matter of providing new knowledge but a matter of "dispositional deflection" and rehabituation of our desires and loves. But we need to drill down even further, for as we've seen, much of my action is generated as a response to a *call* that I sense in my very perception of the world: as soon as I constitute a situation, I have already evaluated it *as* a moral situation that confronts me with certain demands and obligations, a calling—and my dispositions will incline me to act in response to that often unarticulated call. This happens on a register of erotic comprehension and incarnate significance. So if Christian formation (and Christian education) is going to foster Christian action for the kingdom, such formation needs to be nothing short of a sanctification of our perception. And that requires formative measures that are fundamentally aesthetic and imaginative. We need to be moved, not merely convinced.

Historic Christian faith has always intuited this, even if our forebears didn't have cognitive science and social psychology at their disposal. What they did have was a robust theology of creation, an appreciation for the implications of the incarnation, and a sacramental ontology that saw the charged nature of matter that participated in God.[47] The historic practices

46. Ibid.

47. For an important account of these historic Christian intuitions—and the necessity for recovering them today—see Hans Boersma, *Heavenly Participation: The Weaving of a Sacramental Tapestry* (Grand Rapids: Eerdmans, 2011).

of Christian *paideia*—"the church's ancient disciplinary treasury"[48]—have always been a full-bodied, holistic set of disciplines that not only informed the intellect but reformed the very *praktognosia* by which we "feel" our way around the world, reaching the incarnate significance Merleau-Ponty simply called "perception." Indeed, Christian liturgical formation has long understood what Bourdieu finally names: that pedagogies can extort the essential from the seemingly insignificant.

So, for example, Christian worship and spiritual formation have long known and affirmed *in practice* that gestures are not just something we do but that they also do something *to* us—that kneeling for confession is a kind of cosmological act that inscribes in us a comportment to God and neighbor, a way of being-in-the-world that sinks into our bones and becomes sedimented into the core of our being through the crackle of our old knees. The postures of our bodies spill out beyond the sanctuary and become postures of existential comportment to the world. Christian worship has long appreciated the magnitude of practices that marshal the mundane—bread, wine, water—to enact and stage "kingdom come" week after week, giving us a tactile opportunity to rehearse for the consummation of time, and thus go into the meantime of the "not yet" with a different background and different horizon of perception—inhabiting the "not yet" as the fields of the Lord that call for both work and play. As the Story of God's redeeming love sinks down into our imaginative background through practices that are kin/aesthetic, we *perceive* the world differently and thus constitute our environment *as* God's good-but-broken creation. What before would have been vague rumblings and distracting background noises will begin to crystallize into something very different: the cries of the oppressed, the silences of the marginalized alien, Rachel weeping for her children. What was previously perceived with the bright, shiny sheen of "success"—comfort, insularity, accumulation, security—will be perceived anew because it will be constituted within a very different horizon of expectation, a different "background." Conversely, what might have been previously perceived as problems are now constituted as callings. Christian liturgical practices and spiritual disciplines are not just means of personal renewal; they remake the world because they transform the perception of the people of God who not only inhabit the world differently but inhabit a different world, a world constituted as God's creation.

As I've tried to emphasize, Christian worship does this on an aesthetic register: the sanctification of perception is a renewal and restor(y)ing of the imagination, which means that worship is more art than science, more on the order of a poem than a PowerPoint distillation of "the data." However, the (trans)formative possibilities afforded by Christian worship practices are

---

48. Boulton, *Life in God*, 24.

simply not true of all that describes itself as "worship." In other words, not all self-described "Christian worship" will afford the sort of sanctification of perception that I've described above. Here we need to raise a critical, and perhaps uncomfortable, point: *form matters*—not because of any tradition-alism or conservative preservation of the status quo, but precisely because, as Bourdieu showed us, there is a logic to a practice that is unarticulated but nonetheless has a coherent "sense" about it.[49] Form matters because it is the form of worship that tells the Story (or better, *enacts* the Story).

Wide swaths of contemporary Christianity have bought into a specious form/content distinction: we have assumed that Christianity is primarily a "message" and is thus defined by a "content" that is distillable from historical forms. Along with this distinction comes the assumption that forms are basically just neutral containers for the message, selected on the basis of taste, preference, or cultural relevance. With that distinction in place (perhaps unwittingly), we then treat the historical, received forms of Christian worship as a kind of disposable husk that can be shucked (and chucked!) as long as we keep the kernel of the gospel "message." When this distinction and attitude are wedded to our late modern penchant for novelty, we begin to approach Christian worship as an event for disseminating the message and thus look for forms that will be fresh, attractive, relevant, ac-cessible, and so on. In fact, since on this account it is the content/"message" that matters, and since forms are neutral "containers" for the message, we might actually adopt forms that are more familiar and less strange for contemporary "audiences." For example, we might distill the "message" of the gospel and then place it in a "mall" container, or a "coffee shop" container, or a "rock concert" container, or a "rave" container, or what have you. In doing so, we believe that we have in a sense sanctified these forms—taken them up in service to the gospel, all with a "missional" intent.[50]

But as I hope you've already intuited, such strategies are inherently "intellectualist," both because they reduce the gospel to a (propositional) "message" *and* (because of that) completely miss the formative power of the forms themselves. Because such "relevant" paradigms are unwittingly intellectualist,[51] they fail to appreciate that we are liturgical animals shaped

49. Here I'm expanding on some cautions initially articulated in *Desiring the Kingdom*, 151–54.

50. Billings offers a cautionary tale in this regard when he notes that apartheid in the South African Reformed church was initially entertained as a "missional" strategy to expand outreach op-portunities to whites who might not be "comfortable" worshiping with blacks. "Lest we think that the movement [for segregated communion] emerging from 1857 is utterly foreign to contemporary concerns, in many ways it can be understood as an instance where the church was being flexible, evangelical, and 'missional' rather than being rigidly Reformational" (*Union with Christ*, 101).

51. This is the case even if the "worship" (i.e., song service) in such congregations is over-whelmingly emotivist. There is an interesting irony in the ballpark here. Throughout the Cul-tural Liturgies project, I emphasize the importance of affect and emotion, and yet I'm critical of emotiv*ism* as merely expressionist and lacking any strong sense of the *formative* aspects of

by practices that work on our cognitive unconscious. And so they also fail to appreciate that these forms are not neutral; the forms of the mall or coffee shop are not just benign containers that can carry any content. These forms are already "aimed and loaded": they carry their own teleological orientation and come loaded with a complex of rituals and practices that carry a vision of the good life. So while we might think that reconfiguring worship to feel like the mall is a way of making Jesus relevant and accessible, in fact we are unwittingly teaching worshipers and seekers to treat Jesus like any other commodity they encounter in the mall, because the very form of the mall's ("secular") liturgy unconsciously trains us to relate to the world as consumers.

The point isn't that both form and content matter. The point is more radical than that: in some significant sense we need to eschew the form/content distinction.[52] Because worship is not just the dissemination of some content or the expression of an "inner" feeling, the very form of worship tells the Story.[53] The form of worship is the logic of the practice; as such, it has a coherence that is fundamentally narrative, not deductive. The narrative arc of Christian worship is *how* it "makes sense," and it is through our immersion in the implicit narrative logic of the practice that the "practical sense" of the Christian Story soaks into our imagination and becomes part of our constituting background, the Story that governs our *habitus* (as "structured structures" and "structuring structures"!).[54] To be immersed in the irreducible practical logic of Christian worship is like carrying Mark Twain's cat: we thereby learn something we can learn in no other way.

---

worship. The flipside is the irony: it is precisely those forms of worship that are so thoroughly emotivist that are often wed to "intellectualist" construals of Christian faith.

52. One could say something similar by invoking Marshall McLuhan's famous dictum "the medium is the message." As it turns out, this is not just a felicitous overlap. In fact, McLuhan's own conversion to Catholicism and immersion in the liturgy was a significant part of the "background" that informed his theorizing. For some of his reflections on liturgy, and on religion more generally, see Marshall McLuhan, *The Medium and the Light: Reflections on Religion*, ed. Eric McLuhan and Jacek Szklarek (Toronto: Stoddart, 1999).

53. I should note that by "form" I do not mean "style." The form of worship is the *logic* of the practice—the coherence of the story that is rehearsed and enacted by the practice. So the "form" of worship is more about the shape of worship—the elements that constitute the narrative arc of a worship service. Such a form can be instantiated in a number of different styles. So to emphasize a historic "form" of worship is *not* an apologetic for pipe organs over banjos and mandolins.

54. I will not rehearse the specifics of this received shape of Christian worship. For a sketch, see *Desiring the Kingdom*, chap. 5. See also the chart "The Common Shape of Liturgy" in this section, which utilizes Frank Senn's masterful overview of the common shape of Christian worship from pp. 646–47 of *Christian Liturgy: Catholic and Evangelical* (Minneapolis: Fortress, 1997). Senn's parallel overview of the *Roman Missal* (1969), *Lutheran Book of Worship* (1978), Anglican *Book of Common Prayer* (1977), *The Methodist Hymnal* (1989), and Presbyterian *Book of Common Worship* (1993) testifies to a common "shape of the liturgy" that represents the accrued wisdom of the church catholic, led by the Spirit, regarding what we might call "the narrative sense" of Christian worship.

The Common Shape of the Liturgy

Roman Missal 1969	Lutheran Book of Worship 1978	Book of Common Prayer 1977	The Methodist Hymnal 1989	Book of Common Worship 1993
The Order of the Mass	The Holy Communion	The Holy Eucharist	Service of Word and Table	Service for the Lord's Day
Entrance Psalm	(Brief Order of Confession)	(Hymn, psalm, or anthem)	Gathering	Call to Worship
Invocation and Greeting		(Penitential Rite)	Greeting	Prayer of the Day
	Entrance Hymn	(Hymn, psalm, or anthem)	Hymn of Praise	Hymn of Praise
Penitential Rite	Apostolic Greeting	Greeting and Collect	Opening Prayer	Confession and Pardon
(Kyrie)	(Kyrie)	(Gloria or Kyrie or Trisagion)		(The Peace)
(Gloria)	(Gloria or Worthy Is Christ or Hymn)		(Act of Praise)	Canticle, Psalm, Hymn, or Spiritual
Salutation and Collect for the Day	Salutation and Prayer of the Day	Salutation and Collect of the Day	Prayer for Illumination	Prayer for Illumination
First Lesson	First Lesson	First Lesson	Scripture Lesson	First Reading
Psalmody	Psalmody	(Psalm, hymn, or anthem)	(Psalm)	Psalm
Second Lesson	Second Lesson	Second Lesson	Scripture Lesson	Second Reading
Alleluia Verse	Alleluia Verse	(Psalm, hymn, or anthem)	Hymn or Song	(Anthem, hymn, psalm, canticle, or spiritual)
Gospel	Gospel	Gospel	Gospel Lesson	Gospel Reading
Homily	Sermon	Sermon	Sermon	Sermon
	Silent Reflection			
	Hymn of the Day		(Occasional Service)	Affirmation of Faith
Nicene Creed	Nicene or Apostles' Creed	Nicene Creed	The Apostles' Creed	(Pastoral Rite of the Church)
Intercessions	Prayers of the Church	Prayers of the People	Concerns and Prayers	Prayers of the People
			Invitation to the Table	

Roman Missal 1969	Lutheran Book of Worship 1978	Book of Common Prayer 1977	The Methodist Hymnal 1989	Book of Common Worship 1993
	(Confession of Sin)	(Confession of Sin)	Confession and Pardon	
	Greeting of Peace	The Peace	The Peace	(The Peace)
Offering	Offering	Offertory Sentence	Offering	Offering
Offertory Song	Offertory Verse	Offertory Procession	(Hymn, psalm, or anthem)	
Offertory Prayers	Offertory Prayer			Invitation to the Table
Preface and Sanctus	Preface and Sanctus	Preface and Sanctus	Great Thanksgiving	Great Thanksgiving
Canon (9 options)	Great Thanksgiving (5 options) or Words of Institution	Great Thanksgiving (4 options)		
Lord's Prayer	Lord's Prayer	Lord's Prayer	Lord's Prayer	Lord's Prayer
Peace of the Lord		Breaking of the Bread	Breaking of Bread	Breaking of Bread
Lamb of God	Communion	Communion	Giving the Bread and Cup	Communion of the People
Communion (Communion Songs)	(Lamb of God or other hymns)	(Hymns, psalms, or anthems)		
Silent Reflection	Post-Communion Song		Post-Communion Prayer	
Post-Communion Prayer	Post-Communion Prayer	Post-Communion Prayer	Hymn or Song	Hymn, Spiritual, Canticle, or Psalm
	Silent Reflection			
Benediction and Dismissal	Benediction and Dismissal	Blessing and Dismissal	Dismissal with Blessing	Charge and Blessing
			Going Forth	

Frank C. Senn, *Christian Liturgy: Catholic and Evangelical* (Minneapolis: Fortress, 1997), 646–47.

This is just a way of saying that with liturgy, like poetry, we should beware of "the heresy of paraphrase." This notion was first floated by Cleanth Brooks, who resisted modes of poetic criticism that thought they could distill the meaning of the poem into its essential "idea" or "message," which, as you might guess, Brooks considered heresy. A poem's meaning, he contended, is not just a matter of its propositional content—as if the words and form and meter and all of those exquisite aspects of craft were just decorative flourishes that could be dispensed with once you got "the message." No, Brooks argued, the meaning of the poem is ineluctably bound up with its form and is not reducible to what can be propositionalized or paraphrased. A poem is not just a vehicle for ideas; it means both *more* than that and *differently* than that. Brooks summarizes:

> The general point, of course, is not that either poetry or drama makes no use of ideas, or that either is "merely emotional"—whatever *that* is—or that there is not the closest and most important relationship between the intellectual materials which they absorb into their structure and other elements in the structure. The relationship between the intellectual and the non-intellectual elements in a poem is actually far more intimate than the conventional accounts would represent it to be: the relationship is not that of an idea "wrapped in emotion" or a "prose-sense decorated by a sensuous imagery." The dimension in which the poem moves is not one which excludes ideas, but one which does include attitudes. The dimension includes ideas, to be sure; we can always abstract an 'idea' from a poem. . . . But the idea which we abstract—assuming that we can all agree on what that idea is—will always be *abstracted*: it will always be the projection of a plane along a line or the projection of a cone upon a plane.[55]

An apocryphal tale further illuminates Brooks's point: T. S. Eliot reads the entirety of "The Wasteland," and upon its conclusion, someone has the temerity to ask, "What does it mean?" Eliot rereads the poem. Angela Leighton, to get at a similar point, cites a selection from Heather McHugh's fantastic poem "20–200 on 747":

> Given an airplane, chance
>
> encounters always ask, So what
> are your poems about? They're about
> their business, and their father's business, and their
> monkey's uncle, they're about
>
> how nothing is about, they're not
> about about. This answer drives them
> back to the snack tray every time.[56]

55. Cleanth Brooks, *The Well Wrought Urn: Studies in the Structure of Poetry* (New York: Harcourt, Brace, 1947), 204–5. Revisiting Brooks's account, Angela Leighton notes that after Brooks's critique, "paraphrase, as a serious critical idea, has never really made a comeback." Angela Leighton, "About About: On Poetry and Paraphrase," *Midwest Studies in Philosophy* 33 (2009): 167–76 (quote at 168). For rigorous philosophical updating of Brooks's notion, see Ernie Lepore, "The Heresy of Paraphrase: When the Medium Really Is the Message," *Midwest Studies in Philosophy* 33 (2009): 177–97.
56. Leighton, "About About," 169.

The "meaning" of the poem is not some distillable content or idea or message that can be neatly paraphrased and summarized in prose form; *what the poem means is bound up with how the poem means.*[57] Its meaning is intertwined with all of the metaphorical play and resonance that can never quite be named or identified and yet are precisely those elements that do so much literary work. The poem *means* in its cadence and meter, its diction and wordplay, its pauses and line breaks. The meaning of a poem is playing a different game, and means differently, in a way that is inherently bound up with its form. Echoing Bourdieu, Brooks cautions: "We demand logical coherences where they are sometimes irrelevant, and we fail frequently to see imaginative coherences on levels where they are highly relevant."[58] It is those imaginative coherences that are lost in translation when we try to paraphrase the "message" of a poem.

I'm suggesting the same is true with respect to the meaning of Christian worship: the logic of the practice cannot be paraphrased because there is an "imaginative coherence" that is undistillable and yet incredibly significant.[59] We "get" the Story in the form of worship that intentionally rehearses the unfolding of our covenantal relationship to a promise-keeping God, centered in the climax of the covenant in Jesus. While it has been intentionally and communally crafted over time, the logic of historic Christian worship also *means* on a register that exceeds and eludes our conscious appropriation[60]— which is precisely why worship isn't just something that we do; it does something *to* us. The practices of Christian worship mean in a narrative mode: so I "get" worship in ways that will exceed what I'm "thinking" about *when* I worship. This is how Christian worship works, on both a macrolevel and a microlevel. On a macrolevel, the overall narrative arc of Christian worship— gathering, confessing, listening, submitting, communing, sending—tells a story in the background by its very structure and organization, a rhythm

---

57. In the McHugh poem, this includes the sheer verbal play on "about" that constitutes the heart of this poem.

58. Ibid., 202.

59. Or, echoing Zuidervaart's notion of "art-internal" truth (in *Artistic Truth*, 8–9), I'm suggesting that there is a kind of "liturgy-internal" wisdom to Christian worship that is irreducible and even eludes articulation. And yet we *know* it's true. Its truth resonates in the imagination; it is absorbed in our gut. We need to learn to trust our gut. We need to learn to trust those "intuitions" that bubble up from our liturgical formation. And then we need to think about how to "expand" this "liturgy-internal" wisdom across our life together.

60. There is no tension in claiming that Christian worship was intentionally developed and planned and yet can mean *more* than what was intended by those who developed it. The same is true of a poem: the best poetry is the fruit of painstaking craft and intentionality in its creation, and yet its meaning will always exceed what the author intended because the dynamics of metaphor and form elude our control. Indeed, the same dynamic is true of Scripture. For a discussion, see James K. A. Smith, *The Fall of Interpretation: Philosophical Foundations for a Creational Hermeneutic*, 2nd ed. (Grand Rapids: Baker Academic, 2012), 199–221.

and cadence that become part of our own background such that this Story governs our perception of the world in ways we won't realize. In this way, Christian faith, as Bourdieu suggests, is something we come to believe with the body: it is incorporated into us as we are incorporated into the body politic that is the body of Christ. We absorb Christian faith as a mode of "practical sense," not primarily by the didactic dissemination of content, but rather through our immersion in an ethos and an environment, where the Story is in the air we breathe and the water in which we swim, operative in the background in ways we might not always realize. There is a kind of grand poetry about the shape of intentional, historic Christian worship that shows rather than tells. And such a narrative "showing" resonates with our imagination in ways that elude our intellectual grasp.

This is also why the form of worship "works" on us at a microlevel. If historic Christian worship and ancient spiritual disciplines carry the Story that seeps into our social imaginary, this is in no small part because liturgical practices are also intentionally aesthetic and tap into our imaginative core. It is no accident that the poetry of the psalms has long constituted the church's prayerbook, nor is it mere coincidence that the worship of the people of God has always been marked by singing. In these and countless other ways, the inherited treasury of formative disciplines has been characterized by an allusivity and metaphoricity that means more than we can say. There is a reason to our rhymes—a logic carried in the meter of our hymns and the shape of our gestures. Worship innovations that are inattentive to this may end up adopting forms that forfeit precisely those aspects of worship that sanctify perception by forming the imagination.[61] Hence wise worship planning and leadership is not only discerning about content—the lyrics of songs, the content of a pastoral prayer, the message of a sermon—but also discerning about the kin/aesthetic meaning of the form of our worship. We will be concerned not only with the *what* but also with the *how*, because Christian faith is not only a knowing-*that* but also a kind of know-*how*, a "practical" sense" or *praktognosia* that is absorbed in the "between" of our incarnate significance. Because meter and tune each *means* in its own irreducible way, for example, the form of our songs is as important as the content. It is in this sense that to sing is to pray twice.[62]

---

61. This is not to say that there is no room for innovation or improvisation in Christian worship or that affirming the formative wisdom of historic Christian worship requires merely repeating status quo forms. The point is rather that improvisations and innovations of worship *form* need to be attentive to the narrative arc of the form and the unique "incarnate significance" of worship practices. Innovations that are "faithful" will preserve the plot of that narrative arc and deepen the imaginative impact of worship. Unfaithful and unhelpful innovations will be developments that are detrimental to the imaginative coherence of worship.

62. See Brian Wren's unpacking of this famous epigram in *Praying Twice: The Music and Words of Congregational Song* (Louisville: Westminster John Knox, 2000), particularly his

---

To Think About: The Poetry of Prayer

Boulton notes that Calvin's vision for the "reformation of manners" was related to his lifelong passion for the psalms, which eventually yielded the Genevan Psalter, "a compilation of all 150 psalms, the Ten Commandments, and the Song of Simeon, all translated into metrical French and set to new tunes composed not for specialist choirs but for the whole congregation."[1] Why metrical? Because Calvin, with the Christian tradition before him, intuited that we are liturgical animals whose hearts are tuned to sing his praise—and that psalm singing will be a *formative* discipline, not only because of the content of the psalms but because of the form of the song.[2]

1. Matthew Myer Boulton, *Life in God: John Calvin, Practical Formation, and the Future of Protestant Theology* (Grand Rapids: Eerdmans, 2011), 33.
2. For a continuation of this project in the same spirit, see John Witvliet, Joyce Borger, and Martin Tel, eds., *Psalms for All Seasons: A Complete Psalter for Worship* (Grand Rapids: Brazos, 2012). For stories about regular encounters with the psalms, see Kevin Adams, *150: Finding Your Story in the Psalms* (Grand Rapids: Square Inch/ Faith Alive, 2011).

Worship wisdom requires that we be attentive to the practical sense of aesthetic forms, lest we end up singing lyrics that confess Jesus is Lord accompanied by a tune that *means* something very different.[63] Similarly, because our words mean more than their propositional content—and because worship is intended not only to inform the intellect but also to recruit the imagination—we will want to be attentive to the poetic and metaphorical power of words to evoke the world to come, thus resisting temptations to flatten our worship words to the utilitarian pragmatism of the marketplace.[64] In these and countless other ways (we could also discuss gesture, architecture, images, icons, color, vestments, and much more), Christian worship is *more* than its content and means more than it says. Worship that intends to be formative—and more specifically, worship that intends to foster an encounter with God that transforms our imagination and hence sanctifies our perception—must be attentive to, and intentional about, the aesthetics of human understanding. Christian

---

discussion of how hymns "work" as "poems of faith" (253–94). My thanks to Kevin Twit for pointing me to this resource.

63. For a masterful account of these matters, see Jeremy Begbie, *Resounding Truth: Christian Wisdom in the World of Music* (Grand Rapids: Baker Academic, 2007), part 3. For further relevant discussion, see Begbie, "Faithful Feelings: Music and Emotion in Worship," in *Resonant Witness: Conversations between Music and Theology*, ed. Jeremy S. Begbie and Steven R. Guthrie (Grand Rapids: Eerdmans, 2011), 323–54; and Steven R. Guthrie, "The Wisdom of Song," in Begbie and Guthrie, *Resonant Witness*, 382–407.

64. For wisdom on these matters, see Debra Rienstra and Ron Rienstra, *Worship Words: Discipling Language for Faithful Ministry* (Grand Rapids: Baker Academic, 2009), particularly their discussion of metaphor (115–41).

To Think About: Praying a World(view)

How might it impact Christian education if we *prayed* a Christian worldview? If the goal of a Christian education is to form and shape a people who imagine the world otherwise—and act accordingly—then we will need to worship accordingly. We worship in order to worldview. And if we are going to absorb the "true story of the whole world," it's not enough to acquire the theoretical information to *know* this truth; we need a conversion of the imagination so that we "get" this story in our bones. What if the way to do that was to *pray* a worldview? And what if the very *form* of the prayer—the sort of liturgical act it invites and requires—also "said" something about our relationship to God, his world, and one another?

This is John Witvliet's suggestion when discussing education that provides a "comprehensive Christian worldview": "My suggestion," he says, "is that there are few better models for what this can look like than the fully-orbed eucharistic prayers that emerge in the fourth century. They present a theological vision of space, time, good, evil, personhood, salvation, creation and final redemption—all compressed into a prayer that is open to eternity and to the mystery and beauty of God's being."[1] Consider one of his exhibits in this regard: the intercession from the fifth-century Gelasian sacramentary.[2]

The Litany (*deacon*): Let us all say, Lord, hear and have mercy. Father Unbegotten, and Son of God Begotten not made, and Holy Spirit of God, the breath of the faithful, we pray, *Kyrie eleison*.

- For the spotless church of the living God, constituted throughout the whole world, we entreat the riches of divine gifts, *Kyrie eleison*.
- For holy priests and ministers of the Mighty God, and all people worshiping the true God, we pray Christ our Lord, *Kyrie eleison*.
- In particular, for all teaching rightly the Word of Truth, the manifold Wisdom of the Word of God, we pray, *Kyrie eleison*.
- For those who keep themselves chaste in mind and body for the sake of the Kingdom of heaven, and exert themselves in spiritual labors, we pray for plentifulness of spiritual gifts, *Kyrie eleison*.
- For all religious rulers and their soldiers, who prize justice and right judgment, we implore the Power of the Lord, *Kyrie eleison*.
- For agreeable weather and opportune rains and caressing vital winds and the prosperity of diverse times rightly ordered, Lord of the world, we pray, *Kyrie eleison*.
- For those who for the first time into the name of "Christian" are initiated, whom now the desire for heavenly grace inflames, we pray for mercy to Almighty God, *Kyrie eleison*.
- For those who are involved in the weakness of the infirmities of humanity, in envy of spiritual wickedness or various errors of the world, we implore the mercy of the Redeemer, *Kyrie eleison*.

- For those who are of necessity traveling, or are oppressed by the powers of iniquity, or are vexed by hostile hardships, we pray the Lord the savior, *Kyrie eleison*.
- For those deceived by heresy or superstition, we pray the Lord of Truth, *Kyrie eleison*.
- For doers of good works, and those who assist in the necessary labors of brotherly charity, we pray the Lord to have mercy, *Kyrie eleison*.
- For all within this holy House of the Lord, that they may be turned to religious hearers and devout pray-ers, we pray the Lord of Glory, *Kyrie eleison*.
- For the cleansing of our souls and bodies, and forgiveness of sins, we pray the merciful Lord, *Kyrie eleison*.
- For refreshment of faithful souls, particularly of priests of the Holy Lord, who preside over this catholic church, we pray the Lord the spirit and judge of all flesh, *Kyrie eleison*.
- Mortification of sins of the flesh and quickening of the life of faith, *Grant, Lord, grant*.
- Holy fear and love of truth, *Grant, Lord, grant*.
- A pleasant ordering of life and a creditable end, *Grant, Lord, grant*.
- An angel of peace and holy consolation, *Grant, Lord, grant*.
- Here, Lord, the voice of your family who cry for preservation.

As Witvliet comments, this *prayed* "breadth of concern suggests a robust understanding of the scope of divine activity in human lives, institutions, and in creation itself."[3] Here is practice that enables the people of God—in both church and college—to *pray* Kuyper's central claim that there is not a single square inch of creation over which Christ does not say, "Mine!" To articulate this as a prayer is a different sort of speech act: it invites us into the story in a unique way. We become actors in the drama, invested characters on the stage of God's redemptive action. At the same time, to say this *as a prayer* is a practice of dependence: we are asking, praying, pleading, which is a way to practice ourselves out of our penchant for self-sufficient activism and the sort of default Pelagianism that characterizes modern (American) confidence.

What might a college or school look like if such prayers were part of the *ethos* of worship that bathes learning?[4] How might the graduates of such institutions emerge with a different imagination?

1. John D. Witvliet, "Embodying the Wisdom of Ancient Liturgical Practices: Some Old-Fashioned Rudimentary Euchology for the Contemporary Church," in *Ancient Faith for the Church's Future*, ed. Mark Husbands and Jeffrey P. Greenman, 189–214 (Downers Grove, IL: InterVarsity, 2008), 211.

2. Ibid., 193–94, reproducing the text in Marion J. Hatchett, *Seven Pre-Reformation Eucharistic Liturgies: Historic Rites Arranged for Contemporary Celebration* (Sewanee, TN: University of the South, 1973), 48–49.

3. Witvliet, "Embodying the Wisdom of Ancient Liturgical Practices," 195.

4. This particular example is only meant to be catalytic. One could imagine all sorts of worship practices that could have this sort of of "ethos-setting" effect. For example, what if not only chapels but classrooms were adorned with liturgical colors that changed with the church's calendar? Or what if stained glass or banners that "*show*" rather than tell" adorned spaces of both learning and play? The point isn't for Christian learning to *deduce* something from such ethos-setting practices; rather, I'm suggesting that a liturgically shaped ethos will shape the imagination in ways that cannot be articulated but are nonetheless impactful.

worship needs to be an incubator for the imagination, inviting us into "the real world" by bringing us aesthetic olive leaves from the kingdom that is coming, helping us to then envision what it would look like for God's will to be done on earth as it is in heaven. We will absorb this eschatological vision of shalom in ways that elude our awareness, and the Story will be incorporated into our bodies on an aesthetic register. Thus the whole of Christian worship must embody this guiding Story in multivalent ways so that it becomes part of our background and thus sanctifies our perception. Christian worship should send us out with new knowledge and information, as well as a renewed feel for the world, a transformed "practical sense."

In this respect, we might say that Christian discipleship is about not only the acquisition of a worldview but also the inhabitation of a sensibility. To be formed in Christ *for* missional action is to acquire a temperament that guides us beneath and beyond what we think. As David Brooks put it, in order to act justly and rightly, we first need to learn to perceive the world in the right way.[65] And given that our perception is a mode of embodied, kinaesthetic intentionality, a Christian passional orientation to the world will be less like an intellectual grid than a sort of *style* of comportment to the world—a sensibility or temperament that changes *how* we are in the world. That sensibility or temperament, then, will significantly shape how we perceive the world, and hence how we act in it. To be formed as image-bearers of Christ is to acquire a temperament that is indexed to the kingdom of God.

In this respect, it seems to me that a Christian social imaginary is something like the "artistic temperament" that Oscar Wilde extols in "The Critic as Artist." Indeed, Wilde's concern in this dialogue is the nature of criticism, which is very much akin to the sort of practiced judgment we've been discussing. So let's consider Wilde's "critic" as an analogue of the thoughtful Christian, engaging culture; what Wilde describes as "criticism," then, would be an analogue for Christian culture-making. What might we learn from such an analogy?

At the core of his argument is the assertion that "criticism is itself an art."[66] So criticism is not just passive commentary and mere observation; the critic is also a creator, a maker, who in her engagement with the work of art produces her own creative product. We might think of this dynamic as analogous to what we've been describing as "constitution": the way in which we "put together" the world, *make* our world, on the basis of a

65. David Brooks, *The Social Animal: The Hidden Sources of Love, Character, and Achievement* (New York: Random House, 2011), 127.
66. Oscar Wilde, "The Critic as Artist," in *The Portable Oscar Wilde*, rev. ed., ed. Richard Aldington and Stanley Weintraub (London: Penguin, 1981), 81.

background horizon of constitution. To say that the critic is an artist is, in a sense, to say that the critic is *also* a "constituter"—a maker, a creator. It's not just artists who make; to judge art—to be a critic—is also a work of creative constitution.

But if criticism is also a kind of constitution, then we hit upon an important question: what would be the appropriate "background" for criticism? In other words, we need to carefully consider "the artistic qualifications necessary for the true critic."[67] Here Wilde makes a surprising claim. What is most needed for such "true criticism," he suggests, is not merely the right curriculum of study or an encyclopedic knowledge of the arts. Instead Wilde homes in on a surprising qualification: the best critic, he says, will be characterized by an aesthetic *temperament*. "Temperament is the primary requisite for the critic—a temperament exquisitely susceptible to beauty." Which then leads to the question, How is such a temperament acquired? Listen to Wilde's reply and try to keep our analogy in mind:

> To be purified and made perfect, this sense requires some form of exquisite *environment*. Without this it starves, or is dulled. You remember that lovely passage in which Plato describes how a young Greek should be educated, and with what insistence he dwells upon the importance of surroundings, telling us how the lad is to be brought up in the midst of fair sights and sounds, so that the beauty of material things may prepare his soul for the reception of the beauty that is spiritual. Insensibly, *and without knowing the reason why*, he is to develop that real love of beauty which, as Plato is never weary of reminding us, is the true aim of education.[68]

The acquisition of this temperament that is so crucial for "true criticism" is dependent upon an environment. The right environment generates an ethos that cultivates this temperament and sensibility—but it does so "insensibly, and without knowing the reason why." In other words, the temperament is acquired without our realizing it, as part of the "hum and buzz" of an environment, as the constant presence of a background that over time becomes part of *our* background. It is a sensibility that we absorb, a comportment to the good life that is more caught than taught. Temperament is shaped by a sentimental education.

67. Wilde, "Critic as Artist," 120.

68. Ibid. (emphasis added). Gilbert, the voice of Wilde in this dialogue, continues: "I need hardly say, Ernest, how far we in England have fallen short of this ideal, and I can imagine the smile that would illuminate the glossy face of the Philistine if one ventured to suggest to him that the true aim of education was the love of beauty, and that the methods by which education should work were the development of temperament, the cultivation of taste, and the creation of the critical spirit" (121). For a proposal that embraces just such a vision, seeing the unity of the good, the true, and the beautiful, see Stratford Caldecott, *Beauty for Truth's Sake: On the Re-enchantment of Education* (Grand Rapids: Brazos, 2009).

We might say that a sentimental education is an environmental education. Scandalously, Wilde suggests that maybe the most important thing in Oxford is not the professors!

> Even for us [in industrialized England], there is left some loveliness of environment, and the dullness of tutors and professors matters very little when one can loiter in the grey cloisters at Magdalen, and listen to some flute-like voice singing in Waynfleete's chapel, or lie in the green meadow, among the strange snake-spotted fritillaries, and watch the sunburnt noon smite to a finer gold the tower's gilded vanes, or wander up the Christ Church staircase beneath the vaulted ceiling's shadowy fans, or pass through the sculptured gateway of Laud's building in the College of St. John.[69]

The spaces of the environment have their own cultivating effect on the imagination, on the temperament of the emerging critic who, by means of this sentimental education, is imbibing a sensibility that will become the basis for "true" criticism. But Wilde emphasizes that going up to Oxford will be inadequate without a "sentimental" curriculum. Thus, a little later in the dialogue, Wilde praises "a renaissance of the decorative arts"—and in particular the Arts and Crafts movement associated with William Morris—as crucial to this sentimental education. "For the cultivation of temperament, we must turn to the decorative arts: to the arts that touch us, not to the arts that teach us."[70] The art that cultivates an aesthetic sense is not art that you look at, but art that you *live with*. This is why Wilde celebrates the *decorative* arts—those arts that become part of our background, our ethos, our milieu, like the furniture and wallpapers of William Morris or the tapestries of Edward Burne-Jones.[71] As Wilde puts it,

> The art that is frankly decorative is the art to live with. It is, of all our visible arts, the one art that creates in us both mood and temperament. Mere colour, unspoiled by meaning, and unallied with definite form, can speak to the soul in a thousand different ways. The harmony that resides in the delicate proportions of lines and masses becomes mirrored in the mind. The repetitions of pattern give us rest. The marvels of design stir the imagination. In the mere loveliness of the materials employed there are latent elements of culture.[72]

Notice how remarkable Wilde's claim is: it's not just that pretty places are pleasant spaces for learning. Environments that are intentionally well

69. Wilde, "Critic as Artist," 121–22.
70. Ibid., 122.
71. The covers of the Cultural Liturgies trilogy are adorned with a series of tapestries that were the fruit of a collaboration between William Morris and Edward Burne-Jones.
72. Wilde, "Critic as Artist," 124.

adorned are veritable schools for the soul—they create in us both a mood and a temperament.[73] They are part of an embodied *paideia*, a kinaesthetic education. The true critic, then, will be raised in houses with the right wallpaper.

Consider, then, this analogy: If Christian faith is a kind of temperament, then its formation requires the right environment. And if Christian education is going to form our sensibilities, then Christian churches, schools, and universities need the right wallpaper. They need to be environments in which the Story of the gospel is imaginatively woven into the entire ethos of the institution. And while this clearly requires aesthetic and architectural intentionality, more important, it requires incorporating intentional, historic practices of Christian worship as the "wallpaper" of a Christian sentimental education—not as mere pious decoration but rather as precisely the temperament-forming ethos and environment that shapes our affective comportment to God's world. It is the practices of Christian worship that should constitute the milieu in which we teach and learn, regularly weaving for us the tapestry of God's covenant faithfulness, immersing us in the Story so that we absorb it "insensibly, and without knowing the reason why."[74]

Redeeming Repetition: On Habituation

A liturgical anthropology that appreciates the aesthetics of understanding ("the meaning of the body," as Johnson puts it) will encourage new intentionality about the *how* of worship—and as I've just suggested, I think such a model especially encourages us to be attentive to form as that which most resonates with (and hence forms) the imagination. Similarly, I think a liturgical anthropology should engender a new appreciation for repetition. We, especially we Protestants, have a built-in allergy to repetition in worship, though we are quite happy to affirm the value of repetition in almost every other sphere of life, from study to music to sports to art. We affirm the value of ritual repetition if we're learning piano scales or learning to hit a golf ball but are curiously suspicious of repetitive ritual in worship and discipleship. I think this allergy has three causes. The first is part of

73. For a more detailed discussion of religion as a kind of "mood" and attunement, see James K. A. Smith, "Secular Liturgies and the Prospects for a 'Post-Secular' Sociology of Religion," in *The Post-Secular in Question*, ed. Philip Gorski, David Kyuman Kim, John Torpey, and Jonathan VanAntwerpen (New York: New York University Press, 2012), 159–84.

74. And once again, we might learn something from John Calvin's Geneva. For example, Karin Maag notes that students at the Genevan academy rehearsed psalms for an hour each day. See Karin Maag, "Change and Continuity in Medieval and Early Modern Worship: The Practice of Worship in the Schools," in *Worship in Medieval and Early Modern Europe: Change and Continuity in Religious Practice*, ed. Karin Maag and John D. Witvliet (Notre Dame, IN: University of Notre Dame Press, 2004), 123.

the genetic heritage of Protestantism: we associate repetition with dead orthodoxy, "vain repetition," the denial of grace, trying to earn salvation, scoring points with God, going through the motions, and various other forms of spiritual insincerity. Ritual and repetition are bound together in our suspicion of "works righteousness": when it comes to religious devotion, we tend to see ritual observance as mere obedience to duty, a way of scoring points with God and earning spiritual credit. We see repetitive ritual as a bottom-up effort—and it's just that notion of "effort" that starts to sound like "work," and it doesn't take long before this all seems part of an elaborate system of "salvation by works."

Second, after the Reformation, and especially in the wake of modernity, wide swaths of contemporary Christianity tend to think of worship as only an "upward" act of the people of God who gather to offer up their sacrifice of praise, expressing their gratitude and devotion to the Father, with the Son, in the power of the Holy Spirit. Obviously this is an entirely biblical impulse and understanding: if *we* don't praise, even the rocks will cry out. In a sense, we are made to praise. The biblical vision of history culminates in the book of Revelation with a worshiping throng enacting the exhortation of Psalm 150 to "Praise the Lord!" However, one can also see how such expressivist understandings of worship feed into (and off of) some of the worst aspects of modernity. Worship-as-expression is easily hijacked by the swirling eddy of individualism. In that case, even gathered worship is more like a collection of individual, private encounters with God in which worshipers express an "interior" devotion. It is precisely this model that prizes "authenticity" so highly. If worship is only about expression, then sincerity is the highest good, and we have this lingering sense that doing the same thing twice—let alone over and over again—is not sincere. Thus we feel the need to encourage novel modes of expression week after week.

Third, and related to the second point, we have unwittingly bought into the cult of novelty that governs our twenty-four-hour "what have you done for me lately?" culture. We buy into the chronological snobbery that disdains the "old" as "*so* five minutes ago" and thus constantly pursue "fresh expressions." We fall prey to the consumerist mentality, which is also (necessarily) a disposal mentality—doing away with the old in order to partake of the new.

But the wisdom of historic Christian worship runs counter to all three of these assumptions precisely because it sees worship not only as expressive (what we offer to God) but also as *formative* (what God is doing *to us* in the encounter). Indeed, if we demonize repetition we end up abandoning rehabituation. For habituation is a kind of cognitive automation, and such automation only happens through repetition. Only through immersion in the same practices over and over can we hope for the inscription of

---

To Think About: Love's Litany

"In every sphere of life form is the beginning of things." So claims Gilbert in Oscar Wilde's dialogue "The Critic as Artist."[1] He continues in a vein that intersects directly with our concerns here: "The rhythmic, harmonious gestures of dancing convey, Plato tells us, both rhythm and harmony into the mind. Forms are the food of faith, cried Newman in one of those great moments of sincerity that made us admire and know the man. He was right, though he may not have known how terribly right he was. The Creeds are believed, not because they are rational, but because they are repeated."[2] We might be slightly uncomfortable with Wilde's suggestion. And yet, he seems to have intuited from Newman that repetition is the way belief becomes inscribed in the body—that repetition recruits our habits and thus our beliefs, rather than the other way around. Litanies do not just give expression to what we believe and love; they give birth to the belief and love. "Do you wish to love?" Gilbert asks. "Use Love's Litany, and the words will create the yearning from which the world fancies that they spring."[3] The liturgy of Christian worship is the litany of love granted us by the Spirit.

1. Oscar Wilde, "The Critic as Artist," in *The Portable Oscar Wilde*, rev. ed., ed. Richard Aldington and Stanley Weintraub (London: Penguin, 1981), 125.
2. Ibid.
3. Ibid., 126.

---

those "neural maps" that will reconfigure our dispositions. Quite simply, there is no formation without repetition. There is no habituation without being immersed in a practice over and over again. There will be no sanctification of our perception apart from a regular, repeated recentering of our imagination in the Story of the gospel as rehearsed and enacted in the "practical logic" of Christian worship. So it is precisely our allergy to repetition in worship that has undercut the counterformative power of Christian worship—because all kinds of secular liturgies shamelessly affirm the good of repetition. We've let the devil, so to speak, have all the repetition. And we, as liturgical animals, are only too happy to find our rhythms in such repetition. Unless Christian worship eschews the cult of novelty and embraces the good of faithful repetition, we will constantly be ceding habituation to secular liturgies.

Now, we are not talking about repetition for repetition's sake. *What* we're repeating makes all the difference. And *how* we're repeating makes a difference. So my claims about repetition in this section are inextricably linked to the argument about form in the previous section *and* to what I'll suggest in the next section regarding the importance of reflection. The form of worship has to normatively enact the Story, and must do so on aesthetic registers, if the Story is going to sanctify our perception. But if we are regularly and constantly re-immersed in a wise, intentional community of practice normed by the biblical Story, then we'll begin to find that Story becoming part of our background sensibility, becoming part of our "temperament," and engendering action that reflects the shape of the kingdom. And this happens without us realizing it.

Let's consider a case study for a middle-aged man named Alex. Worship at his church is nothing to write home about, as they say; nothing jazzy or innovative or "outside the box." Indeed, to some, worship in this congregation would look quite staid, "traditional," maybe even a bit boring. But as heirs to the wisdom of a liturgical tradition, and submitting their form of worship to that wisdom, the congregation regularly gathers, week in and week out, to effectively rehearse the true Story of the whole world. Alex and his family are faithful worshipers, but when he's honest, there are Sundays he doesn't want to be there. But he is there nonetheless, simply because somewhere along the way Alex has absorbed a core intuition we've been describing: that worship isn't just something we do; it is also a practice in which God does something to us. And so he knows that there is a certain virtue to "going through the motions," even on those days when he's not "feeling it," as we sometimes say. Even on those days when his heart was not in it, he knew that God would keep his promises and meet him in these practices.

Part of the "logic" of this practice includes a crucial, repeated moment each week when the congregation would kneel and confess their sins to God, and then hear the announcement of the good news of forgiveness in the assurance of pardon. Some Sundays the prayer of confession would roll over his tongue pretty much without any active cognition on his part: "We confess we have sinned against you in thought, word, and deed, by what we have done, and by what we have left undone. We have not loved you with our whole heart; we have not loved our neighbors as ourselves. . . . Have mercy . . ."[75] At other times and in other seasons, these words would stop him short; they would be heavy on his lips, and yet they were exactly the words he needed. To recite the prayer was like receiving the gift of tongues, a way for the Spirit to help Alex groan out his own guilt. Then he would hungrily listen for the good news of absolution, eager to be reminded of the mercy of God in the death and resurrection of Jesus Christ. But then again, at other times, even the astounding news of the gospel would sort of wash over him without much awareness on his part. Nonetheless, he was there, and the cadences of the prayer of confession and assurance of pardon would once again ("insensibly") make a dent on his imagination.

But Alex would never realize how formative this seemingly dull, repeated practice was until years later. In the dark evening of a January night,

75. "Morning Prayer: Rite II," in *The Book of Common Prayer* (New York: Oxford University Press, 1990), 79.

Alex and his wife would receive a call: their teenage son was in trouble. Derailed by depression and anxiety, he had spiraled into behaviors that were part defiance and part cries for help. Now Alex was receiving a call he had never been trained for, would make a visit he had never dreamed of, and would have a conversation he never wanted to. Not sure what to expect, Alex inched into an unfamiliar room unsure of himself—dazed, bewildered, disappointed, worried—awash in a sea of emotions and fears. But then he began to imagine what his boy must be feeling, for no matter what his son might be doing, Alex knew who he was, and *whose* he was. And so he became eager to find him, only to then be ushered into a room where his son sat folded into himself in a corner. Upon sight of Alex, his son collapsed and grasped Alex around his waist like he had as a child. Amid the tears and heaves of his sobs, Alex heard his son blubber, "I'm so sorry, Dad. Please forgive me."

And what else could Alex have done? This was replaying a scene he knew only too well: Alex himself had spent a lifetime confessing his sins to a gracious Father who, week after week after week, would announce without condition and hesitation, the complete forgiveness of all of our sins. So without hesitation, and without even having to think about it, Alex just knew what to say and what to do: he gathered up his son into his arms and whispered, "Of course I forgive you." There would be more opportunities for Alex to do the same. There wasn't any particular magic in this heartrending moment. But the regularity and repetition of the practice of confession and absolution had already taught him, on a gut level, that he too was a prodigal son who regularly approached his Father asking for forgiveness—*again*. And again. And again. And every single time the gracious Father, already looking for his arrival, met him at the end of the lane and made the same announcement of forgiveness and mercy. Through his regular and repeated immersion in the practices of Christian worship, Alex had absorbed the temperament of our gracious heavenly Father and so constituted this situation with that story in the background. But such an imaginative construal happened "automatically," as it were, because the repetition of the practice had effectively recruited Alex as a character in the same drama.

If Christian worship is going to be formative, it has to be repetitive.[76] Secular liturgies already know this; yet Christians, especially Protestants, can be suspicious of such "ritualized" repetition. But we need not be. God has created us as creatures of habit and meets us where we are. Indeed, the

---

76. This doesn't mean, of course, that we do the exact same thing week after week. There are macro- and microrhythms of repetition. We might pray the same prayer of confession each week, repeat the church's calendar each year, and work our way through the Scriptures with the help of a lectionary every three years.

Father invites us into union with Christ through Spirit-charged practices that, over and over again, sink us into the triune life. It is in their repetition that the story begins to sink into our imagination, thus sanctifying our perception and engendering action "toward the kingdom."

Redeeming Reflection: On Liturgical Catechesis and Christian Education

The core of my argument has been to emphasize all of the nonconscious ways that we intend our world, and hence the significance of formative practices that "work on" our cognitive unconscious—that shape our background and attune our being-in-the-world in ways that evade conceptualization and even elude our own awareness. *Praktognosia* and *habitus* have been conceptual names I've employed to try to illuminate aspects of our incarnate significance, our embodied being-in-the-world. Appreciating the role that such nonconscious modes of intentionality play in driving our action, I have especially pressed us to be attentive to how our background is formed and shaped and primed to perceive the world, recognizing that we are subject to competing formative practices. I have emphasized these nonconscious modes of meaning largely because they are underemphasized and underappreciated in many discussions of Christian formation and Christian higher education, which is why we are so often susceptible to mis- and de-formation by disordered liturgies that recruit our imagination for a body politic other than the city of God.

However, I want to close by emphasizing that this attention to our unconscious habituation and embodied "feel" for the world is not meant to denigrate or neglect the role of reflection and intellectual analysis. I am not setting up a dichotomy: *either* practice *or* reflection. To the contrary, my hope is to foster intentional reflection *on* practice in order to encourage reflective immersion *in* practice. Consider an example from the very beginning of the book: our proverbial case of reading Wendell Berry in Costco. While ultimately we will close the gap between knowledge and action through rehabituation that operates on our cognitive unconscious (*good* "mindless" eating, as Wansink puts it), there is a moment for reflection here that makes a crucial difference: becoming intellectually aware of what's at stake in my eating practice, and becoming cognizant of how other practices have recruited my habits, will *convince* me to seek new environments and new communities of practice. Being convinced of the importance of practice for "automating" my behavior, I will then *choose* to submit myself to different rhythms and habit-forming routines in order to rehabituate my wants and desires to a different *telos*. Recognizing that my *habitus* has been marshaled by one body politic to ends that I don't want to affirm, I will intentionally pursue the practices of an alternative body politic in order to recalibrate my heart.

We can extend the same principles to how we approach Christian formation—including both the practices of Christian worship and the pedagogies operative in Christian education. Intentionality is important on at least two levels. First, it is crucial that those who are responsible for the shape and form of Christian worship understand the "logic" of the practice in order to know what counts as wisdom *within* the practice.[77] In other words, Christian worship leaders will, in some sense, have to put themselves in the situation of Bourdieu's ethnographer: working with a theory of practice *as* practice, Christian worship planners need to be reflective in order to articulate and analyze the logic of practice so that they can then discern those forms of worship that are consistent with the Story that worship is supposed to invite us into. Worship leaders and planners (and those who teach both) need to be adept in their reflection on that logic of practice that eludes our grasp—precisely so that they can plan worship that invites the rest of us into that *habitus*-forming practice with confidence and trust, because many of the rest of us will not be able to "think about it" like those engaged in worship leadership. For the sake of the community of practitioners, worship planners and leaders need to take on the responsibility of reflexive evaluation of our practices in order to ensure that the imaginative coherences of worship are consistent with the vision of God's kingdom to which we are being habituated.

Second, and more widely, worship requires full, active, conscious participation even if it is also forming us in ways that elude our conscious awareness. If our immersion in the practices of Christian worship is always and only a matter of "going through the motions," then we are not really practitioners—we are more like free riders who float along in an environment without investment or identification. To put it in Bourdieu's terms, we will not be adequately incorporated into the body. However, there are also appropriate degrees of intentional reflection: a child or a new believer or a mentally challenged adult will be "carried" by the practices more than an adult who has been immersed in the faith for a lifetime. Indeed, we might think of the heart of discipleship and faith formation as liturgical catechesis whereby instruction in the faith is primarily focused on helping the people of God understand why we do what we do when we gather for worship. This was the intuition that informed "mystagogical preaching": formational preaching that intentionally invited catechumens into the body

---

77. For an illuminating account of how this should inform the *teaching* of worship (for both worship leaders and worshipers), see John Witvliet, "Teaching as a Worship Practice," in *For Life Abundant: Practical Theology, Theological Education, and Christian Ministry*, ed. Dorothy C. Bass and Craig Dykstra (Grand Rapids: Eerdmans, 2008), 117–48.

of Christ by explicating the sacraments and rites of initiation, "leading" them into the "mysteries" of the faith.[78] But rather than outlining a system of dogma, such preaching and teaching was an excavation and explanation of worship practice. Rather than a curriculum of abstract doctrines, mystagogical preaching was an invitation to reflect on what the people of God *did* week-in and week-out in worship.[79] Commenting on Cyril of Jerusalem's mystagogical preaching, Lester Ruth notes that "Cyril's concern, like that of other early bishops, was to name the different ways in which the various ceremonies had connected the newly baptized to the biblical story."[80] The goal of liturgical catechesis is to invite the people of God to a more conscious, intentional awareness of what we're doing and why we're doing it when we gather for worship—and that intellectual understanding will solidify as a conviction that then moves us to be committed to immersion in the practices.[81]

By equipping the people of God to reflect on worship, we can change how we *enter* worship—change the "angle of entry" into the community of practice that is the worshiping congregation.[82] The angle of entry to worship seems to be a determining factor in the formative power of worship. John Witvliet voices the question that many ask of this sort of "formative" vision of Christian worship: "if liturgical participation shapes us, why in the world are lifelong participants in worship not better people?"[83] Witvliet notes a host of factors that effectively "inoculate" us to the formative power

78. For a classic discussion, see Craig A. Satterlee, *Ambrose of Milan's Method of Mystagogical Preaching* (Collegeville, MN: Liturgical Press, 2002). More recently, consider the case study from Phinney Ridge Lutheran Church, a congregation in contemporary Seattle, as recounted in Paul E. Hoffman, *Faith Forming Faith: Bringing New Christians to Baptism and Beyond* (Eugene, OR: Cascade Books, 2012).

79. The Heidelberg Catechism can be seen in a similar way. Organized around the Creed, the Law, and the Lord's Prayer, the catechism was drawing on what Christians would have rehearsed every week in worship. Insofar as congregations abandon this "spine" of worship practice, the catechism seems abstract, even arbitrary.

80. Lester Ruth, Carrie Steenwyk, and John D. Witvliet, *Walking Where Jesus Walked: Worship in Fourth-Century Jerusalem*, The Church at Worship: Case Studies from Christian History (Grand Rapids: Eerdmans, 2010), 130. This rich volume includes extensive excerpts from Cyril's mystagogical sermons (130–37).

81. Such a goal is obviously germane to congregational life; however, this could also be the legitimate goal of a college chapel program.

82. For a consideration of the affective dynamics related to an "angle of entry," see Sara Ahmed, "Happy Objects," in Gregg and Seigworth, *The Affect Theory Reader*, 29–51. One might also consider an analogous point of "entry" in literature: the suspension of disbelief as a "chosen" disposition in order to inhabit the world of the novel. For relevant discussion, see James Wood, *The Broken Estate: Essays on Literature and Belief* (New York: Random House, 1999).

83. John D. Witvliet, "The Cumulative Power of Transformation in Public Worship: Cultivating Gratitude and Expectancy for the Holy Spirit's Work," in *Worship That Changes Lives: Multidisciplinary and Congregational Perspectives on Spiritual Transformation*, ed. Alexis Abernathy (Grand Rapids: Baker Academic, 2008), 52.

of worship, but one deserves our attention here. "One way to inoculate ourselves against part of worship's power," he suggests,

> is to think of going to church in superstitious terms, as if we are hedging our bets with God. If we participate in worship and simply hope that our being there will cause God to bless us, what we are doing in church really amounts to practicing something other than Christianity. We are practicing superstition, or hypocrisy—in which we sometimes even intentionally learn to say things to God that we do not mean. Spiritually speaking, the sin of hypocrisy is one of the most vexing antidotes to formation. In hypocrisy, our external actions are cut off from internal attitudes. We may even become well practiced at not meaning what we say or do.[84]

The posture or stance we effectively adopt upon "entry" affects our receptivity to the formative power of the practices, and even our openness to the Spirit's operations.

Matthew Boulton suggests that approaching Christian worship practices as merely expressive can also inoculate us to their formative power. "Indeed," he writes, "seeing through Calvin's eyes, we may describe what ails many Protestant churches today as follows: having inherited a treasury of formative exercises, we practice them only here and there, now and then—and still expect and even claim to be getting in shape. Or we expect no such thing, instead interpreting the treasury as a collection not of exercises meant to form us, but rather of activities meant to express, demonstrate, or symbolically establish ourselves as believing Christian beliefs, belonging to a Christian crowd."[85] If our angle of entry can effectively shut down the formative power of the practices, then one of the best things we can do to ensure the transformative, rehabituating power of Christian worship is to foster reflexive intentionality about *what* we're doing and *why*. In short, liturgical catechesis will encourage reflection on worship precisely so we constitute worship *as* that "suite" of disciplines that are habitations of the Spirit, into which we're invited in order to learn how to imagine the kingdom.

Picturing a Reflective, Sentimental Education

If I have celebrated the importance of attending to our "sentimental education," that is not instead of, or at the expense of, an "intellectual" education. The project of formation envisioned here eschews any dichotomy between the two—both because our rational reflection is rooted in affect and because our immersion in affective practice is

84. Ibid., 52–53.
85. Boulton, *Life in God*, 228.

sometimes motivated by intellectual conviction. Our reflection is always already sentimental, and our affective immersion is never untethered from our intellectual being-in-
the-world. So a truly holistic Christian education will be a formation of both heart and
mind, both intellect and affect.

This interplay of intellect and sentiment is wonderfully pictured in Albert Goldbarth's poem "Sentimental." The poem itself effects what it's talking about: it inter-
twines sentimental affect with a reflexive question. The poem poses a question that
we *think* about even as we are carried along by a meaning that eludes our conceptual
grasp and analytic skill. The scene is a writing class in which earnest young poets, devo-
tees of the avant-garde, are on guard for incursions of clichéd schmaltz and kitschy
appeals to emotions and sentimentality. Disciples of modernism, they greet Hallmark
niceties with haughty disdain. Serious poets, they are wary of anything that smells like
the made-for-TV movie. The unforgivable sin is to be sentimental.

But their teacher is going to press them, and it is this thread of the poem that invites
us to reflection. How do you know what counts as sentimental? When have we crossed
the line? And as we're carried along by the affective play of the poem, our confidence
in that line begins to waver, and by the end of it we realize we've been captivated by
sentimentality—and that it is *true*.

> The light has traveled unthinkable thousands of miles to be
> condensed, recharged, and poured off the white white pages
> of an open Bible the country parson holds in front of this couple
> in a field, in July, in the sap and the flyswirl of July
> in upper Wisconsin, where their vows buzz in a ring in the air
> like the flies, and are as sweet as the sap, in these rich and ritual minutes.
> Is it sentimental? Oops. And out of that Bible the light continues
> to rush as if from a faucet. There will be a piecrust cooling
> out of its own few x'ed-out cuts. And will it make us run
> for the picklier taste of irony rolled around protectively on our tongues
> like a grab of Greek olives? My students and I discuss this
> slippery phenomenon. Does "context" matter? Does
> "earned" count? If a balled-up fidget of snakes
> in the underbrush dies in a freeze is it sentimental? No,
> yes, maybe. What if a litter of cocker spaniels? What
> if we called them "puppydogs" in the same poem in that same hard,
> hammering winter? When my father was buried,
> the gray snow in the cemetery was sheet tin. If I said
> that? Yes, no, what does "tone" or "history" do
> to the Hollywood hack violinists who patiently wait to play
> the taut nerves of the closest human body until from that
> lush cue alone, the eyes swell moistly, and the griefs
> we warehouse daily take advantage of this thinning
> of our systems, then the first sloppy gushes begin . . .

Is that "wrong"? Did I tell you the breaths
of the gravediggers puffed out like factorysmoke
as they bent and straightened, bent and straightened,
mechanically? Are wise old (toothless) Black blues singers
sentimental?—"gran'ma"? "country cookin'"? But
they have their validity, don't they, yes? their
sweat-in-the-creases, picking up the lighting
in a fine-lined mesh of what it means to have gone through time
alive a little bit on this planet. Hands shoot up . . . opinions . . .
questions . . . What if the sun wept? the moon? Why, in the face
of those open faces, are we so squeamish? Call out
the crippled girl and her only friend the up-for-sale foal,
and let her tootle her woeful pennywhistle musics.
What if some chichi streetwise junkass from the demimonde
gave forth with the story of orphans forced through howling storm
to the workhouse, letting it swing between the icy-blue
quotation marks of cynicism—*then*? What if
I wept? What if I simply put the page down,
rocked my head in my own folded elbows, forgot
the rest of it all, and wept? What if I stepped into
the light of that page, a burnished and uncompromising
light, and walked back up to his stone a final time,
just that, no drama, and it was so cold,
and the air was so brittle, metal buckled
out song like a bandsaw, and there, from inside me,
where they'd been lost in shame and sophistry
all these years now, every last one of my childhood's
heartwormed puppydogs found its natural voice.[86]

86. Albert Goldbarth, "Sentimental," in *Across the Layers: Poems Old and New* (Atlanta: University of Georgia Press, 1993), 113–14. Used with permission.

Name Index

Adams, Jay E., 64n47
Ahmed, Sara, 188n82
Anderson, Wes, 48n31
Aristotle, 17n38, 19n44, 55n1, 81
Augustine, 5, 7, 17–18n38, 24n52, 27n55, 60n43, 125, 141n83, 152n7
Austen, Jane, 16n32

Bachelard, Gaston, 18
Bailey, Edward, xixn2
Baker, Nicholson, 103–7, 108
Bargh, John A., 6n13
Bartholomew, Craig, 154n12
Baucum, Tory K., 82n15
Baudelaire, Charles, 103n1
Begbie, Jeremy, 33n5, 117–18, 175n63
Berry, Wendell, 8–10, 86n20, 157, 186
Billings, J. Todd, 6n10, 6n12, 15n29, 150n97, 153n8, 168n50
Bloechl, Jeffrey, 124n38
Boersma, Hans, 166n47
Botton, Alain de, xixn2
Boulton, Matthew Myer, 1n1, 15, 152, 154–59, 167, 175, 189
Bouma-Prediger, Steven, 124n38
Bourdieu, Pierre, 33n6, 60n42, 75–100, 108–9, 110, 121n34, 125, 130n58, 133, 134, 137, 142–43, 150, 158, 167–68, 173–74, 187
Boyd, Brian, 38n15, 130nn59–60
Brady, Catherine, 134n76
Brooks, Cleanth, 171–73
Brooks, David, 34, 37, 52, 108n9, 147, 178
Brueggemann, Walter, 160

Bruhn, Mark J., 133n70
Budde, Michael, 162–163
Burne-Jones, Edward, 180

Caldecott, Stratford, 179n68
Calvin, John, 1, 15, 152–58, 175, 181n74, 189
Campion, Jane, 46–49
Canlis, Julie, 15n29
Caracciolo, Marco, 133n71
Carroll, Joseph, 130n59
Caryl, Christian, 139
Cavanaugh, William, 16–17, 20, 138–39
Chrétien, Jean-Louis, 62n45
Clapp, Rodney, 3n2
Cosmides, Leda, 130n62
Crouch, Andy, 5
Cuneo, Terence, xixn1
Currie, Gregory, 17n36
Cyril of Jerusalem, 188

Danto, Arthur, 32n3
Deleuze, Gilles, 128n46
Depraz, Natalie, 18n40
Desmond, William, 17n35
Dewey, John, 37n14, 85n19
DeYoung, Rebecca Konyndyk, 145n90
Didion, Joan, 96, 108, 129, 133n72
Dooyeweerd, Herman, 126n43
Dreyfus, Hubert, 13n24, 32n3, 59n41, 89n26, 91n29, 132
Duby, Georges, 92n30
Dykstra, Craig, 15n27, 65, 187n77
Dyrness, William, 126n44

Eagleton, Terry, 88
Edelman, Gerald, 115

Flaubert, Gustave, 5, 16n33

Goheen, Michael, 154n12
Goldbarth, Albert, 190–91
Gottschall, Jonathan, 130n59
Gregg, Melissa, 31n1
Guthrie, Steven R., 33n5, 175n63

Hauerwas, Stanley, 3n3, 14n26, 36n12, 151n1,
    154n12
Hegel, G. W. F., 86n21
Heidegger, Martin, 17n35, 27n55, 41n18, 51,
    104n4, 137n80
Hemingway, Ernest, 161
Herman, David, 134n76
Hoffman, Paul E., 188n78
Hogan, Patrick Colm, 38n15, 39n16
Husserl, Edmund, 41, 42n19, 56n38, 83n18

Isaacson, Walter, 142n84

Jobs, Steve, 142n84
Johnson, Mark, 17n37, 35, 36–38, 49, 55, 82n17,
    85n19, 110–24, 127n46, 181

Kaag, John, 18, 19n41
Kahneman, Daniel, 6n13, 64n48, 160n28
Kallenberg, Brad J., 144n89
Kant, Immanuel, 77, 106, 119, 127n46, 165n44
Keats, John, 46–49
Kenneson, Phil, 19
Kepnes, Steven, xixn1
Kim, Jaegwon, 32n3
Kosofsky, Scott-Martin, 164
Kramnick, Jonathan, 131–32
Kushner, Tony, 144n87

Lacoste, Jean-Yves, xixn1
Lakoff, George, 117n24, 122n36
Langer, Suzanne, 112
Lanier, Jaron, 149n96
Leighton, Angela, 172n55
Leithart, Peter, 16n32
Lepore, Ernie, 172n55
Lesser, Simon, 132n67
Levinas, Emmanuel, 124n38
Lewis, C. S., 24n52
Lipsky, David, 21n46
Lloyd-James, Sally, 160n30

Maag, Karin, 181n74
MacIntyre, Alasdair, 16n32, 19n44, 55, 108,
    109n12, 112n19, 139
Malick, Terence, 116
Max, D. T., 26n54
McCarthy, Cormac, 91n28, 161
McCullers, Carson, 98–100
McGilchrist, Iain, xvi, 11n22, 31n2, 34–35,
    44n24, 117n26, 118n26, 118n30, 124n39,
    128n47, 133, 134n74
McHugh, Heather, 172
McLaren, Peter, 94
McLuhan, Marshall, 75n1, 169n52
Mele, Alfred R., 32n3
Merleau-Ponty, Maurice, 19n44, 41–73, 83, 85,
    108–10, 125–26, 128n48, 136, 157, 167
Milbank, John, 46n27
Mitchell, Nathan D., 60n42, 119n31
Mlinko, Ange, 118n26
Morris, William, 180
Moseley, David, 33n5
Mulder, Mark, 140n82
Murphy, Francesca, 14n26

Neruda, Pablo, 116
Newman, Cardinal John Henry, 88, 183
Nichols, Shaun, 17n36
Núñez, Rafael, 122n36

Ochs, Peter, 164–66

Percy, Walker, 22, 43n21
Phelan, James, 130n61
Piper, John, 140n82
Pippin, Robert, 86n21
Plantinga, Cornelius, 6n14
Proust, Marcel, xii–xiii, 40–41, 73, 95

Rashkover, Randi, 165
Recker, Joyce, 136
Richardson, Alan, 133n70
Ricks, Christopher, 47–49
Ricoeur, Paul, 117n25, 128–29, 135
Rienstra, Debra, 175n64
Rienstra, Ron, 175n64
Rivera, Joseph, xixn1
Robinson, Jenefer, 38n15
Ruth, Lester, 188n80

Satterlee, Craig A., 188n78
Schalow, Frank, 17n35, 18n40
Seerveld, Calvin, 5n8, 118, 126n43, 134n73,
    159n27, 161, 163n36

Siegworth, Gregory J., 31n1
Senn, Frank, 169n54, 170–71
Shteyngart, Gary, 148–49
Smit, Laura, 15n29
Smith, Christian, 109n12
Smith, James K. A., xixn1–2, 3n5, 6n11, 7n15,
    8n16, 15n30, 33nn5–6, 46n27, 95n34, 105n7,
    109n12, 111n16, 122n35, 126n42, 127n44,
    137n80, 151n2, 154n15, 165n44, 173n60,
    181n73
Smith, Zadie, 146, 149
Sosa, Ernest, 13n25
Steenwyk, Carrie, 188n80
Stump, Eleonore, 19n44, 91n27

Taylor, Charles, xiiin4, 9, 13n24, 16n34, 32n3,
    33n6, 43n22, 82n14, 109n12, 126n41, 146–
    47, 154n15
Tooby, John, 130n62
Trilling, Lionel, 158–59
Twain, Mark, 14

Varela, Francisco, 18n40
Venema, Henry, 117, 128–29

Walker, Jeanne Murray, 120–21
Wallace, David Foster, 21–27, 103, 108, 130,
    146–47
Walsh, Brian, 124n38
Wansink, Brian, 9–10, 186
Ward, Graham, 152n4
Wells, Samuel, 3n3, 14n26, 151n1
Wilde, Oscar, 178–81, 183
Wilfred, Thomas, 116
Wilson, David Sloan, 130n59
Wirzba, Norman, 9n18
Witvliet, John D., 3n4, 175, 176–77, 187n77, 188
Wren, Brian, 174n62
Wright, Christopher J. H., 5n7, 151–52n3
Wright, N. T., 127n45, 154n12, 163n37
Wolfe, Thomas, 40
Wolterstorff, Nicholas, xixn1, 155n16
Woods, James, 14n26, 188n82

Zuidervaart, Lambert, 134, 135–36, 173n59
Zunshine, Lisa, 133n71

Subject Index

affect, 31, 35–36, 112–13, 162, 168n51, 188n82
analytic theology, 19n44, 91n27
anti-intellectualism, 11n21, 32
antithesis, 126n44, 156
apartheid, 168n50
artificial intelligence, 59n41
artistic truth, 134, 136, 173
attunement, 70, 72, 87, 108, 137n80, 157, 159, 181n73

benediction, 2, 5, 153, 171
Brantwood, 71

Cartesianism, 49
centrifuge, church as, 157
chicken sexing, 52
cognitive narratology, 132–33. *See also* literary Darwinism
cognitivism, 17n36, 59n41
compatibilism, 84
constitution, 50–51, 56n38, 62–63, 71, 81, 113, 129n55, 178–79
counseling psychology, 64n47

dispositional deflection, 157–58, 161, 166
divine action, 15, 152
Downton Abbey, 21
drones. *See* unmanned aerial vehicles

emotional prefocusing, 38
emotions, 32, 35–39, 95n34, 120
emotivism, 168n51

Eton, 96
evolutionary psychology, 130–31

Facebook. *See* social media

Genevan Psalter, 175

habit, habits, 9–10, 12, 33, 36, 38, 57–58, 79–81, 86n21, 125, 132, 138, 144, 145, 166, 183, 185
habituation, 33, 51, 93, 98, 105, 140, 181–86. *See also* rehabituation
habit-body, 44, 45, 69, 115, 138
habitus, 79–98, 125–27, 138–39, 141–42, 157, 158, 169, 186–87
heresy of paraphrase, the, xiiin4, 91n27, 171–74
holiness, 113
Holy Spirit, 2, 3, 5, 6n12, 14, 15, 20, 33, 45, 65, 102, 111, 113, 136, 150, 152–56, 169n54, 176, 182, 183, 184, 186, 189

imagination, 14n26, 15–20, 32, 36, 39, 56, 59, 62, 88, 105, 108–9, 124–50, 158, 160–81. *See also* social imaginary
implicit religion, xixn2
improvisation (in worship), 174n61
innovation (in worship), 174n61
intellectualism, 20, 25, 27, 32, 39, 43n22, 53, 55, 58, 77, 80–81, 94
iPhone, 142–44

kinaesthetics, 15, 20, 101, 109, 124
know-how. *See praktognosia*

197

libertarian freedom, 84, 86n21
literary Darwinism, 130–32. *See also* cognitive
    narratology

magnum monasterium, 155
metaphor, 97, 117–37, 173, 175
    conceptual, 110, 118–20, 123–24
    primary, 119–20
microhabits, 143
micropractices, 110, 143
missio Dei, 4, 5, 151, 153, 156
missional institutions, 157–58, 166
motor intentionality, 53–56, 59–60, 66
mystagogical preaching, 187–88

narrative theology, 14n26

operative intentionality, 42n19

pedagogies of desire, 13, 96, 137
plasticity, 114
poetics, 15, 18n39, 20, 49, 101, 109, 117n24,
    124–37
pragmata, 51, 104n4
praktognosia, 56–61, 83, 123, 126, 157, 167,
    174, 186

rehabituation, 53, 65, 66, 166, 182, 186. *See also*
    habituation
repertoires, 115–16
Romanticism, 17n35, 46–49, 71, 88, 133n70

secular liturgies, xviii, xixn2, 4, 7, 9, 10, 15, 19,
    20, 39, 58, 80, 94, 97n35, 101–2, 103–7, 109,
    110, 122, 123, 126n44, 137, 139–41, 163,
    183, 185
self-consciousness, 145–50
sin, 60n43, 140–41. *See also* temptation
social imaginary, 16n34, 94, 96, 126n41, 138, 143,
    148, 149, 174, 178. *See also* imagination
social media, 143–50
Spirit. *See* Holy Spirit
story logic, 134

temptation, 20, 101, 140–42
    phenomenology of, 140–42
Twitter. *See* social media

unmanned aerial vehicles (UAVs), 138–39

wallpaper, 180–81
worldview, 7–11, 21, 84, 98, 119, 138, 176, 178